DECISION
at the
CHESAPEAKE

DECISION
at the
CHESAPEAKE

Harold A. Larrabee

Clarkson N. Potter, Inc./Publisher, New York

119828

To my grandchildren:
Peter, Amy Noël, and Judith Wyman

TABLE OF CONTENTS

LIST OF MAPS

FOREWORD

The interest that prompted the inquiry from which this book has come was aroused in Paris forty years ago, while the author was studying in France on a Rogers Traveling Fellowship of Harvard University. In the course of writing a doctoral dissertation on the philosophy of Henri de Saint-Simon (the Saint-Simonian), the discovery that three members of this family (a marquis, a baron, and a count) were present at the battle of Yorktown awakened curiosity about that campaign. Further investigation resulted in two articles: the first (titled before "collaborator" had become a nasty word) was "A Neglected Collaborator in the Victory of Yorktown: Claude-Anne, Marquis de Saint-Simon (1740-1819)" in the *Journal des Américanistes* for 1932; and the second: "Henri de Saint-Simon at Yorktown: A French Prophet of Modern Industrialism in America" in *The Franco-American Review* (Autumn, 1937).

There followed an interruption of many years due to pre-occupation with the college teaching of philosophy, until retirement made possible a resumption of historical research. The conviction had been growing that although innumerable histories of the events of the American Revolution have been published, the significance of some vital contributions to the cause of American independence, both by inept bungling on one side, and by deft co-operation on the other, had been largely over-looked. Either too little credit was given to the French navy and army for their part in the final victory, or else they were praised for the wrong reasons. The chauvinists among American historians have been concerned to glorify Washington, Greene, and

the land campaign. Americans are notoriously fond of being
loved for themselves alone, and tend to rebuff the idea that it
was hatred of England, and not love of our ancestors, which
prompted the French. The sentimental Francophiles, stirred
deeply by the two more recent world wars, have portrayed
General Rochambeau and Admiral de Grasse as convinced
crusaders for the rights of man, which they were not. May it not
be possible to draw up a balance sheet of our unquestioned debt
to France which will come closer to recording what actually
happened, and why?

A possible key to such a reappraisal offered itself in the form
of a strangely forgotten naval engagement which decided the
outcome of the Revolutionary War. A short account of it, called
"A Near Thing at Yorktown," was published in *American Heritage* for October, 1961, to whose editor, Oliver Jensen, thanks
are due for permission to incorporate some of its material in this
much fuller recital. To center attention upon the decisive battle
is not, of course, to minimize the many preceding achievements
which enabled it to be decisive. A just and accurate view of any
war can be obtained only by viewing it from many perspectives.

The aim in writing this book has not been to find out a great
deal that is new about the battle of the Chesapeake, but to bring
together from many sources, some of them obscure, most of what
we know about it, and to explore its historical background. The
principal object is understanding: insight into the familiar and
the unfamiliar from a somewhat novel point of view. The form
chosen is broadly dramatic, because the pace of events and the
astonishing rise of American fortunes from the depths of despair
in 1780-81 have all the elements of drama.

When a historian writes of events he did not witness his reliance upon the records of others is total, so that no one should be
surprised at the multitude of quotations from sources. The temptation to indulge in fiction of the "Washington must have felt on
this occasion . . ." variety is strong, but has been resisted. It is
true that the annals we have are incomplete, but the historian
has no right to invent his own substitutes. Excerpts from letters are not traced back to the manuscript collections where
they are located, but are deliberately cited from secondary

sources available to readers who have access to a fairly well-stocked public or college library.

It is probably true that every author has at least one ideal reader in view as he writes. It is painful to have to invoke only the memory of an avid and judicious connoisseur of naval history, the late President John F. Kennedy, in this connection. But one would love to think that he would have enjoyed reading these pages. No formal acknowledgment can fully express the writer's debt to past and present historians (see Notes and Bibliography) or to present librarians, may their tribe increase! Among the latter are to be numbered the entire staff of Union College's Schaffer Library, headed by Professor Helmer L. Webb and his successor Professor Edwin K. Tolan. Mr. Charles F. Wilde has been tireless in facilitating inter-library loans from the Library of Congress, the State Library in Albany, and the Cornell University Library. Mrs. Catherine G. Stanley has helped in all matters pertaining to circulation. Only authors and their wives will understand how much this one owes to the patience and presence of Doris Kennard Larrabee.

H. A. L.

Schenectady, New York

INTRODUCTION

"The Battle of Chesapeake Bay was one of the decisive battles of the world. Before it, the creation of the United States of America was possible; after it, it was certain."
—Michael Lewis, *The History of the British Navy*

On the afternoon of September 5, 1781, off the Capes of Virginia, two and a half hours of cannonading between warships of the British and French navies determined the outcome of the American Revolution. It was the one decisive engagement of the bitter six-year struggle of the thirteen colonies against England, and it could have gone either way. Not many Americans have ever heard of it; yet "few naval actions," says Professor Randolph G. Adams, "have decided more." In the judgment of a European historian, the late Emil Reich, it deserves the name of "British naval Waterloo off Cape Henry."

The reasons that the encounter has been noticed only in the detailed histories of the war are not far to seek. Everyone concerned, apparently, had motives for wanting to forget it. The British did not wish to call to mind the egregious blunders which destroyed their chances of victory. Only seven months later the French admiral who defeated them was thought to have disgraced himself by losing the battle of the Saintes and being taken prisoner to England. Americans have been understandably reluctant to face up to the fact that their status as a nation was decided by an engagement at which no Americans were present.

Fought out of sight of land, the conflict had only its active participants as eye-witnesses, and few of them took the trouble to write about it. Such accounts as exist have remained hidden in the naval archives of England and France, or have been published in the form of articles and monographs. The meeting of the two fleets does not even have a name that is generally accepted. You will find it called the Battle of the Chesapeake, of Chesapeake Bay, of Lynnhaven Bay, of Cape Henry, and of the Capes of Virginia.

Almost no one, at the time, seems to have grasped its full significance. George III called it "a drawn battle"; Rear Admiral Thomas Graves, "a lively skirmish"; Rear Admiral Sir Samuel Hood, "a feeble action"; and George Washington, "a partial engagement." As modern battles go it was a small affair. Probably less than ten thousand men came under fire on each side, and the total casualties did not exceed six hundred. In a conversation with the Marquis de Lafayette some years later, Napoleon Bonaparte is said to have scoffed at the smallness of the armies and navies that were engaged in the battles of the American Revolution. "It was the grandest of causes," replied Lafayette, "won by the skirmishes of sentinels and outposts."

One of the many paradoxes about the Chesapeake struggle is that one of the greatest naval victories of all time was decisive because it was indecisive. Not a single ship was taken or sunk during the battle itself, although the British were forced to burn one afterwards; and neither admiral was driven from the field. Yet the result was as crushing to the hopes of General Earl Cornwallis as if every British warship had been sent to the bottom. To save his army of seven thousand men, the British fleet had to win control of Chesapeake Bay. This it failed to do. England lost naval supremacy just long enough to insure the winning of American independence. Once the sea-approaches to the Chesapeake were sealed the siege of Yorktown and Cornwallis's surrender were foregone conclusions.

In view of the extremely dim prospects of the American cause only five or six short months before, the Yorktown campaign constituted a dramatic and glorious reversal of form and fortune. Hopes which had been deferred for six long years were suddenly and unexpectedly realized. The goal of victory, which looked so remote in January, 1781, was substantially achieved by the month of October, even though the treaty of peace was slow in coming. Seen in retrospect, Yorktown appears as an inspired model of strategy and timing, as if a chess-master had been pitted against a third-rate opponent. Yet the Grand Design of the Franco-American allies was devised in detail only a few weeks in advance of its execution, and it might have gone haywire at a dozen points. If it had done so, America would hardly have been restored to its former colonial dependence, but complete freedom from British rule might have been a long time in coming, if at all.

The fact of the matter is that for the rebels everything clicked. In addition to superior generalship the allies had all the luck, their enemy almost none. Many of our pious forefathers interpreted this as distinct partiality on the part of the Deity, displayed in what Washington in his proclamation called "such re-iterated and astonishing interpositions of Providence."[1] Others agreed with Henri Doniol that "the complicity of things decidedly deserted the British." In the opinion of Captain Dudley W. Knox, U.S.N., "There are a hundred circumstances connected with the Yorktown campaign which could only be adequately explained either by a fatalist or a confirmed believer in the God of Luck."[2]

There was, however, a great deal more than sheer good fortune involved in the battle of the Chesapeake. Its outcome flowed from an intricate combination of causes, some of them buried deep in the social systems prevailing on both sides of the Atlantic. It will not do, in contemplating it, to forget Allen's Law, first stated by the late Frederick Lewis Allen, long the editor of *Harper's Magazine*: "Everything is more complicated than it appears to be." There is also high drama in the way in which the Yorktown plot unfolded. From the American and French points of view, it is a classic example of a struggle in which, as the vernacular has it, "the good guys finally got all the breaks."

Where, then, is that essential dramatic ingredient: suspense? College students sometimes shun courses in American history on the ground that "they already know how it comes out." That is certainly true of the American Revolution if the only question to be answered is: who won? But the suspense and uncertainty come back into the picture if one raises such vexing issues as: Ought Britain to have won the war "hands down"? Did she lose it primarily by her own mistakes? Did the Americans win their own independence? Or was it substantially a gift from the French? It is just such controversies that are still open for debate. As for more specific queries, there are at least two dozen "ifs" connected with Yorktown about which historians have disagreed.

Readers who are impatient for action may be dismayed by the amount of space devoted to setting the stage and introducing the actors in Chapters 1 and 2-9 inclusive. The setting requires attention because eighteenth-century warfare was carried on for reasons which we find strange, and with weapons which are even stranger. Both the ideas of a frankly exploitative empire and a ruling aristocracy, on the one hand, and the horse and sailing ship as the speediest means of transport, on the other, are decidedly out of date.

As for the actors, if it is true that action flows out of character, we cannot know too much in advance about the men who are to make the key decisions. Not, that is, if we wish to understand them, and not just observe them. In the theater, of course, such knowledge has to be acquired from the program notes and an Act I, Scene I conversation between the butler and the parlormaid. A drama in book form may be permitted greater scope. It should be noted especially that the sketches of the actors in Chapters 2-9 do not extend beyond their careers up to the year 1780, when this account begins.

The recounting of the naval action, and the land campaigns before and after it, presents some problems of overlapping, since the Yorktown campaign involved the convergence of armies and fleets from long distances, beautifully synchronized by the French and the Americans. First it is essential to understand why and how Lord Cornwallis got to Yorktown in the first place, and decided to remain there (Chapters 10-14 inclusive). Then the scene shifts to the West Indies with the coming of Admiral de Grasse, and his decision to come north to the Chesapeake (Chapter 14). The next phase, enacted in the same locale, comprises Admiral Rodney's failure to cope with the French threat, and his sending of Rear Admiral Hood to the rescue in his place (Chapters 16-17). After the detailed recounting of the battle of the Chesapeake (Chapters 18-20), the words

are "Too Little, Too Late" as Rear Admiral Graves and
General Sir Henry Clinton try in vain to play a return engagement with De Grasse (Chapter 21).

Having recounted the moves in the decisive naval battle, the
narrative returns to land and to the North, temporarily, telling of
the earlier genesis of the Grand Design and its modification by
Rochambeau; Washington's great march south with him; and
the siege and surrender which the victory at sea had made inevitable (Chapters 22-24). Some reflections upon the merits of
the violent controversies which broke out among the participants
and their partisans are added, although at that point the undis-
couraged reader should have reached conclusions of his own
(Chapter 25).

1

THE STAGE—
AND SOME PROPERTIES

"A great empire and little minds go ill together."
—Edmund Burke

The struggle which decided the independence of the United States of America was enacted upon the waters at the entrance to Chesapeake Bay. But it was only a part of a much wider conflict, a duel for empire between Great Britain and France, whose stage was a triangle stretching across the Atlantic Ocean. Its apex was the English Channel, with one side reaching the North American coast and the other the islands of the West Indies. The distances involved, in terms of those to which Europeans were accustomed, and of the means of transport then available, were vast: three thousand miles or more for the long sides of the triangle, and over one thousand miles along its base. It was a stage large enough to dwarf all but men of exceptional vision, rare in any age.

There was only one method known by which the great distances could be traversed, and that was the sailing ship, built of wood and usually displacing from three hundred to twelve hundred tons. It was propelled by the winds and the ocean currents, and was completely dependent upon them, both for its ability to move at all and for its speed when in motion. With westerly winds prevailing in the North Atlantic, a voyage from England to North America took two months, and about one month in the opposite direction. The trip from the West Indies to New York was a matter of from three weeks to more than a month. This meant, as Major General J. F. C. Fuller says, that "letters took so long they often confused the operations they were intended to assist."[1] Adverse winds could hold a ship in port for weeks at a time. Sudden calms in mid-ocean might immobilize it for days. Equally sudden hurricanes could drive it hundreds of miles off its course, or pile it up on some reef or rocky shore.

Of the two imperial protagonists, England and France, the latter was markedly superior in area and population with upwards of twenty-four million people as compared with nine million in Britain. Both nations had acquired footholds in the three main colonial areas of the world at that time: the East Indies, the West Indies, and North America. In colonial population, however, the thirteen English colonies were by far the largest, with nearly three million inhabitants. "Three-quarters, and perhaps seven-eighths of them lived in a central strip about five hundred miles long from the northern boundary of Massachusetts to the southern edge of Virginia, nowhere extending more than one hundred and fifty miles westward from the Atlantic, and throughout most of its length ending less than a hundred miles from salt water."[2]

Viewed from London, the North American colonies seemed to consist of a few seaports, "the vertebrae of the whole colonial social structure," situated upon the fringe of a wilderness which could be disregarded. Nearly everywhere roads were bad and bridges and ferries inadequate, so that transport depended largely upon the bays and rivers. To strangle colonial trade seemed therefore to be a simple matter, in spite of the long coastline, provided enough warships could be spared from duty in the richer regions of the Caribbean.

What is overlooked in most discussions of the American rebellion is the cardinal fact that, in immediate monetary returns, the North American colonies could not compare with the relatively tiny islands of the West Indies. A single successful voyage from England to the Antilles for sugar, tobacco, cotton, rice, or indigo could make a man a fortune. It was the West Indies which constituted "the world's greatest commercial prize" of that era; and in consequence they were a much stronger magnet than North America for attracting battleships. Their great drawback for sailing ships was the annual hurricane season lasting from

July to October, when vessels were well-advised to go elsewhere.

In judging the worth of a colony trade was given first place by all but religious zealots. The search for religious liberty was indeed a powerful motive in establishing many of the American settlements. But for most persons in the mother country, "Trade was the soul of empire." A colony was a large investment which was expected to show a profit. It was the age of mercantilism, when each nation regarded its colonies as properties to be "milked" by those who financed them, and by no one else. It was deemed far more important to sell and to carry than it was to buy; and much energy was expended in hampering the trade of rivals. A country was believed to be rightfully entitled to an absolute monopoly of the products and sea-trade of its colonies: English goods could be carried only in English ships, French goods in French ships and so on.

With several powerful maritime nations engaged in competitive empire building on such a basis, it soon became apparent that each one of them must have not only its own large merchant marine, but the means of protecting it against hostile attacks. It was pointless to conquer territory and set up a colony, and then find that at any moment one might be denied access to it. In the words of Daniel Defoe: "Naval power and commerce, like twins, are born together and not to live asunder." Thus the seventeenth and eighteenth centuries saw the growth of ever-larger navies, and the rise of a new conception, that of "command of the sea."

Since it was precisely the loss of her command of the sea which occurred at the battle of the Chesapeake, costing England the loss of America, the idea is worth further examination. At first it was envisaged in terms of land power, as something localized, the conquest of water territory in which a country desired to trade freely. But water territory is not like land territory; and the doctrine simply did not work at sea, since trade routes remained open to neutrals, and no navy could subsist upon the ocean alone. Sea-borne commerce is not something which can be controlled by permanent zones of influence marked off and guarded by naval forces.

Gradually statesmen came to understand that there could be no balance of power upon the seas of the world similar to that which had been, and still was, so carefully guarded on the continent of Europe. If it is true that "the sea is one," then the all-or-none principle prevails. Either a nation has the freedom to trade wherever it pleases or else it can do so only upon the sufferance of others. The essence of sea command is "commerce prevention"—the denial to others of the freedom to trade wherever they please, reserving that privilege for oneself alone.

For a time the rulers of Europe tried to keep their strictly colonial rivalries from interfering with their domestic concerns. But before long they became convinced that command of the sea was capable of affecting the balance of power on land. The colonies became enmeshed in the prosperity of the home-economy: about one-third of France's exports and imports were West Indian, and English merchants were said to reap a profit of a million pounds a year from trade with America. Colonial possessions were becoming important pieces upon the European diplomatic chessboard; and men began to wonder whether it might not be true that "he who is master of the sea is master of the land," although, as Admiral Rodney discovered among the islands of the West Indies: "Ships cannot take mountains."

What did come about was a new state of political tension, in all the courts of Europe, between the demands of land power and those of sea power. Which was to have priority, the army or the navy: the defenders of landed estates, or of overseas trade? An empire was discovered to have within itself a built-in conflict between domestic needs and those of the periphery, the colonies. In Britain during the American war this took the form of home defense against invasion *versus* the holding of trade advantages in the West Indies and the Mediterranean. On September 13, 1779, George III went so far as to write to Lord Sandwich: "Our West Indian islands must be defended at the risk of an invasion of this island. If we lose our Sugar Islands it will be impossible to raise money to continue the war . . ."[3]

In France there was perpetual competition between her continental and her maritime ambitions. She had two "front doors" on the Atlantic and Mediterranean, and also many "back doors" on her land frontiers. France had no encircling "moat" like that which shielded England, whose soil was seldom threatened. Except during the period of the American Revolution England could always count upon some other European power or combination of powers to keep France preoccupied on land. *Le sol de France* always came first in the minds of her rulers. French interest in naval affairs was only spasmodic, whereas the state of her army gave her constant concern. Of England just the reverse was true. Her navy was of primary and continuous importance, while her army was only employed in Europe at intervals.

The prize that beckoned to all the aspiring colonial powers in the later eighteenth century was "the overlordship of the ocean," called by Liddell Hart "the deadliest weapon which any nation has wielded throughout history." The securing of it turned out to be an expensive business, for it called for the building and maintaining of battle squadrons numerous enough and powerful enough to sweep the seas of the world. Spain and Holland had fallen behind in the contest; only England and France seemed to have the vision and will and resources to strive for the grand award. In the years when the American revolt was brewing, England's rulers supposed that she had already won permanent possession of it by the terms of the treaty which ended the Seven Years' War in 1763. Her navy and her merchant marine were the world's largest, and were soon to be neglected for that very reason. In the eyes of General George Washington on May 28, 1780, it seemed (as he wrote to Governor Reed of Pennsylvania) as if "the maritime resources of Great Britain are more substantial than those of France and Spain combined and her riches are greater . . . in modern wars the longest purse must chiefly decide the issue. I fear that of the enemy will be found the longest."[4]

France's navy was about to display remarkable recuperative powers, but it was inferior to that of Britain and was obliged to adopt the tactics of a challenger who is not yet ready for a showdown. Where English admirals were eager to provoke a decisive engagement, their French counterparts were preoccupied with preserving their inferior numbers, keeping their fleets in being, and avoiding destructive cannonades. This defensive posture became such an ingrained habit of the French naval service that when, on several occasions, the French actually possessed naval superiority their admirals hesitated to take vigorous offensive action. In effect, this repudiated the concept of command of the sea.

The cost of empire in the 1770's and 1780's had to be reckoned in the currency of battleships and their crews. The ship of war had increased in size until it seemed to have reached the limit of usefulness in the three-decker. This veritable floating fortress carried one hundred or more guns. Only a handful of such naval behemoths were in commission, and most of them were British. The really effective weapon in the hands of an admiral, however, was not any single ship, no matter how powerful, but his "line of battle." This was composed of a file of warships of sixty guns or more in bowsprit-to-stern formation. In that way only, since all their guns fired in broadsides, could they cover one another and, with luck, maneuver and engage as a unit.

The workhorse of the battle line was the standard seventy-four-gun ship, which carried on the lower of its two gun-decks 28 cannon firing thirty-two-pound shot, with 28 more loaded with twenty-four or eighteen-pound cannonballs on its upper deck, and 18 nine-pounders on its upper works. The French favored heavier guns and more of them, and had built a number of eighty-gun ships, as well as the largest fighting machine of all, De Grasse's flagship, the one-hundred-and-ten-gun *Ville de Paris*. A line composed of seventy-fours and sixty-fours, with one or two three-deckers in the center, could only be challenged by a similar line roughly equal to it in length and fire power.

In order to provide the platform for so many heavy guns, ease of handling had to be ruthlessly sacrificed. The ships of the line were great tub-like hulks, "bloody floating barns," some called them, one hundred and seventy to one hundred and ninety feet long, with a beam ranging from fifty to seventy feet. Their three masts rose to heights almost equal to their water-line lengths. To manipulate the billowing canvas they carried took great amounts of both skill and muscular strength. Battleships were notoriously "dull and heavy" in responding to the helm. The straight lines of ships that are shown in the diagrams of naval battles are largely imaginary. Such lines, even in good weather, were very hard to form. The process might take hours; and sometimes it proved impossible to get balky ships into formation at all.

At one cable's length apart (seven hundred and twenty feet) a battle line of twenty ships extended for some three and a half nautical miles. At such distances, and with a primitive system of signalling (the French excelled the British in that department), there was constant trouble in transmitting the orders of the admirals to their subordinates. Instead of signal flags standing for letters and spelling out words, each flag stood for a particular maneuver and might have another meaning if hoisted at a different point on the ship's rigging. Such flag signals were often obscured in the smoke of battle, and messenger frigates had to dash up and down the line with the admiral's orders.

As a fighting machine, the warship of the period stood in almost constant need of repairs. It was said that the repairing of a wooden ship began on the day it was launched, and never ended. The hull was vulnerable, unless coppered, to dry rot and the attacks of the sea worm. In the tropics marine growths steadily cut down a vessel's speed, so that frequent careening was a necessity. Masts and rigging were not only subject to heavy damage in battles and storms; sometimes "one had but to fire a gun and a mast went by the board." Halyards and cables were made of hemp, which changed in length according to the amount of moisture in the air, sometimes tearing away the ironwork fastenings. Ropes of more than twenty inches in diameter and heavy when watersoaked took so much time to heave in that cables had to be cut when there was any need for haste. It was always a question how long a naval vessel could stay at sea without having recourse to a dockyard. One of the greatest deficiencies of the North American coast, from the naval point of view, was its lack of well-equipped naval bases. Halifax, Nova Scotia, was the lone British exception. As for the French, their best port for refitting was Boston.

Naval gunnery had only begun to become an exact science, and at the hands of the French. The British still aimed their cannon largely by guesswork. But since the range at which fleets engaged was ideally that of a musket shot, so that all arms could be brought to bear, and since the target presented by an opposing ship and its sails was about one hundred and eighty feet square, one could hardly help hitting something. In a single battle a three-decker might fire as many as three thousand cannonballs. Since no wooden ship had any armor, and because its decks were frequently crowded with soldiers as well as the six hundred to nine hundred sailors of its crew, the destruction wrought by a broadside could be fearful indeed. In Campbell's words: "The havock produced by a continuation of this mutual assault may be readily conjectured by the reader's imagination: battering, penetrating and splintering the sides and decks, shattering and dismounting the cannon; mangling and destroying the rigging; cutting asunder or carrying away the masts and yards; piercing and tearing the sails so as to render them useless; and wounding, disabling and killing the ship's company."[5]

Battle casualties of 20 to 30 percent or more were not uncommon when the range was short. Ships could engage at twenty five hundred to two thousand yards, and bring all their guns to bear at fifteen hundred to one thousand yards. "A close cannonade" would usually decide the issue between opposing ships before they came close enough to board. A ship's captain had the obligation, by strict naval etiquette, to display "extreme gallantry" (and also to avoid a court-martial) by fighting his craft to the last extremity. Only when totally dismasted, his guns silenced, and his decks running with gore, was a commander entitled to strike his colors with honor.

One perpetual source of worry at sea was the supply of food and drink, most of which had to be brought from long distances. This meant an endless battle to preserve salt meat and hard bread from decay; and references to "crawling, maggotty food" in naval documents are plentiful. "The sailor," says Michael Lewis, "had an invincible stomach which, ostrich-like, could well digest iron. He had to be like that, if he were to eat at all." The habitual refuge from salt food was drink, supplied to the crew in the daily grog, a mixture of a half-pint of rum with water. As for the officers, Hannay notes that "indulgence in fiery liquors had something to do with the prevalence of gout and stone among naval men." Water constantly became foul, and stayed that way. The failure of the beer supply to arrive was considered a valid reason for delaying an important sailing.

A diet so unbalanced by any standards brought on the disease which was the scourge of the sea-farer, the scurvy. According to testimony in the House of Commons in December, 1760, two-thirds of all sailors raised for the sea service in the last war (130,000 out of 185,000) had died of the scurvy and other diseases. The reliance for scurvy-prevention, while they lasted, was placed upon a ship's supplies of "beer and sour crout"; although it was known that "Peruvian bark, lemon and orange juice," lime juice and "good, sound, rough cider" were "great and peculiar antiseptics" for the purpose.[6] On a long voyage it might be expected that one-third to one-half of a ship's company would become scorbutic, and wind up in hospitals ashore, if they were fortunate enough to survive.

A man-of-war's accommodations below decks were incredibly cramped; and the stench which arose was, to a landsman, literally overpowering. As described by Fleming MacLiesh and Martin L. Krieger: "The men slept in hammocks some fourteen inches apart . . . A sailor lay there in his soaking wet clothes in the cold and darkness—no fires were permitted below—and the darkness dripped, because all wooden ships in fair weather or foul, continually leaked. There was a stench compounded of the reeking water in the bilge, of an accumulation of rotting refuse which was often swept into the ballast, of wet, close-packed men, lousy and flea-infested, who practically never changed their clothes, who seldom washed and for whom there were no facilities for bathing, a stench compounded by the decaying carcasses of drowned rats and other vermin below."[7] Perhaps the best comment on the state of affairs in the sailors' part of a warship is the astonishment which greeted Admiral Anson's announcement that he was going to make an inspection of his entire ship. It was said to be almost unprecedented for a commanding officer in the Royal Navy to descend into the body of his ship.

It is not surprising, then, that the navy became known as the "dread refuge of the disobedient and profligate," or that the men who manned the ships expected to be systematically swindled by those in authority. They lived in an age of both petty and large-scale corruption, when greedy men in high and middle places lined their pockets at the expense of those below them.

But the stage upon which all these men acted called for political and military and naval thespians of tall and broad dimensions. By the year 1780 the police action of 1775 in Massachusetts had spread to all the colonies, and "from America to Europe, from the English Channel to the Baltic, from the Bay of Biscay to the

Mediterranean, from the West Indies to the Mississippi, and ultimately involved the waters of the remote peninsula of Hindoo-
stan."[8] It had become a struggle of empires, the "fifth Anglo-
French war," and it called for statesmen, generals, admirals, and
men in lower ranks whose stature was imperial.

2

THE ACTORS—
THOUGH NOT IN ORDER
OF THEIR APPEARANCE

"Not one of the English statesmen in whose hands lay deci-
sions of policy affecting America had ever set foot upon
American soil."
                                              —Erich Eyck

In recent decades there has been a strong reaction against the
practice of earlier historians who recounted wars almost exclu-
sively in terms of kings, ministers, generals, and admirals. What
about the men in the ranks who did most of the actual fighting
and dying? The century of the common man has developed an
increasing curiosity about the common soldier and sailor, and not
without reason. What did they think about what they were doing? What were the motives and opinions of the men in the
lower echelons? Would that we knew more about what they
were in 1780-81!

The sad truth is that it was the men at the top who left most
of the records of what occurred, and of what they thought
about it. Part of the attractiveness of the eighteenth century for
many minds today lies in its pronounced individualism. In those
days, one feels, what a single leader thought and did really made
a difference. Thus with all the democratic good will in the
world, it is difficult for the chronicler to break away from the
ancient aristocratic pattern which portrays the general as winning the battle, not his troops; the admiral routing the enemy
fleet, not the gunners on his ships.

One reason for the rarity of accounts of battles written by
lowly individuals in the army and navy of the 1780's is that most

of them apparently felt that their views did not count for much. It was an age when the crucial decisions were made in secret by a small number of persons who believed themselves appointed to rule and command. Unlike their counterparts today, the holders of high office employed no corps of public relations officers to cosset the citizens. Admirals and generals were not obliged to take any great account of the opinions of their inferiors. They assumed that the ordinary seaman and the private soldier would gripe and grouse at them, of course; but when it came to orders the King and his appointed deputies had to be obeyed on pain of death.

A high percentage of the crew of any ship in the Royal Navy in 1780 had been dragooned into the service in one way or another. About half of them had probably been pressed, that is, had fallen victim to one of the savage press-gangs that roamed wherever seafaring men were to be found. They made their largest hauls from merchant ships, in which seamen preferred to serve because of the higher pay. A merchant sailor just in sight of home after a long voyage might find himself pressed, and an almost perpetual prisoner on a warship. Although the pressmen were not supposed to molest bona fide landsmen, they frequently snatched one off to sea, where he might be kept for six or seven years. Naturally such individuals sought to escape at the first opportunity.

The remainder of the crew was likely to be made up of hopeless debtors who had chosen the Navy as an alternative to prison, rogues, vagabonds, and other undesirables, aliens, with here and there a volunteer who had succumbed to the lure of a bounty. As Admiral Vernon once said: "The men on whom depended the liberties of our country were the only people who had no liberty at all."[1] Or, as Dr. Samuel Johnson put it, "Being in a ship is being in a jail, with the chance of being drowned."

Sailors and naval officers alike were the victims of a violent endurance contest with the elements, their harsh shipboard surroundings, and each other. As a class, able seamen were an uncouth lot, superstitious and extremely conservative in their adherence to custom, but daring in times of stress. Henry Fielding described them as thinking themselves "entirely discharged from the bonds of humanity" and glorying in "the language and behavior of savages" when on land, but "perfect masters of their business" at sea. Life in the forecastle reflected many of the worst characteristics of unrefined existence ashore: bad sanitation, loose morals, and a savage penal system. Discipline on shipboard was little short of ferocious; and at the hands of officers who were often as violent as their men. Their authority was absolute; and they made free use of both the gag (with a marlinspike) and the lash. A court-martial could condemn a sailor to be hung, or to be flogged to death (five hundred lashes). In 1775 flogging had been curbed somewhat by Article Four of the *Naval Rules*, which stated: "No Commander shall inflict any punishments upon a seaman beyond twelve lashes upon his bare back with a cat-o'-nine-tails."[2] Severer penalties should still be meted out by a court.

A famous "Naval Person" of our century, Sir Winston Churchill, has summed up life in the navy of this period as consisting of "Gin, women, and the lash." A more drastic form of escape than the first two of these was supplied by desertion, which reached fantastic proportions in the Royal Navy during the American war. No words can be more eloquent on the topic than the figures for the years 1775-80. During that period, the number of men "raised for the King's navy" was 176,145, of whom only 1,243 were killed by the enemy, while 18,543 died of disease and other causes, and 42,069 deserted. In attempting to account for this extraordinary total, Dr. John Campbell noted that it was "during a war with people who spoke the same language, and bore the same general features and character . . ." so that "it was found extremely difficult to prevent the desertion of our seamen."[3]

Lest it be supposed that the naval officer occupied a vocational bed of roses, it should be pointed out that he shared many of the grueling conditions of life at sea with the crew; and also had problems of his own. One of them was "employment" by the Admiralty, possibly leading to promotion in rank, which in both the British and French navies was painfully slow. When not on board ship, the commissioned officer was entitled to a "retainer" in the form of half-pay. The crews were paid off at the end of each voyage; the officers remained in service, and naturally came to believe that they *were* the Royal Navy.

But in time there came to be many more individuals holding
the various rankings, all the way from midshipman to full admiral, than there were posts to be filled, especially in time of
peace. Of sixty admirals in 1780 only twenty were employed.
Thus there was intense competition for active-service appointments; and an officer had to summon all the influence he could
muster in order to secure a post, hold onto it, and advance in it.
In England, this could be done most expeditiously by "procuring the influence" of one of the great families. The country was
ruled by those who owned its land, the "gentlemen of estate";
and, according to Professor J. H. Plumb, "Church, army, navy,
the Plantations, the Court and the administration had become a
vast racket that provided relief to needy younger sons and dependent cousins." Ships and regiments and seats in Parliament,
too, "were property—property that belonged by divine, hereditary right to the ruling classes."[4] In France it was much the
same. There the choice naval appointments were believed to be
determined similarly by "friends at Court."

British naval officers of high rank frequently complicated matters of preferment by seeking election to the House of Commons, thereby mixing politics and war. Nearly all the famous
admirals of the century—Anson, Hawke, Keppel, Howe, St.
Vincent and Rodney—simultaneously held House seats and sea
commands. This was made possible by the spasmodic character
of their active service; there was plenty of time for most of them
to be both admiral and politician. An officer with direct political
influence made his position at sea more secure. When there was
washing of the navy's dirty linen in public he could defend his
professional conduct against partisan attacks. In the long run,
however, the political admiral had a ruinous effect upon naval
morale. When employment by the Admiralty became a partisan
matter some of England's best naval leaders were kept idle solely
because they held the wrong political views.

British naval officers were supposed to be the sons of gentlemen, and strenuous efforts were made to attract scions of noble
families, but with relatively scant success. Service in the army
was far more attractive to the young lord. As Professor Graham
indicates: "The English people of the sixteenth century had no
great tradition of the sea to compare, for example, with that of

the Scandinavians . . . The forbears of the Hoods, of Nelson, St. Vincent, Howe, Collingwood and Blake, were country gentlemen, solicitors, or parsons, with no great sea record behind them."[5]

The crews of eighteenth-century battleships were not the only ones who were subject to discipline. If they feared their officers, and if the lower ranks of officers feared the higher, even the admirals were not exempt from fear of the court martial and its consequences. For it was an era when, according to the naval historian W. L. Clowes: "The British Navy was honeycombed with distrust, falling little short of panic." This was because the rigid enforcement of the *Fighting Instructions* and the Articles of War "in the letter rather than the spirit" had convinced most of the high-ranking officers that blame was what was to be avoided at all costs.

The *Fighting Instructions*, which had become "as narrowing as a pair of handcuffs," had originated in Henry VIII's *Orders to be Used by the King's Majesty's Navy* in 1530. They had merely instructed his admirals "to apply to get the wind of the enemy," leaving "each captain free to choose any antagonist that he considers an equal match." Not until 1653, under Cromwell, did the key doctrine of the "line-ahead" come to the fore. "All the ships of every squadron," said the rule, "shall endeavor to keep in line with the chief" under penalty of "severest punishment."[6] Along with this dogma of the line-ahead went a tight restriction of the previous maxim "Choose every man his bird"; for each ship was now obligated to engage its opposite number in the enemy line, beginning with the van, flagship against flagship, and so on to the rear. A numerically inferior fleet must extend its line to become conterminous with that of the enemy, for fear of being "doubled," that is, having its rear attacked on both sides by the "extra" enemy ships.

These rules were promulgated as obligatory by Charles, Duke of York, as Lord High Admiral in 1665, and further revised by Vice Admiral George Rooke in 1703, remaining in force with little change for nearly a century. They were by no means confined to the British Navy. French admirals and captains received *Instructions* in 1765 that were just as detailed and rigid as those which prevailed in England. Admiral de Grasse himself is credited with the dictum: "As long as men-of-war carry their main armament in broadside batteries, there could never be any battle order but the single line ahead."[7]

In both countries the established code had become sacrosanct, and had the force of law. The result, says Chatterton, was "formalism, conventionalism, lack of imagination . . . a naval officer considered it almost better to fight and lose a battle 'according to instructions' than to win one on disapproved principles. It was all as prim and perfunctory as a minuet; as stiff as the manners ashore were insincere."[8] Any unauthorized departure from what was ordained could receive punishment all the way from a public reprimand to death before a firing squad. The eighteenth century was dotted with such courts-martial, the most fearsome of which was the execution of Admiral the Honorable John Byng in 1757 for "negligence" against the French off Minorca, principally because he departed from the orthodox line-ahead.

There were reasons, of course, for this exaggerated reverence for the line. It was rooted, as De Grasse said, in the fact that a ship's guns could fire only at right angles to its course. If a formation was to be handled as a unit, and was to engage the enemy to the best possible advantage to itself, its commander must be able to count upon each of his captains to hold his position in line, so that its aggregate fire-power could be aimed in the same direction. The alternative was a grand melee over which the admiral felt he would have no control.

But the great disadvantage of the line ahead was pungently stated by the future Lord St. Vincent to Hood: "I have often told you that two fleets of equal force can never produce decisive events unless they are equally determined to fight it out, or the commander-in-chief of one of them *bitches* it so as to misconduct his line"[9] (Italics his). The privilege of deciding whether or not to attack was confined to the squadron to the windward; but the ships to the leeward enjoyed the counter-privilege of bearing away and escaping, unless they were slower sailers than their opponents. The French were notorious for preferring the leeward position, parrying the attack and saving their ships.

3

ARCHITECTS OF DEFEAT:
GEORGE III AND LORD NORTH

"None of these names will be pronounced with enthusiasm by posterity." —Sir Nathaniel William Wraxall

Every time another American takes the trouble to read the whole of the Declaration of Independence, the public image of King George III as a contemptible tyrant and arch-enemy of liberty is refurbished. And this in spite of all the corrective efforts of historians on both sides of the Atlantic. Even during his own lifetime, that monarch had a bad press; and after his death his detractors got a big head start on his defenders, since the papers of the opposition were the first to become available and the Whig historians made the best of their advantage. During the last hundred years there have been marked revisions in posterity's estimate of "the King who lost America." He has become, as one historian put it, "the historians' whetstone." Some even suggest that the whitewashing of George III has gone too far.[1]

Speaking with legalistic strictness, everything that any Britisher did in uniform during the American Revolution was the act of his king. But no one any longer thinks of George III as an absolute despot, a sort of British Nero, with an insatiable lust for personal power over the colonists. The king was actually a strange mixture of Tory and Whig, for he believed himself to be a constitutional, that is, a self-limiting monarch, the incarnation of the true will of his people. But he thought of the latter as being constituted by the ruling, or propertied, class who were fully entitled to enjoy their aristocratic privileges. And he did become an active chief executive of his realm, especially in the choosing and retaining of his ministers, who must also have the backing of a majority in Parliament.

Everything seemed to favor the grandson of George II when he came to the throne in 1760 at the age of twenty-two. Unlike the preceding Hanoverian kings, he had been born and educated in England, proudly felt himself an Englishman, and had no competing heir in sight around whom an opposition clique might rally. He had, however, as Wraxall says, been brought up "in a state of almost absolute seclusion from the world" by his mother the Princess Dowager in the hope that he might escape contamination by the evil influences of young men of his own age. His mother has been described as "a narrow-minded intriguing woman, with the Continental notion of the relations between royalty and the rest of mankind . . . . ambitious to see her son govern as arbitrarily as the Elector of Saxony."[2] She "kept him in the nursery till within two years of the time he mounted the throne." His principal tutor was Lord Waldegrave, who later testified that he "found His Royal Highness uncommonly full of princely prejudices, contracted in the nursery, and improved by the society of bedchamber women and pages of the backstairs."[3]

The results of this sort of royal education were summed up in one of the letters of "Junius": "Secluded from the world, attached in infancy to one set of persons, and one set of ideas, he can neither open his heart to new connexions, nor his mind to better information. A character of this sort is the soil fittest to product an obstinate bigotry in politics and religion . . ." At the same time the king's schooling did produce a few public and many private virtues. George III was "shy and backward, not a wild, dissipated boy, but good-natured and cheerful, with a serious cast on the whole . . . he was genuinely religious, exceedingly abstemious in his habits, and entirely decorous in his mode of life."[4] But, as Sir Lewis Namier has pointed out, "The biggest blunders in the world are committed by men with serious faces who feel uncomfortable in their own minds, talk a great deal, and never enjoy themselves." George III was conscientiously well-intentioned to the point of acute self-righteousness. He was so aware of his own rectitude that he could not bear the thought of defeat by those whose intentions were so obviously evil. Unfortunately, as time went on, this purity of purpose with regard to ends did not always extend to his choices of means, for he proved to be "willing, when it came to the point, to fight corruption with corruption."

The sad truth about the king was that the purity and integrity of his intentions did not keep him from being ignorant, narrow-minded, and unimaginative in his approach to the practical politics of doing what he thought was good. So he became, in the words of W. Bonham Dunne, "a blunt, busy, shrewd, but not very sagacious man; one well acquainted with public business—better versed in it indeed than many of his advisers—a restless, inquisitive man . . . rising early, and, when work was to be done, sitting up late . . . punctual, even minute in his transacting of business . . . a good hater."[5] Among the things which he hated, and for which he also had an utter contempt, were innovation, America, Catholics, and France. "Like tens of thousands of his ale-swilling subjects," says Pemberton, "he took one redcoat to be a match for any three mounseers, and any British frigate more than a match for the finest ship of war as ever put out from Cadiz harbor."[6] As for the Americans: "They are a sad nest."

Coming to the throne just before the triumphant ending of the most successful war in British history, George III was said to possess finer prospects than any king since Charles II had returned from exile exactly one hundred years earlier. Yet "never was a youthful dream so turned to ashes, never was a noble purpose so twisted and torn as it began to move and assert itself in the world of concrete things—began to struggle in a world of tricks and chances."[7] For it was not long before this promising and virtuous young sovereign was being ridiculed as "Farmer George"; and Byron could write in *The Vision of Judgment:*

> A better farmer ne'er brushed dew from lawn,
> A worse king never left a realm undone!

What can account for this astonishing reversal of judgment? From 1714 to 1760 England had been ruled by an oligarchy of the great Whig families governing through relatively supine monarchs in the name of the Glorious Revolution of 1688. With

the accession of George III there came a social, economic, and
political change of atmosphere which historians have exhaus-
tively debated, especially since the application of "structural
analysis" to the problem by Sir Lewis Namier and his followers.
Was the new king simply determined "to rule as well as reign"
by expanding the royal prerogative? Or was he merely trying to
rescue the just powers of the monarchy from the intrenched
abuses of an overweening oligarchy?

Now it is not necessary to decide whether his grandfather
George II had actually been "enslaved" or "enchained" by the
Whig grandees who wanted "to make a pageant of the throne"
to the point where that sovereign protested that "Ministers are
kings in England." What counted was George III's *belief* that
something like that had occurred, and that it was high time that
the king was set free. The important thing was his own resolve
never to endure involuntary domination of any kind from any
quarter. He thought that he was merely recovering the lost constitutional powers of the throne: to be served by ministers of his
own choosing without regard to party, and directly responsible
to himself. But the catch was that, at least after George I's day,
the king's ministers must also be backed by a majority in Parliament. It was George III's fate to come to power in the middle of
a transition toward a mixed form of English government which
was to be both personally royal and at the same time parliamentary, although not yet the rule of a collective cabinet.
Furthermore, his government had to be operated by an aristocratic ruling class slowly emerging from feudalism and unwit-
tingly on its way toward increased responsiveness to middle-class
public opinion. Among these proud patricians George III would
have to find ministers possessing absolute loyalty to him, popularity in Parliament, and talent in administering a complex and
far-flung colonial empire. But it was his tragedy that there was
not among them a war leader of even moderate ability, since
during his reign, "mediocrity and incapacity prevailed in the
councils of State."[8]

It was this ambiguity in the constitutional positions of the
King, Parliament, and people which enabled George III to
arrive at his conception of the proper royal role in government,
and to talk, as Namier remarks, "flapdoodle of the most innocent

kind about the Constitution." For it was his firm belief that, in exacting loyalty and obedience to the Crown, he was really demanding it in the name of Parliament, which was to him the voice of the only people who counted, namely, the propertied class. Actually Parliament, says Guttridge, "consisted at the time almost entirely of a small governing class monopolizing the seats in both houses. Closely connected by birth, by education, and by interest, the vast majority of members reflected in their outlook the complacency natural to an aristocracy that had seen the country victorious far and wide . . ."[9]

When the American rebellion flared in 1775, the prevailing British idea of empire was that of the author of the Stamp Act, the Honorable George Grenville: "a supreme center and subordinate parts." The apex of the hierarchy of power was the Crown; but it was "the *Parliamentary* right inherent in the mother country to tax her American colonies" (italics mine) which George III saw to be at stake. On this point there could be no compromise; for it was the order of things established by God Himself, and in preserving it, the King "relied above all upon the assistance of Divine Providence." The monarch had an almost mystical belief in the complete unanimity of the virtuous King and a free and independent Parliament, together constituting the sovereignty of Great Britain. As he wrote to Lord Sandwich on July 1, 1775: "My fixed resolution is either to bring the colonies to obedience to the legislature of the mother country or to cast them off."[10]

Some Americans believed for a time that independence might be obtained by playing off against one another the three sources of their oppression: the "tyrant" king, his "wicked" ministers, and the "corrupt" Parliament. After all, there was no written constitution to tell them which one of the three was robbing them of their liberties as Englishmen. But George III stoutly resisted any attempt to separate himself and his servants from what he regarded as the voice of his people, although some historians have held that he might have come to advantageous terms with his transatlantic subjects by so doing. Instead, he doggedly regarded himself as "King of America by Act of Parliament"; while the American rebels, thanks mainly to John Locke, did not see him in that light at all. To their enlightened minds he was, until the Declaration of Independence, "King of America by virtue of a compact freely entered into between their ancestors and the former kings of England." The terms of that contract they said, he had grievously violated, thereby rendering it null and void.

George III could hardly be blamed for failing to recognize himself in any such role. Consciously or not, he had chosen for himself the part of Bolingbroke's "Patriot King," fighting "the battle of the legislature" on behalf of his people, and not of himself. His empire must be preserved in a state of proper obedience by ministerial servants chosen by himself without regard to party, and Parliament would naturally provide them with a stable majority. This dream of a "purified" and incorruptible non-partisan government gained in attractiveness at a time when political jobbery was rife and party labels had become indistinct. Whiggism in power looked much the same as Toryism; and when the Whigs were in opposition in 1780, says Guttridge, they attacked "the machine created by their own party under George II."

What had happened was that England had evolved a multi-party political system composed of numerous "connections" grouped around powerful leaders. Such a situation cried out to be managed. But George III preferred not to do his part of the managing by meeting with a collectively responsible Cabinet. He preferred to transact business with individual ministers to whom he gave audience in one of the rooms or closets of his palace. This meant that access to "The King's Closet" became a matter of the highest political privilege and importance. It gave to the royal personage all the advantages of privacy and strictly oral agreements; and it emphasized personal loyalty of the ministerial servant to his master to the point where George III spoke of Lord North's eventual resignation as "desertion."

When it came down to the practical politics of maintaining a supposedly "nonpartisan" majority for the King's measures in Commons, the high-minded George III found himself relying in actuality upon a new political party which he himself had created, "The King's Friends." All other groupings were denounced as mere "faction." Professing to put an end to Whig bossism and corruption, the King himself wound up as an "ignoble Parliamentary boss" of a "brute majority" kept tractable by every known variety of "influence." What George III had done was to take over the only known way of managing Parliament, the old Whig system of place and patronage, thereby involving himself in the same corrupt methods the Whig oligarchs had used. He did not, in Namier's words, ever leave "the safe ground of constitutional government, but merely acted the *primus inter pares*, the first among the borough-mongering, electioneering gentlemen of England." As Trevelyan said, it was not that the King initiated corruption, but he "protected and prolonged a bad system which, but for him, would have died an earlier death by at least sixteen years."[11]

Once having managed to assemble a majority in Parliament who agreed that, in the American revolt, their authority, identical with his own, was being traitorously challenged, the whole conflict became a matter of national and individual honor. "As between gentlemen of the 18th century," says Pemberton, "there was only one way by which such niceties could be settled—the sword, as between nations it seemed almost hopeless to expect any milder alternative."[12] This relieved the King and his supporters from any obligation to understand the actual grievances of the Americans. It was enough that they had defied royal, lawful authority. As George III himself said: "Blows must decide." It was his personal resolution, he declared, "to part with his life rather than suffer his dominions to be dismembered."

Having taken this intransigent stand, there could be no turning back for a king of George III's disposition. The kindlier among his critics have said that "frequently he adhered too pertinaciously to his determinations"; while the less kindly disposed have spoken of his "immature, unbalanced, passionate obstinacy."[13] His tutor Lord Waldegrave had observed that in his youth, George III "did not want resolution, but it is mixed with too much obstinacy. . . Whenever he is displeased . . . he becomes sullen and silent and retires to his closet." These tendencies he did not, unfortunately, outgrow. In the early stages of the American rebellion, he expressed the hope to Lord Sandwich on January 11, 1776, that "the English lion, when roused, has not only his wonted resolution, but has added the swiftness of the racehorse." Throughout the war the King was very impatient for quick results: "I sigh for action," he said. On another occasion he commented: "Decision is the joy of my life . . . when once those rebels have felt a smart blow they will submit."[14]

George III took a great personal interest in the Royal Navy on parade, and evidently enjoyed the sort of deafening uproar which greeted him on the occasion of his review of the fleet at Spithead on June 29, 1773, commencing with "a triple discharge of 232 pieces of cannon, followed by 21 guns from each of the forts, from each of 20 ships of the line, repeated when the Royal Standard was raised on the *Barfleur*, given again by all ships as the Queen's health was drunk, and again for the King's and the same salutes on his coming out as on his coming in." The King never failed to "express the highest approbation of the good order and discipline of his fleet; the excellent condition of the dockyard, arsenals, and garrison, and the regularity with which everything was conducted." As one of his princess-daughters remarked: "The dear old King was very fond of his Navy."[15]

This enthusiasm did not, unfortunately, make the king a very good judge of the performance of his ministers who were directly responsible for the conduct of the war. What he chiefly demanded of them was wholehearted agreement with his policy of coercion of the colonies by force of arms. This made partial hypocrites out of some of his ablest lieutenants. But its effect upon the opposition was nothing short of disastrous. Once victory over the Americans had been made a patriotic issue involving the honor of the Crown, there could be no truly loyal opposition to the King. Anyone who ventured to suggest that independence might be granted to the Americans in any conceivable circumstances was immediately branded as unpatriotic and even traitorous. Those critics of his ministers, and they became fairly numerous, who went so far as to rejoice at the news of American victories seemed to George III to be wantonly exposing Britain to contempt and a loss of national prestige.

It will not do to press the matter too far, but there was to be some truth in the contention that it was at Yorktown that the Whig opposition triumphed over George III.

LORD NORTH

Frederick North, the eighth Lord North, was born about two months after George Washington in 1732. His family had belonged to the peerage for about two centuries, but his title was a courtesy one until the death of his father, the Earl of Guildford, in 1790. This permitted Frederick to stay in the House of Commons with all the extra advantages of noble birth. He had arrived upon the scene at a time when the British aristocracy was coming to the peak of its influence. "Never at home did it enjoy," says W. Baring Pemberton, "such uncontested reversions to the thousand and one places and sinecures which made the task of governing congenial and in not a few cases made existence possible."[16]

On his way to an assured political career, Frederick North passed through Eton and Trinity College, Oxford, and, like other young men of the ruling class, made the Grand Tour of European capitals before returning to a safe seat in the House of Commons from Banbury. In 1756 he married an unprepossessing heiress named Anne Speke, aged sixteen, said to enjoy an income of four thousand pounds a year, with expectations of a greater legacy to come, which did not materialize. A contemporary describes North as having "large legs, walks heavily, manners clumsy, very large features, thick lips, wide mouth, high forehead, large nose, eyes not lively." The lack of physical beauty in both Lord and Lady North was legendary, and became for him a source of merriment. For North was nothing if not amiable. That trait accounts in part for his extraordinary personal popularity in Parliament. Few leaders have been subjected to more vituperative abuse than North, but he seemed to be able to absorb unlimited punishment. He was a hard man to ruffle; and there were times when he seemed to carry the day by his sheer facetiousness. "Happen what will," said Mr. Thomas Townsend, "the noble Lord is ready with his joke."

George III's accession to the throne in 1760 began for Lord North a twenty-year period of domination by a stronger will, which left him with the reputation of having been little more than a royal puppet. It revealed the greatest flaw in his character:

his incurable tendency to rely upon the judgment of others whom he believed to be superior to himself. Among them, he assumed that he owed supreme fidelity to his sovereign, who in turn was committed to constitutional, that is, to royal-Parliamentary government as then practiced.

North entered public office as a junior Lord of the Treasury, where he made a solid reputation for both competence and prudence, and was already marked down as a young man to watch. In October, 1767, he rose to become Chancellor of the Exchequer, and prepared the next fourteen budgets for his country's finances. At almost the same time he took over the leadership of the House of Commons, which he was to retain for the same period. His domination of the House for this long tenure in times of trouble has been attributed to a combination of "leadership, imperturbable affability and a sense of humor."

In 1770 North became George III's First Minister, inaugurating the so-called "King's system of government," in which the test of patriotism was not party, but personal loyalty to the Crown. There also began a scheme of administration by separate, self-contained and "equal" departments, "whose point of contact was [the King's] Closet rather than Downing Street." North insisted upon regarding himself as only one among the King's servants, preferring to call himself "the King's agent or man of business." This meant that there was, in the modern sense, no Prime Minister; which is another way of saying that George III attempted to become his own Prime Minister and largely succeeded.

As for the other members of the Cabinet, said Wraxall, "they were in fact rather North's co-equals than his subordinates, as they ought to have been; and the public service often suffered, as I well know, from their want of union, or from their clashing interests and private animosities." North did not undertake the vital "superintending duties" of the King's First Minister; he did not, "like the great Earl of Chatham, sufficiently coerce the other members of the Cabinet."[17] It could be said that he did not coerce them at all; for on one occasion North boasted: "I have never interfered with any of their departments." As Dundas remarked in a Commons debate on December 12, 1781, "Lord North lacked only one quality to render him a great and distinguished statesman, I mean, a more despotic and commanding temper."

Given North's personal qualities, "his well-known indolence, his conciliatory disposition, his disinclination to make decisions," the result was a fatal amount of sheer inaction at a time when action was imperative. As the Lord Chancellor, Lord Thurlow, railed in exasperation at North's inactivity: "Damn him, nothing can goad him forward, he is the very clog that loads every-thing."[18] It was often the case that what North and other ministers failed to do, simply did not get done. In time of peace, this might be tolerated; but as John Robinson, M.P., his right-hand man, wrote to Lord Sandwich on August 18, 1777: "War can't be carried on by departments."[19] As the conflict broadened and deepened, the government's sins of omission became more numerous and more serious. With the mounting pressure of events Lord North became subject to fits of depression, moody silences and a near-paralysis of the will. He remained in office because his fidelity and tenacity had made him indispensable to the King, and because his debating skill along with Germain's insured a "brute majority" in Parliament.

Much has been made of the corrupt and non-representative character of the House of Commons in North's day. "It was, to say the least," says Pemberton, "not a high-minded age," nor a heroic one. The First Minister himself has never been accused of profiting directly from what went on, but it has been widely implied that North's majorities over the years were bought by various forms of "the King's influence" or worse, that is, by outright bribery. There were, in fact, in Parliament around two hundred placemen from the so-called "rotten boroughs," who were morally (or immorally) bound to do their patron's bidding. Much money was spent on certain elections; but the total num-ber of all votes that were purchasable by some variety of pay-ment never amounted to a majority of the five hundred and fifty-eight members of the House. The noble Lord's majorities were solidly and prosaically based upon "the independent country members," the "stolid foxhunters," the "squires anxious to get back to their gun-rooms."[20] Their interests for the most part were not imperial, but parochial. They simply regarded Lord North as the best qualified and most honest person in

sight to be the King's chief hired man. The sad fact is that the
leadership he provided was also stolid and parochial, too preoccupied with narrow interests to govern an empire.

As First Lord of the Treasury, North was also predisposed to
strict economy. In pursuit of that goal he allowed his hopes for
a cheap peace to obscure his vision of the future. Obsessed with
the urgent necessity of paying off a large slice of the national
debt, in 1772 he held out the hope that one and one-half million
pounds could be devoted to that purpose. Moreover he proposed
to take about half of that sum from the budget of the Royal
Navy. That would have obliged the decommissioning of four
of the twenty guardships, "the very cornerstone of Britain's
naval might." To justify such a step, he said that "he could not
recollect to have seen a more pacific appearance of affairs than
there is." Only firm opposition by Lord Sandwich and others
prevented North's plan from being carried out in that year; but
in 1774 came a step called "imprudent to the point of folly."
This was the reduction of the Navy's personnel from twenty
thousand to sixteen thousand men. Nothing could have contributed more drastically and fatally to Britain's unpreparedness
for war only one year later. In the Royal Navy, especially, the
cry for more seamen became deafening, and it continued
throughout the war.

When it came to the point of peace or war with the American
colonists North was anything but a jingo. After it was virtually
all over, on December 12, 1781, he told Parliament that the war
"had never been a favorite of his; he had always considered it as
a war of the most cruel necessity, but at the same time as a war
founded upon a truly British basis: a war instituted in support
of the just rights of the Crown and of the Parliament of Great
Britain."[21] As minister he was always hoping for moderation
and conciliation; but "he saw America in the same half-light as
the King . . . It is one of the grimmest jests in history," says
Pemberton, that North took the measures which brought on the
Boston Tea Party; and then discovered that force must be used to
restore the "just dependence of the colonies upon the Crown and
Parliament of Great Britain." The misguided colonists must be
taught a lesson. It mattered little that he also declared that "no
method of punishment ever came from him but with great

regret." Once he had committed himself to coercive measures, he saw that they must be pressed far enough to be effective. This made him, with his conception of absolute loyalty, the secure prisoner of George III's obstinacy. Before he knew it, North found himself bracketed with his royal master and Lord Germain as a symbol of a "never-independence-for-America-under-any-circumstances" doctrine, probably against his own better judgment.

It never occurred to any of these exalted aristocrats that some form of federation might have been negotiated that would have kept America within the British empire. The very notion that "the inhabitants of His Majesty's Plantations were to be considered in any sense the equals of the governing classes at home would have been taken as a joke in very poor taste." The idea "of sitting down on equal terms with the Adamses, the Rutledges, and the Otises would to England's patrician statesmen have appeared as ludicrous as the proposal that they should marry their mistresses."[22]

4

ARCHITECTS OF DEFEAT: LORDS GERMAIN AND SANDWICH

"Lord George Germain and the Earl of Sandwich mark the nadir of British military competence." —J. H. Plumb

"The man primarily responsible for Britain's defeat in the American Revolution" was, according to the book jacket of a recent English biography of the gentleman, Lord George Germain. That may be a slight exaggeration, yet he is certainly a promising candidate for the grim distinction. Lord North's recent biographer, W. Baring Pemberton, agrees that Germain "may be said to have contributed as much as any one man" to the result of the war.

Germain was the third son of the seventh Earl of Dorset (later Duke), and during his life had no less than three different legal identities. He was born Lord George Sackville in 1716, and bore that name until 1769, when he received an estate and a large legacy from Lady Betty Germain on condition that he adopt her family name. From that time on throughout the American war he was Lord George Germain, until his much-debated elevation to the House of Lords as first Viscount Sackville in 1783, a title he bore until his death in 1785.

Lord George grew up in that "fortress of aristocratic security," the great house of Knole, with its fifty-two staircases, three hundred and sixty-five rooms, and four acres of buildings. Of the Earl of Dorset's three sons, he was esteemed "the most talented and steady," capable of "hard work when the mood struck him." At an early age he developed that air of arrogance toward most of humanity, and those capacities to drink, gamble, and swear which were expected of a proper lord. His schooling at West-minster ended at fourteen, when he went with his father, the new Lord Lieutenant, to Ireland, where George attended Trinity College, Dublin, described as "half beer garden, half brothel" until he was eighteen years of age.

Soon he entered the army and began to move upward. At twenty-five he was a lieutenant colonel, and went with George II as aide-de-camp on a campaign against the French. He was seriously wounded in the breast at the battle of Fontenoy in 1745; and in the next few years he served under the Duke of Cumberland in Scotland and on the Continent. When not in the field, he sat in the House of Commons for Dover and made a good impression as an incisive speaker. At age thirty-four he was back in Ireland with his father again, this time as Secretary at War for that unhappy country. At the time, Dublin society was noted for its excessive eating and drinking, and "the love of the sexes," we are told, "was much indulged in . . . Horns sprouting abundantly."

By this time Lord Sackville had acquired a lasting reputation for cold haughtiness. As Horace Walpole observed: "He never had the art of conciliating affection . . . His pride, which was naturally very great, grew into a most intolerable insolence."[1] In 1754 he achieved "the stabilizing propriety of marriage" with Diana Sambrooke, adequately well-born and well-to-do, who bore him five children before her death at forty-seven in 1778. The family's second tour of duty in Ireland ended in unpopu-larity to the point of mob violence over the control of taxation, which drove father and son back to London, and resulted in the Duke's dismissal.

But Lord George was now a major general; and his military prestige could hardly be impaired by a merely political fiasco. He was anxious for service on the Continent, "where military reputations were won," and men fought according to the book, rather than in wild America, "where they were easily lost." Nevertheless it was in Germany at Minden on August 1, 1759, that Lieutenant General Lord George Sackville was suddenly to lose his own burgeoning military prestige. He was second in command to the Duke of Marlborough, who was serving under

Prince Ferdinand of Brunswick, the allied commander-in-chief. Lord George was in charge of the British cavalry behind a ridge on the right wing; and when the French infantry gave way, he was given repeated orders by Prince Ferdinand to attack at once. Sackville became confused; there was a half-hour's delay; and the almost certain destruction of the enemy was thereby prevented.

Lord George was brought to trial by court-martial. Throughout the proceedings he assumed "a dictatorial style to the court . . . browbeat witnesses, and used the judge-advocate with contempt." He was found guilty of disobedience, and "adjudged unfit to serve His Majesty in any military capacity whatsoever." It is said that George II struck him off the Army List and the Privy Council books with his own hand, and dismissed him from all his various State employments netting him over six thousand pounds a year.

It was a sentence of which Germain was to be reminded again and again by Opposition speakers and editors for all the rest of his active life. By this prodigious fall from royal favor and professional position, he found himself "in Coventry with eight-tenths of England"; yet he refused to hide or go abroad. He never forgave those who brought about his downfall; and the experience seems not to have taught him the least degree of spiritual humility. Even though Shelburne said that "No man would be seen to speak to him in the House of Commons,"[2] he was determined to brazen things out by standing for re-election and by attending the sessions.

Most of all he placed his hopes of climbing (or crawling) back into favor upon the then Prince of Wales. When the latter became King George III, Germain, still "proud, haughty, and desperate," saw his chance to obtain some kind of civil employment for his restless talents. The rebellion of what he called "the American peasants" was brewing; and Lord George was shrewd enough to see that George III was eventually bound to welcome anyone who would champion the right of Crown and Parliament to rule the colonies by force of arms. He had by this time acquired the name of Germain, which had the advantage of not reminding everyone that he was "the coward of Minden." He had also substantially decreased his personal unpopularity by a duel with Captain George Johnstone, an M.P. who had in-sulted him; so that, as Walpole commented, in some eyes "Lord George Germain is a hero, whatever Lord George Sackville may have been."[3]

With the benefit of this partial rehabilitation, Germain went to work to demonstrate the soundness of his claim to the leadership of the "war party" against America, avoiding factional entanglements in the process. The fact that he knew almost nothing about the Americans did not deter him from being "at his most authoritarian, vociferous, and inflexible" in rejecting their every protest. Such ungrateful children of the mother country must obviously be chastised "with Roman severity" and brought back to their senses, and their duties, by military force; and that was exactly the doctrine of the King. According to Walpole, Germain won George III's favor by invoking "fire and sword against the Bostonians." He would offer them only two alternatives: ruin or submission. After Bunker Hill, Germain was all for "exerting the utmost force of this Kingdom to finish this rebellion in one campaign." Plainly here was a man after the King's own heart.

By the sheer reiteration of his demands for extreme measures against the rebels, Germain came to be regarded in Parliament as something of an expert on American affairs, as well as one restored to good standing at Court. Fortunately for him, Lord North found himself sorely in need of an effective spokesman in Commons to meet the attacks upon the King's aggressive American policy. A majority of the members were willing to go along with a firm assertion of their supremacy over the colonists, but relatively few were as truly enthusiastic as Germain at the prospect of waging a civil war. As time went on, Lord North, who himself regarded the suppression of the American rebellion in the light of a regrettable necessity, became more and more impressed with Germain's imposing, self-assured manners and imperious strength of will as qualifications for office. The choice was Lord North's, but it had the approval of the King.

On November 10, 1775, Lord George Germain was appointed to "relieve" the hesitant Lord Dartmouth, who had a distaste for coercing the Americans, as Secretary of State for the Colonies. That office soon became known as the Secretary of State for American Affairs, largely responsible for the direction of the overseas war. The disobedient general of Minden was now the virtual commander-in-chief of the armies of England and the principal determiner of their strategy. Not everyone had forgotten his earlier misstep, for the contemporary historian Belsham commented: "The most odious of tasks was assigned to the most odious of instruments."[4]

But Germain's rise to top military power did not happen overnight. He had first to fight to establish his "third" secretaryship on a par with the two "ancient" ministries of state held by the Earl of Suffolk "for the North" and Lord Weymouth "for the South." The colonial secretaryship had only been in existence since 1768. Edmund Burke explained its creation by saying: "The two secretaries are doing nothing, so a third was appointed to help them."[5] That was a partisan exaggeration, but it did betray a principal reason for setting up a third ministry, namely —to create additional fees and patronage. But the senior ministers were extremely jealous of their new colleague, who drained away some of their fees and sinecures, and whose office they ardently hoped to abolish. Every move by Germain was regarded as an encroachment upon their domains.

The principal point at issue in their running feud with the new minister concerned his right to give orders to the Admiralty and the War Office regarding the transport of troops to and from the colonies, a function previously exercised by the Southern department. Whoever wielded this power could direct the course of the war in America. Germain never thought of himself for one moment as anything but the equal of the other two Secretaries of State. He refused to allow himself to be boxed in by the narrow interpretation of colonial or American affairs, which would have permitted him to control the soldiers and sailors only *after* their arrival overseas upon the orders of some other department. With cold aggressiveness he seized control of the areas under dispute and would not be dislodged. In point of fact it was he who gave most of the orders for the sending of troops, ships, and supplies to America throughout the war. This does not mean that he made the decisions unaided, since matters of high strategy were usually discussed with the King, Lord North, and the Cabinet at its weekly meetings.

Since during the early years of the struggle with the colonists,

American affairs were paramount in British politics, Germain became not only the equal of his ministerial colleagues, but actually their superior. Thanks to the vacuum created by Lord North's failure to take the lead and the King's strong backing, Germain became, as Temple Luttrell said in Parliament, "the chief minister for the civil war." This came close to making him "the principal Secretary of State," for his department was "the pivot upon which the entire organization of resistance to colonial independence turned."[6] By comparison, Lord Barrington as Secretary at War had very little real authority.

Germain had won his battle for ministerial supremacy, but this did not mean that he had found the ideal formula for administering a colonial war. For his department could not function effectively without the close co-operation of the other departments whose chiefs he had antagonized. Lord North's *laissez-faire* policy of decentralized departments left each minister free to withhold co-operation for any one of a number of petty reasons. There was endless bickering over fine points of precedence and jurisdiction among the department chiefs. There was no one to step in, knock their heads together, and insist that they work harmoniously, or even that they work at all.

Common to all the branches of George III's government was the chronic "failure to expedite business." Papers were lost; letters were not written, or not delivered; payments were months and even years in arrears. This state of affairs was caused by a whole list of eighteenth-century administrative maladies that were regarded as normal and incurable: nepotism, favoritism, sinecures, inequalities of compensation, fee-grabbing, downright stealing, and an incredibly bad system of communications by a totally inadequate messenger service.

The truth of the matter was that England in the 1770's was trying to govern an empire with machinery and ideas that were deficient in time of peace, and hopelessly unequal to the demands of war. This was especially true of a war that had to be fought three thousand miles across an ocean, and which required the closest co-ordination of land and sea forces. The war effort in America, if it was to be successful, cried out for a single directing hand. But the more George III and Germain attempted to supply that need, the worse the results. For what they contributed was ignorant and wrong-headed overdirection of the commanders at the front. In the words of Munro and Fitzroy: "the movements of troops were badly prepared and ill-concerted, the organization and equipment unsuited to the character of the campaigns, and the officers in command lacking in energy and resources."

All these deficiencies came together in 1777 at Saratoga, whose "ultimate cause," in the judgment of Lucas and other historians, "was Lord George Germain."[7] After giving rigid and detailed orders to the hapless General Burgoyne, Germain's casual neglect to send vital directions to Generals Howe and Clinton almost defies explanation, as does his disingenuousness in blaming everyone but himself for the catastrophe. One would have thought that Saratoga would, in General Carleton's words to Burgoyne at the time, "have prevented in future ministers from pretending to direct operations of war in a country at three thousand miles distance, of which they have so little knowledge as not to be able to distinguish between good, bad, or interested advice, or to give positive orders in matters which from their nature are ever upon the change."[8]

Nevertheless Germain, as the strong man of North's government and the key figure in the conducting of the war, went right on alienating his own generals and admirals for five more years. In the words of William Eden: "Germain contrived to lose the esteem and reliance of every description of men civil and military, who are to serve with him or under him."[9] Some of this may be attributed to his haughtiness in official discourse and his exacting temper toward his subordinates. He gave small credit to anyone who defeated the Americans, because "the spirit and intrepidity of the King's troops" must necessarily make short work of such cowardly, boorish, and depraved "peasants." How Englishmen, merely by emigrating, could have evolved into such a lower order of beings he could not imagine. Nor could he see why his generals in the field could not strike the single decisive blow against them that would promptly end the war.

Germain stood out among North's ministers for his swiftness in doing business when once he applied himself, but this became a handicap when it produced snap decisions, and when his slavery to punctuality caused him to leave before his work was done. He is described as alternating between hesitancy in accepting some responsibilities and recklessness in matters where he felt optimistic and sure of himself. Professor Guttridge sums up his stature as American department head in these words: "His ill-balanced disposition and his resentment of criticism made him totally unfit to conceive and direct broad schemes based on a broad statesmanlike outlook; and the unfortunate scandal of his military career led to opposition and personal animosities which were increased by his quick temper and thwarted ambitions."[10]

LORD SANDWICH

Since the decisive battle of the American Revolution was lost by the Royal Navy, much of the blame has been assigned to the man who was First Lord of the Admiralty throughout the war. He was John Montagu, fourth Earl of Sandwich (1718-92), who earned the reputation, for a number of reasons, of being "the most unpopular man of his time." His numerous critics in Parliament were known as "Capulets." John Montagu had become an earl at the age of eleven, and at fifty-four described himself as "a very old man." He was educated at Eton and Trinity College, Cambridge, and after the conventional Grand Tour of the Continent took his seat in the House of Lords as a Bedford Whig. The followers of the Duke of Bedford disagreed with the Rockingham Whigs, who doubted the wisdom of attempting to coerce the American colonies. Lord Sandwich was a pillar of "The King's Friends" party, and bears to later generations all the earmarks of a Tory.

On three different occasions he occupied the position of First Lord of the Admiralty: from 1748 to 1751; for five months in 1763; and from 1771 to 1782. In his own day he inspired the most contradictory estimates of himself. On the one hand he was called:

> "Too infamous to have a friend,
> Too bad for bad men to commend"

and on the other hand it was said that "In 1771 he was, by his experience and knowledge of naval affairs, better fitted to be the First Lord than any other statesman in either house." Yet

Sandwich's critics never ceased to harp on the fact that he was "an ignorant landsman" conducting "a general naval war," adding that it would be as sensible to "give the direction of a band of music to an ignorant cobbler."[11]

The Earl's unpopularity with the public began with his action in 1763 when, as one of the Secretaries of State, he participated in the prosecution of one of his former associates in revelry, John Wilkes, for "impious libel." Sandwich and Wilkes had been fellow members of the Medmenham Fraternity, composed of "the most rip-roaring roués and blasphemous sinners of London"; and Sandwich had just been expelled from the Beefsteak Club for blasphemy. Wilkes had had privately printed a bawdy *Essay on Women* by another member of the Fraternity, and Sandwich got hold of a copy by "means morally, if not actually, criminal." Then before the House of Lords Sandwich, "whose own private life gave him of all people the least right to raise his hands in pious horror . . . had the effrontery to recite this essay obviously not intended for publication, in order to brand Wilkes as a corrupter of good morals and unworthy of the honor of being a member of Parliament."[12]

Wilkes was expelled from Commons, but repeatedly re-elected by his resentful constituents; while Sandwich's barefaced exhibition of hypocrisy won for him the nickname of "Jemmy Twicher," after a character who peached on Captain McHeath in *The Beggar's Opera*. Sandwich never made any secret of his private career as a rake. Besides a legitimate heir by his wife Dorothy, daughter of Viscount Fane, he had several offspring by his mistress for sixteen years, Martha Ray, who was murdered in April, 1779, by another of her lovers, James Hackman.

As for Sandwich's administration of the Navy, it is the verdict of Sir John Knox Laughton that "by no one has the patronage of the First Lord been so abused as it was by Sandwich, and by that abuse the Navy was brought to its lowest pitch."[13] Between 1755 and 1778 he received about six million pounds for the service, not including the pay of the men, and he had little to show for it. "Offices were bought, stores were stolen, and worst of all, ships unseaworthy and inadequately equipped, were sent to fight the battles of their country." It was, says Captain James, "a long story of administrative jobbery and corruption: estimates falsified, ships counted twice, ships commissioned to please political supporters, and not for active service."[14]

Horace Walpole wrote that Sandwich's "supreme talents were the artifices of a spy," which was probably too caustic a view. "It is difficult," says Valentine, "to be sure of the character of the Earl, since he was a chief target of Whig virulence, but in a weak and devious Ministry he was one of the most devious and perhaps though not the weakest, deserved the later description of Sir John Fortescue as 'a politician of evil reputation and inveterate jobber.' " The effect upon Navy morale, when political hostility was added to personal distaste, was devastating. "It became a point of honor that no Whig admiral should accept command from Lord Sandwich; and this was a serious matter, since by chance the ablest flag officers, with the notable exception of Rodney, were Whigs almost to a man."[15]

So fascinated have many historians become by the private scandals attached to the name of Sandwich that his genuine accomplishments as administrator have been scanted somewhat. He did insist upon copper sheathing for the Navy's ships; upon some slight improvements by Kempenfelt in the antiquated system of signalling; and upon the arming of the upper decks of the larger ships with carronades.

In his defense it must be said that he did not inherit from his predecessors at the Admiralty a navy in fighting condition. After its principal rival, France, had been crushed at Quiberon Bay in 1759, the British fleet had been allowed to deteriorate. "When I came to the Admiralty," Sandwich said, "we had not above fifteen ships fit for sea." In the early 1770's Lord North could see no war clouds anywhere on the horizon; and was afraid that "great peace establishments will, if we do not take care, prove our ruin." He "flinched from the cost of preparation for war," and called upon Sandwich at the Admiralty to exercise "a judicious economy." North's mind was on the heavy burden of national debt which had been piled up during the Seven Years' War, and he was grimly determined to pay off a substantial amount of it in time of peace. He seemed to think, also, that by a policy of not preparing for, and thus not provoking a naval arms race between France and Britain, war could be indefinitely postponed or avoided altogether.

Not only was the Royal Navy in those crucial years kept woefully short of ships and seamen; there was also a steadily diminishing supply of the materials for ship construction. The accelerated building of vessels during the Seven Years' War had used up the reserve supplies of oak in the English dockyards; and the American war was soon to cut off the flow of New England pine for masts and spars. Ships had to be constructed of inferior Baltic oak with only a quarter of the length of life and often unseasoned, while the mast ponds were frequently all too empty. Some of the blame rests upon those who did not have the foresight to plant English oaks a century before to replace those which had been cut down. But in the judgment of Professor Robert G. Albion, "By neglecting the material conditions of the ships and by alienating the Whig admirals, Sandwich probably did more damage to the Navy entrusted to his care than any hostile French admiral had ever done," When he gave Parliament "the impression of such a surplus of stores that the dockyards could not accommodate them, Sandwich lied outright."[16]

His arrogant over-confidence about Britain's strength in the 1770's may have been due in part to his underestimation of the seriousness of the American rebellion and his utter contempt for Americans in general. When it was brewing, Lord Sandwich, like most of the English ruling class, treated it as a provincial uprising rather than a war between nations. As such, it must of course be suppressed. On August 25, 1775, Sandwich wrote to Admiral Samuel Graves, then commanding the North American station: "The nation here is unanimous against America in their resolution to crush the unnatural rebellion that has broke out in America by force of arms," although in a later version of the same communication he inserted the qualifying clause "except some factious and interested opponents."[17]

When it came to reviling Americans Sandwich rivalled Germain, calling them "the most treacherous, infamous, worthless race of men on earth." Shall we, he asked, "be afraid of a body of *fanatics* in New England, who will bluster and swell when danger is at a distance, but when it comes near, will like all other mobs throw down their arms and run away?" (Italics his.) To rout such obvious cowards would not require very much in the way of either time or resources. As Major Pitcairn wrote from

Boston in February, 1775: "The Americans will see that they are very insignificant when opposed to regular troops." Sandwich himself expressed the hope that thirty or forty thousand Americans, instead of twenty thousand, might join their army, for "the more rebels, the greater the stampede when they come up against the British." The Royal Navy would have an easy task with no real resistance: a mere police action along the Atlantic seaboard against unarmed commerce, the almost nonexistent patriot navy, and a few privateers. This need not involve Sandwich's precious ships of the line at all: frigates and sloops could do the job. But soon it was discovered that more than the New England provinces were involved, and that the coastline of the thirteen colonies was very long and difficult to patrol. There were never frigates and sloops enough to do the job; and the first naval forces sent across the Atlantic, says James, were both "totally inadequate" and badly commanded.

But the home fleet of line ships could be kept intact and not "wasted in America." To Sandwich the safety of England was paramount, even if it cost the outright abandonment of the American colonies. Always lurking in the background was the specter of the Bourbon Family Compact and the possibility of a two-power naval war. As Sandwich stated the problem in a memorandum to Lord North on August 3, 1777: "I lay down as a maxim that England ought for her own security to have a superior force in readiness at home to anything that France and Spain have in readiness on their side."[18] Unfortunately for England, Sandwich's actions did not match his own sound maxim. At the very moment of stating it he could not honestly maintain that the nation had more than thirty-six capital ships available, or that more than thirty of them had complete crews, as against a probable Franco-Spanish fleet of forty-four. Yet in November of that same year he was boasting in the House of Lords that "our whole naval force fit for actual service consists of fifty-four line ships and nearly two hundred frigates and sloops, etc., a force superior to what France and Spain could bring against us."[19] When obliged to make good on such rash promises, when France (and then Spain) sailed against Britain, Sandwich found himself embroiled in a controversy with Germain.

The two dominating Cabinet personalities clashed over the

policy of using the bulk of the home fleet to contain the French
navy in their ports *vs.* the strategy of letting them out to go in
hot pursuit. Sandwich argued strongly for the latter policy,
declaring that with the limited number of lineships available,
the coasts of England must not be left undefended by attempts
to bottle up D'Estaing. In this stand he was backed by Admiral
Keppel, who insisted upon keeping the whole home fleet together in a force superior, he hoped, to any possible combination
of invaders.

Germain contended just as forcefully that what was most
important was to win the American war, even at a certain risk.
"In all military operations of importance some risk must be
run," he wrote in April, 1778, "and it is more meritorious to
suffer in a vigorous and necessary exertion of our forces, than
to submit to the loss of our detached fleets, armies, and distant
possessions, which must infallibly draw after it the absolute
ruin of Great Britain,"[20] Lord North found himself uncom-
fortably in the middle between two dynamic individuals; and as
usual wound up with a timid, dilatory solution, giving first Sandwich his way and then Germain. D'Estaing was first set loose and
then pursued by Admiral Byron, who promptly solidified his
reputation as "Foulweather Jack" by running into a violent
storm. Sandwich's wrong policy prevailed just long enough to
prevent Germain's right policy from being effective.

As the French threat was seen to be becoming more formidable, Sandwich took refuge behind an array of excuses. There
was "the unexpected magnitude of the naval force collected by
the united House of Bourbon," as George III described it,
omitting to point out that the Admiralty's intelligence must have
been faulty. Then "it was answered that England till this time
[September, 1779] was never engaged in a sea war with the
House of Bourbon thoroughly united, their naval force un-
broken, and having no other war or object to draw off their
attention and resources. We unfortunately have an additional
war on our hands . . . and no one friend or ally to assist us . . ."
And finally, it was not the sole responsibility of the First Lord
to provide the proper number of ships. "Do my lords imagine
that the First Lord of the Admiralty equips fleets whenever his
own fancy leads him to do so? . . . it is the business of the King's

administration at large to judge when it shall be advisable to put the nation to the expense of that equipment."[21]

By his own folly in pretending to a naval readiness and superiority which did not exist, Sandwich placed his ministry constantly on the defensive. The first attempt to remove him from office was made by Vice Admiral the Earl of Bristol in April, 1779, and, like several others, it was defeated seventy-eight votes to thirty-nine. Charles James Fox declared that Sandwich's greatest crime was the concealment of shocking conditions which he ought to have known and admitted. The First Lord could not be blamed for the economy budgets which had starved the Navy; but he was responsible for many deficiencies which he tried to keep out of sight. He was also guilty of unwise appointments of incompetent admirals, such as Marriott Arbuthnot, of whom Lord Germain said that no one believed in his competence except Sandwich.

5

ARCHITECTS OF DEFEAT: GENERALS CLINTON AND CORNWALLIS

"Cornwallis planned badly, but until the final crisis in Virginia he acted audaciously ... Clinton's response was to make elaborate plans and then wait." —William B. Willcox

No one doubts that one of the principal reasons that England failed to subdue her rebellious American colonists was the internecine strife which prevailed among her principal commanders on both land and sea. There were not merely differences of opinion about strategy and tactics; there were truly venomous personal animosities directed against fellow officers in both services. Nobody made a higher score in that unpleasant category than Sir Henry Clinton (1738-95), commander-in-chief of the British armies in America from 1778 to 1782.

Clinton's father was an admiral, the Honorable George Clinton, younger brother of the Earl of Lincoln, and related to the politically powerful Pelham family. Henry's father gave up the sea in 1743 to become Governor of New York, where the son began his army career in the New York militia. On returning to England in 1751, he was gazetted a lieutenant in the Coldstream Guards, and in 1758 became a lieutenant colonel in the Grenadier Guards. When his father died in 1761, his estate consisted mainly of tracts of land in New York and Connecticut which were later confiscated. His only son Henry was left anything but rich by aristocratic standards, and money worries harassed him for most of his life.

On his first active service under Prince Ferdinand of Bruns-

wick in 1760, Clinton distinguished himself for gallantry in
action and became a colonel. Shortly after, in August, 1762, he
was wounded at Johannisberg. Peace kept him relatively inactive;
but in 1772, having become a major general, he entered Parliament through the patronage of his cousin, the second Duke of
Newcastle, remaining a member until 1784, although he was out
of the country most of the time. He underwent a severe personal
crisis when his wife Harriet died in August, 1772, having borne
him five children in five years. After a trip to the Balkans to visit
the Russian army front against the Turks in 1774, he received
orders to go to America on the *Cerberus* with Generals Howe
and Burgoyne.

They reached Boston in May, 1775, just after the fighting at
Lexington and Concord. All three were major generals (Howe
was Clinton's senior, Burgoyne his junior) Clinton said of the
voyage: "At first (for you know I am a shy bitch) I kept my
distance, seldom spoke till my two colleagues forced me out."
This troublesome aloofness, however, was combined with an
equally irritating counter-tendency to suggest alternative plans
to his superiors. With a minimum of tact, Clinton tried that
gambit on General Gage, and also on Sir William Howe, with
whom he was soon at odds for "speaking too freely." Yet Clinton
played a notable part, though somewhat outside the letter of his
orders, at Bunker Hill, winning a promotion to local Lieutenant
General.

Lord Howe then sent him on a fruitless expedition to Charleston, South Carolina, with Vice Admiral Sir Peter Parker. It was
Clinton's first independent army command, but unfortunately
the vice admiral was equally independent of him, and no one had
taken the trouble to give one of them supreme authority in case
they disagreed, which they promptly did. Clinton's policy, then
and afterwards, says Professor Willcox, was that of "minimum
risk—which in the long run is the riskiest policy of all."

What Clinton acquired from the Charleston fiasco was a
multiple grievance: first against his naval colleague, which he
ventilated in his report to Lord Germain; and then against Germain for publishing an account in the official *Gazette* which
seemed to reflect upon Clinton's military competence. He got
leave to go to England to defend his honor, enlisted the aid of

Charles James Fox, who was only to glad to attack Germain for his "infamous libel on the character of a gallant officer." Clinton had to be mollified, and silenced, by being made a knight, but from that time on, according to Valentine, "he never liked or really trusted Lord George Germain."

After a short stay in England, Clinton returned to New York with three thousand reinforcements and a commission as second-in-command to Howe in August, 1776. His unsolicited suggestions to his superior multiplied, but now they were exceptionally good ones, only a few of which Howe adopted. Clinton played a notable part in the battle of Long Island and the subsequent occupation of New York City. Once more back in England, and not intending to return, he complained to a friend in July, 1777, that "The Minister [Germain] has used me so ill that I can no longer bear with life."[1]

Already Sir Henry Clinton had shown himself an almost incredibly touchy and sensitive individual, whose impulse, when frustrated, was "to avoid self-reproach by reproaching others." Some light has been thrown upon the complexities of his character by an analysis of it in terms of modern psychology. On the basis of an examination of some two hundred volumes of Clinton papers in the Clements Library of the University of Michigan, Professor William B. Willcox, a historian, and Professor Frederick Wyatt, a clinical psychologist, wrote an article entitled "Sir Henry Clinton: a Psychological Exploration of History" in the January, 1959, issue of the *William and Mary Quarterly*. They found Sir Henry a bundle of neurotic paradoxes, an "obsessive-compulsive personality," harried by conflicts of ambition and shyness, audacity and timidity, self-assertion and self-distrust. The crux of his conduct, they believe, "was an unconscious conflict over authority," which he both craved and dreaded. When he did not have it, he sought it; but when he attained it, he tried to get rid of it. One result was a proverbial tardiness.

His cure for his own self-doubts was "the transfer of his internal conflict to others." This led him to incessant quarrelling and the preferring of charges, as well as to the elaborate fabrications by which he defended himself. The need for absolute self-justification was overwhelming. When he wrote his *Narrative* defending his every act in America, he declared flatly that "none of the misfortunes of the unfortunate campaign of 1781 can, with the smallest degree of justice, be imputed to me." He had what amounted to a persecution complex with regard to his associates, by whom he was perpetually being "wronged." Unlike Rodney, it was directed against his superiors or equals, rather than against his subordinates. This made him "aloof, sensitive, and petulant"[2] in his personal relationships with men who were themselves not exactly models of forbearance and equanimity.

For it must be confessed that, in addition to Clinton's imagined grievances, he had sound reasons for believing himself harshly treated by George III, Germain, General Howe, and fate. When Burgoyne was named to command the invasion of New York from Canada, for instance, a post which Clinton had done nothing to secure, thinking that as Burgoyne's senior it was his for the asking, he had a grievance against Burgoyne, for whose success he was to show little enthusiasm. Back in New York in response to the pleading of the King and Germain, he was further shocked to discover his own role in the operation. While Burgoyne was coming from the North, and Howe was sailing off to Philadelphia in search of laurels in the field, he was to remain a mere garrison commander in New York.

Quite sensibly Clinton explained to Howe "the superior advantages to be derived . . . from co-operation of his whole force with General Burgoyne on the River Hudson"; but instead Howe took fourteen thousand men by sea to attack Philadelphia, leaving Clinton with less than nine thousand of whom only half were regular troops. The latter set about the task that was soon to become his principal obsession, and which was to affect vitally the outcome of the Yorktown campaign—the defense of New York against an expected attack by Washington. Clinton was left angry and frustrated, "with nothing but vague orders, heavy responsibilities, and troops inadequate to meet them." Howe added insult to injury by writing him while at sea on July 30: ". . . if you can make any diversion in favor of General Burgoyne's approaching Albany (with security to King's Bridge) I need not point out the utility of such a measure."[3]

Clinton delayed any move up the Hudson until reinforcements arrived from England, then acted skillfully but too late to help

Burgoyne. Any chance of pushing on to Albany was stopped by
Howe's call for reinforcements to be sent southward. Clinton believed that he had done everything that could be expected of a
prudent garrison commander poorly informed about the larger
strategic situation. "When it called in reality for improvisation,"
writes Willcox, "he remained the general of regular approaches."

"Never," said Sir John Fortescue, "was there a finer example
of the art of organizing disaster,"[4] than the Saratoga campaign.
England paid the high price of an entire army for the capture
of Philadelphia, and the even higher price of France's entry into
the war. Sir William Howe left under a cloud; and Sir Henry
Clinton inherited the post of commander-in-chief, from which he
began resigning even before he was confirmed. His orders were
most discouraging: to evacuate the just-conquered city of Philadelphia, and even New York and Rhode Island under desperate
circumstances, retiring to Canada if necessary, while the Carlisle
Commission made a vain attempt to buy peace by granting
everything except its indispensable condition: the independence
of America.

In one of his strange reversals of form, Clinton seemed invig-
orated at being told to lead from weakness rather than from
strength. He marched Howe's army, swollen to eighteen thousand men, and encumbered by twelve miles of baggage wagons,
from Philadelphia to New York, attacked Washington's harassing columns skillfully if not decisively at Monmouth Court
House (his only battle command of the war), and then co-
operated with Admiral Lord Richard Howe in thwarting D'Estaing's expedition against New York. Clinton "never showed to
better advantage," says Willcox, than in his weeks of collabora-
tion with the energetic Admiral Howe.

One might have thought that the appearance of a superior
French fleet, combined with Clinton's passion for security, would
have combined to remind the latter of the absolute necessity of
maintaining British naval superiority in coastal waters. Howe's
ships and transports had had a very narrow escape from D'Estaing's twelve of the line as they were returning from the Delaware. Clinton was, after all, the son of one admiral and the
brother-in-law of another, and might have been expected not
only to realize how complete was his dependence upon the

Royal Navy, but to act upon it. When establishing a standard by which to judge Vice Admiral Arbuthnot in 1779, he listed high among the latter's duties "the preserving at all times free and ready communications between the several posts of the army . . ."[5] Clinton also seems to have appreciated the value of the Chesapeake and the Hudson as lanes by which sea-based armies could bite deeply into the American interior. But he did not manage to cope with all the risks of land campaigns in the interior, cut off from the ocean supply lines, or the perils of divided armies and commands with uncertain communications until it was too late. Otherwise he would peremptorily have ordered Cornwallis to avoid them. He was never tired of telling how much he counted upon the Navy and its promises to do its part; but he did not seem to grasp fully how vital to his own existence the presence of the King's ships was, until they were defeated. Even so, he was far in advance of any other British army leader in these respects.

What D'Estaing did accomplish by his coming was the placing of Clinton on the defensive, impelling him to evacuate Rhode Island in October, 1779. The British general remained in New York, strengthening its fortifications and making occasional forays into the surrounding country. For nearly a year, neither he nor Washington accomplished anything of consequence. Then came Clinton's greatest hour of triumph, followed by two long personal vendettas with Vice Admiral Arbuthnot and Lord Cornwallis. His attempt to command those two chieftains was, as Professor Willcox has said, "to guide a wild horse while carrying the Old Man of the Sea." But, above all, "his nemesis was himself."[6]

LORD CORNWALLIS

Charles Cornwallis, the second Earl Cornwallis (1738-1805), was the sixth child and eldest son of the first earl, who had made a fortunate marriage with Elizabeth, daughter of Lord Townshend and niece of Sir Robert Walpole. Young Charles attended Eton, where he suffered an eye injury in hockey at the hands of the later Bishop of Durham, Shute Barrington. He then went up to Clare College, Cambridge, before entering the army as Ensign in the Grenadier Guards in 1756 as Lord Brome. In the summer of 1758 he found out that the Guards had been ordered to Germany to join Prince Ferdinand of Brunswick, and hastened there six weeks ahead of his regiment, becoming an aide to the Marquis of Granby. He was present at Minden, the scene of Lord Germain's downfall.

In January, 1760, he was elected to the seat in Parliament for Eye, which had been in his family for about three centuries. In the following year he got a lieutenant colonelcy in the 12th Regiment of foot, which was hotly engaged at Kirch Donkern and elsewhere. On the death of his father, he succeeded to the title and estates, taking his seat in the House of Lords in 1762. There he sided with the Whig peers against Lord Bute, and, when Lord Rockingham became Prime Minister in 1765, Cornwallis was rewarded by being made aide-de-camp to the King, a Gentleman of the Bedchamber, and Colonel of the 33rd Regiment of foot.

While he took no part in active political life, Cornwallis acquired a reputation for personal integrity and independence. He refused to approve the ministerial action against John Wilkes, and was one of four peers who backed Lord Camden's stand against the resolution affirming the right of Parliament to tax the Americans. This exposed him to the later charge of inconsistency at the hands of Wilkes himself, for when Commons debated a vote of thanks to Cornwallis for his victory at Camden in November, 1780, Wilkes denounced the latter's "Inconsistency in drawing his sword to maintain a cause which, a few years earlier, he had reprobated publicly in the House of Peers . . ."[7]

Although Cornwallis gave up his offices in 1770, with the exit of his friend Lord Shelburne, George III did not have the same distrust and dislike for him which he entertained for the other Whigs, and made him Constable of the Tower. When the American rebellion broke out Cornwallis did not refuse to accompany his regiment, in spite of the entreaties of the wife, Jemima Tullikens, whom he had married seven years earlier. He was placed in command of Howe's reserve division, and took part in the battles of Long Island and White Plains, capturing Fort Lee from General Greene.

It was a different story at Princeton, New Jersey, when Corn-

wallis chose to wait a day "to bag the fox," meaning General
Washington, and was nearly bagged himself when the American
general stole around his flank during the night. At dawn the surprised Cornwallis heard fighting in his rear, and fell back to
protect a supply depot. When Howe made his misguided expedition against Philadelphia, Lord Cornwallis won back some of
his lost laurels by routing General Sullivan on the American
right wing at the battle of Brandywine. After helping to cover
Clinton's retreat from Philadelphia to New York, Cornwallis
hastened home because of the dangerous illness of his wife, who
died on February 16, 1779. He was back in America again, now
a permanent lieutenant general, in August, 1779, relieved to find
that at last Sir Henry Clinton, the commander-in-chief, was preparing to carry the war into the Carolinas and Georgia.

Lord Cornwallis was capable of making himself over in more
ways than one. "Junius" had said that politically "he shifted his
company as well as his opinions": and now he was to behave
quite differently under Clinton from the way in which he had
acted under Howe. He began to strike out for himself as both
policy maker and tactician, ridiculing Clinton's cautious "wear-
ing-out" policy of attrition as mere "tobacco-stealing." Instead
of small predatory expeditions to wear down rebel resistance in
the manner of Clinton, Cornwallis began dreaming of landing
the knockout blow that would really end the war. But he must
first acquire from a jealous Clinton a Southern army large
enough to insure the final victory.

6

ARCHITECTS OF DEFEAT: ADMIRALS RODNEY, HOOD, AND GRAVES

"Keeping the commanders on Barbados, Jamaica, and the American station independent of each other, whereby each is induced to starve the service committed to the others, that he may have more officers to make, and prize money to receive." —Letter signed "Cato Censor," *Political Journal,* January, 1782

George Brydges Rodney (1718-92) came from a solid Somersetshire country family, and made his way in the Navy through the Brydges connection with the Duke of Chandos. After a brief stay at Harrow, he entered the service at the age of thirteen as a King's letter boy, "with a better right to be made lieutenant than others." Indeed he was the last man to enter the Royal Navy through that particular channel of favoritism.

His rise was rapid. By the appointment of Admiral Mathews he skipped a grade and became captain of the *Plymouth,* 64 guns, at the age of twenty-three. In October, 1747, Rodney made the first in what was to be a long series of complaints against a fellow officer, accusing Captain Fox of the *Kent* of "hanging back" and showing lack of zeal against the French. Fox was tried for misconduct, dismissed, restored by the King, but denied further employment. In the following year Rodney was named to his first post in America as Governor of Newfoundland in the *Rainbow,* 40 guns, where he stayed for five years. On his return to England, he married Lady Jane Compton, by whom he had two sons and a daughter before her death in

1757. Already he was suffering from the disease of that hard-drinking century, the gout.

While in London in 1756 he was ordered to sit as a member of the board at the famous, or infamous, court-martial of Admiral John Byng, but Rodney was excused on account of "a violent bilious colic." He was then the captain of the *Monarch*, 74 guns, which he commanded until a few weeks before its quarterdeck was the scene of Byng's execution. Thus Rodney had no hand in the judicial murder of that admiral, "one of the worst miscarriages of justice in recorded British history."[1] Rodney's intense dislike for half-hearted leadership of any kind led his biographer David Hannay to conclude that his subject did not disapprove of the Byng verdict; but there is evidence to the contrary. When Captain Augustus Harvey made a last-minute attempt to prepare a petition for mercy on Byng's behalf, Captain George Rodney assisted him in soliciting the signatures of members of the court and of Parliament.

A patron had enabled Rodney to sit for Saltash in "the best club in England," the House of Commons, in 1751. As he wrote to his second wife in May, 1780, "A man in our country is nothing without being in Parliament." For eight years before he hoisted his flag, he had been "a political admiral," but simply in order "to push his fortunes," and not to promote any political principles or convictions. He owed his seat to the Duke of Newcastle's government, and voted for whatever his patron directed. In 1768, however, the Duke of Newcastle died; and Rodney was obliged, if he was to stay in Parliament, to campaign for Northampton at his own expense. The cost of winning that election was said to have reached thirty thousand pounds, which, together with Rodney's inveterate passion for gaming, plunged him into "a debt that hung around his neck for years."

From 1761 through 1764 Rodney served his first tour of duty as commander-in-chief of the Leeward Islands station in the West Indies. In 1764 he was made a baronet; and was married for the second time, to Henrietta Clies by whom he had two sons and three daughters. In 1765 he became the good-natured governor of Greenwich Hospital, "a hotbed of the dirtiest conceivable jobbery and thieving of the lowest type of the eighteenth century," for which his friend Lord Sandwich was ultimately responsible. In 1771 Rodney was sent to Jamaica to counter a Spanish threat which did not materialize, and was dressed down by Sandwich for nearly provoking a war. He had hoped to retain his Greenwich Hospital emoluments along with those of his sea command, and thus to climb out of debt. Sandwich would not permit this, and a coolness developed. Rodney felt further aggrieved by being refused the Governorship of Jamaica at the end of his three-year tenure as commander there. When he struck his flag at Plymouth in September, 1774, he faced the unpleasant prospect of meeting his army of creditors on an officer's half-pay. Bitter at Sandwich, Rodney betook himself to Paris, ostensibly to economize, at any rate to escape the incessant dunning.

In Paris he did not economize, but went right on wasting money that he not possess. "An admiral who could rule his fleet with an iron will," says E. Keble Chatterton, "he was incapable of controlling his private affairs."[2] This was because, as Wraxall remarked: "Throughout his whole life, two passions, both highly injurious to his repose, the love of women and of play, carried him into many excesses." His person was "more elegant than seemed to become his rough profession. There was something that approached delicacy and effeminacy in his figure . . ." He was attractive to women; and, says Wraxall, who often indulged in gossip, "It was universally believed that he had been distinguished in his youth by the personal attachment of Princess Amelia, daughter of George II," and "that a living evidence of the former connexion existed, unless fame had recourse to fiction for support."[3]

Rodney's participation in the dissolute life of Parisian society added fresh obligations to his English indebtedness. When his written pleas to Lord Sandwich for employment were coldly ignored, Rodney sent his wife, and later his son, to London in October, 1776, to present his case in person. Sandwich's written reply to Lady Rodney said: "If Sir George will consider the thing impartially, he will see that, though his merit as a sea officer is undeniable, there are reasons that make it impossible for me to prevail on His Majesty to appoint him to take command of a foreign squadron . . . As a man in office, your husband has deprived me of the power of being useful to him."[4]

To an officer who had spent his whole life in the Navy, Rodney's continuing exile in Paris was galling indeed. His French creditors were only restrained from taking extreme measures against him by the protection of the Lieutenant of Police. When in 1778 France joined the American colonies in their struggle for independence, an idea which Rodney detested, he was frantically eager to get into action against the new allies. Yet he seemed to be condemned to spend the American war in the capital of the hereditary enemy as the prisoner of his own reckless extravagance, if not as a literal prisoner for debt in case the protection of the police should be withdrawn.

Lady Rodney had also attempted, early in 1777, to "procure a subscription to be opened among the members of the club at White's" for her husband's financial relief, but his erstwhile associates at the gaming tables showed no enthusiasm for her project, and "after much ineffectual solicitation among Sir George's former friends," it was abandoned.[5] Deliverance came suddenly, and from an extraordinary source. The aged Marshal de Biron, well knowing "how formidable an opponent he was restoring to the service of Great Britain," offered Rodney a loan of one thousand *louis* to make him solvent again. This magnanimous and quixotic offer was twice refused, until all other efforts to obtain relief turned out to be fruitless. Four years later a Paris mob was to threaten the old Marshal with violence for his part in making possible De Grasse's defeat by Rodney in the battle of the Saintes.

Thus "ransomed" by the enemy, Rodney returned to England in March, 1779; and a voluntary loan from the Drummond family of bankers enabled him to repay his Parisian benefactor. He was full of acrimony against Sandwich, who by that time was hard up for admirals of Rodney's ability and political orthodoxy. Not until the end of 1779 would the First Lord relent and grudgingly offer Rodney a second tenure of the Leeward Islands command, this time including Jamaica and the freedom to intervene on the American coast. It may have been that no other flag officer of Rodney's experience and standing would accept the post at Sandwich's hand. "It was a time," says Mundy, "when a strong party spirit pervaded the fleet as well as the nation at large, for the war being with our colonies, partook somewhat of the nature of a civil war, political opinions being divided regarding the justice of it."⁶

Rodney had not the slightest qualms about repressing the rebellion. He agreed with his sovereign that the Americans were nothing but pirates to be hunted down and subdued. He credited his own opportunity to take a major part in the operation, not to Sandwich, but to George III, whose servant he regarded himself henceforth "in a peculiar degree." Sandwich's language in finally recommending Rodney to the King indicated fears about the admiral's dealings in money matters which were prophetic of his difficulties at St. Eustatius one year later.

"I omitted to mention to Your Majesty," Sandwich wrote, "that if Sir George Rodney should from his indigence have any temptation to make advantage of purchasing stores or anything else of that sort, he will have no means of doing it at present as there will be a commissioner on the spot through whose hands all that business must be transacted."⁷ It was said that the West Indian merchants disliked the appointment, and tried to get it for Vice Admiral Palliser instead.

Rodney was sixty-one years old, "tormented with gout and gravel," with a thin, lined face looking older than his years. He had spent nearly half a century in the Navy without achieving any resounding success. This lack he proceeded to remedy in a spectacular fashion. On his way to his station in the Antilles with twenty-one sail of the line and a convoy of three hundred merchant ships, he had been ordered first to relieve Gibraltar, which was then being closely blockaded by Spain. On January 16, 1780, just beyond Cape St. Vincent, he surprised an inferior Spanish squadron of eleven of the line under Admiral Juan de Langara heading for Cadiz. Night and a rising gale did not prevent Rodney, "a fine gambler," from ordering a General Chase in such a manner as to place his ships between the Spaniards and the land. Lying ill in his berth as the fight began, Rodney told his flag captain: "Lay me alongside the biggest ship you can see, or the admiral, if there be one." Too late, the enemy tried to flee "like a shoal of frightened porpoises a swarm of sharks pursue." The result of the Moonlight Battle (as it was called) was a complete British victory; of the nine enemy ships engaged one blew up, two escaped, and six were captured, including the wounded

Admiral de Langara's splendid flagship *Fénix*, which was rechristened *H.M.S. Gibraltar*. "The Spanish men-of-war we have taken," Rodney explained to his wife, "are much superior to ours." Even such a sweeping success, however, could not keep Rodney from making bitter criticisms of his captains.

Both Gibraltar and Minorca were relieved. The Tory admiral was the toast of London, was made a Knight of the Bath, and received the freedom of the City of London in a gold casket. George III was especially delighted; and, with what Laughton calls "sublime impudence," Sandwich congratulated Rodney, and himself: "The worst of my enemies now allow that I have pitched upon a man who knows his duty, and is a brave, honest, and able officer."

Rodney reached his assigned command in the West Indies on March 28, just a few days after his opposite number, Admiral Count de Guichen, arrived at Martinique. There followed a series of three bloody but inconclusive artillery duels between the two nearly equal fleets: Rodney had twenty-one sail of the line, and De Guichen, twenty-three. In the first engagements, Rodney's flagship *Sandwich*, 90 guns, fired three thousand two hundred and eighty-eight cannonballs at the enemy, using one hundred and sixty barrels of powder. Neither side gained any ultimate advantage from the savage cannonading.

It is evident that Rodney expected much more of the encounter on April 17, 1780, which he called "the great opportunity of my life" to crush the French. He alleged that it was missed because "the British flag was not supported" by some of his veteran ship captains. He was enraged by what he called "the base and infatuated conduct" of officers who chose to be "passive lookers-on, keeping aloof in a dastardly manner," thereby enabling De Guichen to escape destruction. The principal culprit, in his eyes, was Captain Robert Carkett of the *Stirling Castle*, leading ship of the van, who, when ordered to "lead down and every ship to steer for her opponent" in the French line, obeyed the letter of the twenty-first Article of the regular *Additional Fighting Instructions*, and went off hunting for the first ship of the enemy van, rather than the one "at that time abreast" of the *Stirling Castle*, as Rodney intended. The real trouble, which was to dog Rear Admiral Graves at the battle of the Chesapeake, says

Hannay, was a faulty code of signals and "the foolish system which compelled an admiral to fight in chains imposed by standing orders."

Rodney continued to heap abuse upon his captains, who did not know what was on his mind, and whom he did not trust. The complete autocrat, he was determined to bring them to heel. He gave "public notice to his captains that he expected implicit obedience to every signal made, under certain penalty of being instantly superseded." When Rear Admiral Joshua Rowley, another object of his wrath, questioned the meaning of an order, Rodney told him that obedience only was required of inferiors, "the painful task of thinking belonged to me." He threatened to transfer his flag to a frigate to police his line closely. "It is inconceivable," said Rodney, "in what awe it kept them."[8] He found that the results of this brand of intimidation were excellent. Without regard to rank, he said, "I taught them to be what they had never been before—Officers . . . My eye on them had more dread than the enemy's fire," he wrote to Lady Rodney, "they knew it would be fatal."

Rodney did not lead men by enlisting their personal loyalty or affection, but by fear. As Hannay says: "He lived apart from his captains, neither asking for their friendship nor giving them his . . . His relations to his subordinates were always strained." As one of them said succinctly: "He despises them, and they him." Another of his officers, Commodore Hotham, wrote to Lord Sandwich: "I can no longer wish to serve in this country, where the chief in command will assume merit to himself, and aim to aggrandize his own reputation by depreciating indiscriminately the character of every officer below him."[9]

Although assigned to command the Leeward Islands station, Rodney alone among the British admirals seems to have envisaged the war as a whole, and to have itched for what should have existed, an Atlantic supreme command. He had long had his eyes on the New York station, and seized the pretext of De Guichen's possible move there with "ten or twelve sail of the line" (which did not materialize) to go there himself. He argued that the French admiral was about to give De Ternay at Newport a naval superiority that would surely spell the "overpowering" of the ten British ships at New York. On his own responsibility Rodney sailed for that city with ten of the line, arriving on September 13, 1780, "unexpected and unwelcome to friends and foes alike."

The commander of the North Atlantic station was Vice Admiral Marriott Arbuthnot, almost seventy years of age, and very tired after fifty-three years of constant service. He was described in the *Morning Chronicle* for May 18, 1781, as "a coarse, blustering, foul-mouthed bully," one of Sandwich's very worst appointments, perhaps a deliberate move on his part to provoke Sir Henry Clinton to the point of resigning. Rodney outranked him, and announced "I will be the admiral" at New York. This infuriated Arbuthnot, for it meant that Rodney took over the commander-in-chief's share of all prize money. Shortly after his arrival, a frigate brought in a vessel loaded with arms and stores for the rebels, and Rodney calmly pocketed his share down to the last sixpence—three thousand pounds. To Jackson he explained that he could have made much more by cruising the Spanish main, but that stern duty had called him to New York.

Arbuthnot complained bitterly about Sir George's "unlimited licentiousness" in subverting "without either reason or necessity" his own arrangements, by ordering ships to sea, appointing officers, and "in no one instance" doing anything "conducive to His Majesty's service." The irascible vice admiral betook himself to Gardiner's Bay to watch the French, refusing to come to New York until Rodney departed in November. At that time Arbuthnot suspended all the appointments Rodney had made; but his bitter complaints to Sandwich got nowhere. George III commented that "Sir George Rodney's conduct seems as usual praiseworthy. I am sorry Vice Admiral Arbuthnot has lost his temper; the insinuation that prize money has occasioned it seems founded."[10]

Rodney reached New York just as the Benedict Arnold betrayal was about to come to fruition, and the cause of the patriots was flagging perceptibly. He said that his coming produced "the utmost dismay" among the rebels; and he hoped to take advantage of it by recovering Rhode Island. In this dream he was frustrated by Clinton and Arbuthnot, each blaming the other because Rhode Island had been evacuated in the first place, and was now too strongly fortified to be stormed with success. Just before leaving, Rodney summed up his views regarding "the manner in which the war is carried on" in America, writing to Sandwich that "there appears to me a slackness inconceivable in every branch of it; and that briskness and activity which is so necessary, and ought to animate the whole and bring it to a speedy conclusion, has entirely forsaken it."[11]

Rodney then went on to outline his conception of the proper British strategy: "It is now turned to a war of ports . . ." Clinton had given up the best one, Rhode Island, which was "the most fatal measure that could possibly be adopted." That left only the Chesapeake, "which our troops have twice taken possession of and evacuated . . ." as the place where a large British fleet could be stationed during the winter months.

The admiral's physical health had not improved during his stay in New York, most of the time ashore cursing the cold, damp climate. But his financial well-being, thanks in part to the influx of prize money, had shown a marked upturn. For one thing, a petition to the King submitted by his friends with what Hannay calls an "almost incredible want of taste," since it "made much of Rodney's notorious pecuniary embarrassments," resulted in the granting of a pension of a thousand pounds a year payable to Lady Rodney in the event that she survived him. What was more immediately important to the admiral was his being able to send funds to Lord Sandwich with which to purchase a seat in Parliament for Westminster.

Meanwhile Sandwich was having his troubles with another problem, writing to Rodney on July 14, 1780: "I know not what to do to find a good second-in-command for you . . . a person who I think will be likely to second you properly and with proper subordination." Besides all the political factionalism which had created suspicion throughout the Navy, Rodney was known to be subject to violent explosions of temper and the possessor of a biting tongue. He had made many enemies in his profession, since, although "he talked much and freely upon every subject," he had a strong tendency, said Wraxall, "to make himself the theme of his own discourse . . . and to conceal nothing in the course of conversation, regardless of who were present, dealing his censures, as well as his praises, with imprudent liberality."[12]

REAR ADMIRAL SIR SAMUEL HOOD

After several rather desultory inquiries regarding other admirals, the man Lord Sandwich finally selected as Rodney's second in command was Sir Samuel Hood, later first Viscount Hood (1724-1816). He was "understood to be on friendly terms with Sir George," under whom he had served as midshipman in the *Ludlow Castle* in 1743, and again as captain of the *Vestal* during the Seven Years' War. Sir Samuel was the son of a vicar, and had entered the navy as a captain's servant, had become an able seaman, and then had made the difficult ascent into the ranks of the officers. His first voyage across the Atlantic was as a lieutenant in 1748, and he went again in 1759. Because of a severe bilious disorder he sought assignment to a milder climate, but was sent back to America in 1765 and 1767-68, when his ship *Romney* visited Boston to allay "the mischievous humors of the populace."

In January, 1778, his active service as ship captain seemed to be at an end, for he was appointed Commissioner of Portsmouth Dockyard and Governor of the Naval Academy. It was commonly supposed that these posts offered honorable retirement. This notion about Hood seemed to have been confirmed when George III on his visit to the dockyard made him a baronet. Consequently there was great surprise in naval circles when, in September, 1780, Sir Samuel was suddenly promoted to the rank of Rear Admiral and hoisted his flag in the *Barfleur*, 90 guns, as Rodney's second in command.

The choice had not been an easy one for either Sandwich or Hood. The First Lord had written to Rodney: "It has been difficult, very difficult, to find out proper flag officers to serve under you. Some are rendered unfit from their factious connexions, others from inferiority or insufficiency, and we have at last been obliged to make a promotion in order to do the thing properly."[13] For his part, Hood first rejected, on Saturday, September 16, 1780, Sandwich's "very flattering offer of my flag and going to the West Indies," asserting that "those bodily infirmities with which I have been afflicted for near twenty years, are of late become so very heavy and severe that I have no spirits left and can scarce keep myself upon my legs and should only be the shadow of a flag officer." But on the following Monday, "feeling myself so much better than I was on Saturday . . . and flattering myself that a warm climate will tend more towards removing my complaints than any assistance I can get at home," he accepted.[14]

Hood's extreme reluctance is somewhat hard to explain in the light of his earlier pleas to be sent to sea. In March, 1780, he had maintained that he had not become Commissioner at Portsmouth "from inclination, but from a desire of giving accomodation to Government." He spoke of "my very great desire of hoisting my flag and serving in the military line," and his "mortification of seeing my juniors placed in the road to glory and preferred to distinguished employments."[15] It is altogether probable that Hood on Saturday was more concerned about braving the rough side of Sir George's tongue than he was about the buffeting of the elements.

By temperament Hood was not fitted to be second in command to anyone. In the opinion of Dorothy Hood, his biographer, "Subordination was not his forte . . . he carried no oil for troubled waters in his locker." Yet as the most recently promoted Rear Admiral of the Blue, he found himself junior to everyone: to Rodney at the Leewards, to Parker in Jamaica, and to Graves in New York. Vehement, passionate, and well aware of his own considerable powers of insight and initiative, he was a harsh judge of his superiors. "It is rarely," writes Hannay, "that he has a good word for anybody, or that his criticism is not pointed by contempt . . . his inclination to sneer was strong . . . he was always on the lookout for an occasion to find fault." Friction between two such gifted fault-finders as Rodney and Hood was inevitable, and when it came it was violent, at least on Hood's part.

Hannay concludes that Hood "had not been five months in the West Indies before we find him writing of his superior in a tone of acrimonious contempt. . . . He detested his commander-in-chief . . . toward Rodney his natural censoriousness is reinforced by something which amounts to hatred." He is at something of a loss to explain Hood's incessant backbiting at Rodney's expense. He recognizes that Hood was Rodney's social inferior and touchy about it, at the same time that he excelled his admiral professionally and knew it. Combined with no little aristocratic insolence, Hannay finds in Rodney "an air of breeding, a fine distinction of manner, which his able subordinate [Hood] entirely lacks."[16] Perhaps this consisted in writing charmingly to Sir Samuel on his appointment that there was no one he would have preferred to have as his second, while assuring a friend in conversation that "They might as well send me an old applewoman!"[17]

REAR ADMIRAL THOMAS GRAVES

The man who commanded the British fleet at the battle of the Chesapeake was Thomas Graves (1725?-1802), the second son of Admiral Thomas Graves of Thanckes, Cornwall, by his second wife Elizabeth. He entered the navy at an early age, and served in the *Norfolk* commanded by his father, becoming a lieutenant at age eighteen in 1743. He remained in that rank for the next ten years, but then advanced quickly from commander to captain in 1755. While in command of the *Sheerness*, a 20-gun frigate, in 1756, he encountered a French Indiaman which he mistakenly took to be a ship of the line, and avoided action. For this he was court-martialed, the verdict being that he ought to "have attempted to discover her force by going down and engaging her," although he had "not avoided coming to action through negligence, disaffection, or cowardice under the 10th, 12th, or 13th Articles of War." His offense was owing to "an error in judgment" under the 36th Article; and he was sentenced to be reprimanded publicly by the president of the court.

This episode had a "peculiar interest" for Graves because it was handed down at Plymouth on the very same day that Admiral John Byng was condemned to death by a court-martial at Portsmouth under the 12th Article for "negligence" rather than for "an error in judgment." Historians generally have since concluded that Byng's offense was indeed only an "error in judgment," and that his plight at Minorca was due to criminal negligence on the part of his accusers.

Thomas Graves might have advanced even more rapidly in his profession, had it not been for a clerical error by Sandwich. When Thomas's uncle, Admiral Samuel Graves, who has been described as "a corrupt admiral without any shadow of capacity," was recalled from America in 1777, he felt entitled to a *douceur* from the First Lord, which was furnished in the form of "provision" for three of his nephews, Samuel, John, and Richard Graves, all of them young and aspiring naval lieutenants. The trouble was that Admiral Samuel had a fourth nephew, Thomas Graves, the eldest and most esteemed by him of them all, but who was left out of consideration because Lord Sandwich got the names mixed.

In spite of this oversight and the early blemish on his record, Thomas Graves advanced to the command of frigates during the Seven Years' War, and held the Governorship of Newfoundland from 1761 to 1763. During the peace which followed, he had only the captaincy of a Plymouth guardship. In 1778 he went out to America as captain of the *Conqueror*, 74 guns, in Admiral Byron's fleet that was tardily ordered there in pursuit of D'Estaing. He became separated from Byron in an Atlantic storm, and arrived at Sandy Hook in a disabled state. Having been made a Rear Admiral of the Blue on March 29, 1779, he was recalled to England, and sent out as a "fifth admiral" to Sir Charles Hardy's home fleet, then consisting of four divisions.

When it became known that a French squadron under the Chevalier de Ternay was to go to American waters, Rear Admiral Graves was ordered there to counter him with eight of the line, later reduced to six. Most of his ships had just come from the relief of Gibraltar, they were short of supplies and men, and their men were short of pay. Graves expected trouble; and it came on April 8, 1780, when the signal was given to leave Spithead, and five of the eight did not move. Their crews shut themselves between decks with all the ports down. Believing, as he wrote to Stephens, that "mutiny was to be suppressed at the instant, though it might cost some lives," Graves ordered the men "forced into the daylight . . . if any man venture to oppose by violence, put him to death."[18]

The display of force succeeded, and the mutineers gave in on April 11. After a ten-day trial of sixteen of them, two were sentenced to five hundred lashes each, one-half of which were given "to strike some terror into the fleet," and the rest remitted. They escaped hanging only because it was proved that "in strictness of the Act of Parliament," their wages were actually due to them. Graves got his squadron of six of the line to Plymouth, where they were weatherbound for a month. They were finally able to sail on May 17, and reached New York on July 13, an unusually swift passage. This was just two days after Commodore de Ternay landed Rochambeau's contingent at Newport, although he had left Brest some sixteen days before Graves sailed from Plymouth.

But Graves found himself in hot water, and over the touchy subject of a prize ship, the rich French East Indiaman *Farges*, which he had captured at sea and which arrived at New York eight days later. Complaints immediately arose that he had wasted time in taking and towing this valuable conquest. Admiral Rodney, who came to New York so unexpectedly two months later, was sure that Graves's delay had prevented Clinton and himself from getting to Rhode Island ahead of De Ternay. Perhaps for the purpose of cutting off criticism in Parliament, Vice Admiral Arbuthnot was ordered to investigate Graves's conduct. This implied, said Graves, who was furious, "a suspicion of negligence and delay by a greater attention to the preservation of a prize than to the public service." Lord Sandwich assured him that he had been cleared of any such charges; but a grievance still lingered, and was revived after the battle of the Chesapeake.

So great was the anxiety at the Admiralty regarding the wintering of Arbuthnot's reinforced fleet of ten ships of the line that the Cabinet on September 14, 1780, voted a peremptory order to Graves to take five of them to Rodney at the Leewards; only to cancel it on October 11. Clinton had been trying by every known method to get rid of the decrepit Arbuthnot, who by February, 1781, had "lost almost totally the sight of one eye, and the other is but a very feeble helpmate . . . Besides," said that admiral, "I have lately been seized with very odd fits . . . almost instantly I faint, remain senseless and speechless sometimes four hours and sometimes longer . . . with cold sweats for two or three days after . . ."[19] To Clinton's immense relief Arbuthnot finally turned over the command to Graves on July 12, 1781.

Nearly all the estimates of Graves's character portray him as courteous, kindly, and rather dull, though by no means lacking in courage. Professor Willcox is of the opinion that he "was conscientious, polite, easy to work with, fitted to command a squadron which was comfortably superior to the enemy. But he was not the man for a crisis, and he was plunged without warning into the worst naval crisis of the war. He tried to meet it bluntly, by a battle in which he displayed more courage than skill. He failed, and failure seems to have left him with no further resources in himself."[20]

7

ARCHITECTS OF VICTORY:
LOUIS XVI, CHOISEUL,
AND VERGENNES

"The presence and work of the French fleet gave America her independence."　　　　　　—J. Franklin Jameson

Why should the oldest and least democratic kingly realm in Europe make common cause with ragged republican rebels against another monarchy? The actions of Louis XVI and his advisers in 1778-83 seemed quite inexplicable to Englishmen, who found it hard to believe that any monarch in his right mind would deliberately encourage armed defiance of the very principle upon which his own power rested: the divine right of kings. To them it was "an unnatural alliance" of Papist and Protestant (or Deist), aristocrat with republican, traditional enemy with recent foe. Accustomed as we are to explaining alliances in terms of ideas, it seems difficult, even today, to account for the actions of the French noblemen, just ten years before they were to be wiped out by their own revolution, in ideological terms. Yet in 1931 the Comte de la Loge d'Ausson found it logical to publish in Paris a book entitled (in translation) *How Monarchist France Liberated America*.

Credible or not, the decision was ultimately made by the French King Louis XVI ((1754-93), who was much closer to being an absolute sovereign of his realm than George III of his, although he took a much smaller part than the English king in determining his country's policies. Louis XVI came to the throne in 1774 at the age of twenty. When the American Revolution began, therefore, he was an inexperienced ruler who quite naturally deferred to the already established policies of his ministers. His own intellectual attainments were modest, to say the least. He had little interest in the details of royal administration, preferring such pastimes as hunting and the making of locks. The only serious subject for which he "displayed an uncommon passion," says Wraxall, "was geography. It is well-known that none of his ministers equalled him in that branch of knowledge. Before 1778, when the French Cabinet embraced the injudicious determination to aid the Americans by sending out D'Estaing with a fleet to their support, the King had rendered himself so perfect a master of the topography of the trans-Atlantic continent, that from the River St. Lawrence to the southern extremity of Florida, not a headland, a bay, a river, or almost an inlet, were unknown to him."[1]

This lively interest in geography extended to voyages and ships, and so to France's navy. One of its historians, Claude Farrère, has said that "Louis XVI was the only one of all our kings who was not ignorant of the navy and who was not ignorant of the advantages to be reaped by it."[2] Another area of knowledge in which the monarch was well versed was that of dynastic politics. He was keenly concerned for the honor of the house of Bourbon, resenting his new role as "unheeded onlooker," and was determined to restore France's dominant position on the continent. She must also retain her remaining colonial possessions. The blame rested upon England for the harsh terms which ended the Seven Years' War in 1763. Louis XVI was naturally reluctant to involve his nation to the point of war by intervening in an Anglo-American "family quarrel," but he was receptive to arguments based upon revenge and long-run self-defense. To King Charles III of Spain, he explained that he was "seeking reparation for the insults to the French flag" and the salvation "of an oppressed people who had thrown themselves into my arms."

It is impossible today to accept any longer the oversimplified notion that the French Court was swept into the American alliance on a wave of liberal enthusiasm inspired by the heroic example of the young Marquis de Lafayette. Undoubtedly there was unrest with the "gilded servitude" of life at Versailles, and a profound thirst for military glory among many of the courtiers. Among the intellectuals there was unquestionably a good deal of sentimental sympathy for the "unspoiled" Americans as exemplified by the immensely popular Doctor Benjamin Franklin. But, as the late Professor Corwin pointed out: "The idea of intervention came, in the first instance, not from the *salon* but from the Foreign Office . . . It was shaped, not by philosophers, but by professional diplomatists."[3]

In the later stages of the war, generosity mingled with calculation, but at its inception, the Franco-American alliance had all the earmarks of a hard-headed economic and political bargain. For Louis XVI and his ministers the problem was not simply a matter of vengeful punishment of England for her humiliation of France. It was not even a simple transaction involving the payment of "two or three million in aid to save three hundred million in sugar islands." The peace of 1763 had upset the balance of power in Europe in a manner unfavorable to France. The process of restoring the Bourbon dynasty's lost status had already been begun under Louis XV, whose Foreign Minister from 1758 to 1770 had been the able Étienne François, Duc de Choiseul. The kings of France had an absolute right to choose their ministers, and did not have to worry about whether or not they could maintain parliamentary majorities.

Consequently the choice of a minister often depended far more upon "the favor of the King's favorite" than upon a candidate's political ideas. It is said that the Duc de Choiseul, for example, gained the good graces of Madame de Pompadour by procuring for her some of the letters the King had written to his cousin Madame de Choiseul in the course of an intrigue with her. But however he may have reached high office, Choiseul showed himself to be a man of extraordinary vision and energy. It was he who perceived that the great obstacle in the path of any restoration of French prestige was the maritime colossus across the Channel, and that England's principal source of strength lay in her commerce with her colonies. That view was amply confirmed by Lord Chatham in a speech to Parliament on November 18, 1777, just after Saratoga, when he said that "America was indeed the foundation of our wealth, the nerve of our war strength, the nursery and basis of our naval power." The theme was echoed and re-echoed by George III and Germain and other last-ditch opposers of independence for the colonies on the ground that it would spell the absolute ruin of Great Britain.

"The true balance of power," Choiseul wrote to France's ambassador to Sweden on March 21, 1759, "really resides in commerce and in America." Trade in turn must rest upon naval supremacy, which is a matter of having a navy powerful enough to go where it will. Hence if France is to regain her status in a world where Britain rules the waves, it will not be enough to win battles on the continent of Europe. France must achieve naval supremacy; and the first step must be to bring about the downfall of England. That must be accomplished by fighting "the true war, the war upon the seas and in America."[4] Furthermore, the aim of that American naval war must be independence. It will not be enough to carry on a war to win autonomy for the thirteen colonies *within* the British empire. To be of any real value to France, it must be a war for outright independence of the mother country. In a memoir which Choiseul with considerable impertinence submitted to Louis XV in 1766 after his dismissal from office, he wrote: "But the American revolution that will come, but which we probably shall not see, will reduce England to a state of weakness in which she will no longer be an object of fear."[5]

Choiseul not only argued for sea power, but, aided by his cousin Praslin, he set about to lay the keels of a new and powerful French navy, setting as his goal eighty ships of the line and forty-four frigates. He aroused the patriotism of French men, women, and children to the point of donating all manner of contributions, large and small, to the building and equipping of warships, the providing of arms and uniforms, and the training of officers and men. Among the latter he reorganized a corps of ten thousand expert naval gunners who drilled once a week.

France had long been in the lead in applying science to the arts of war and ship design. Her yards could turn out a three-decked ship in fourteen months against the three years required by English shipwrights. "The average French ship of the line," says Graham, "was the product of skilled architects, and was capable of heavy fire-power without loss of weatherliness. The same could not be said of English-built ships of similar rating."[6] The French navy, however, had long been weak in officer morale and discipline, thanks to the gulf between the *officiers rouges* of the nobility and the volunteer *officiers bleus*. Among the nobility, all officers of various ranks were "equal," but felt themselves far above the non-nobles, the tabs of whose uniforms were blue instead of red. Choiseul tried to alleviate this extreme class feeling, but without much success.

In line with Choiseul's concern for commerce and America, secret agents, among them Baron de Kalb, were sent to the colonies as early as 1764. Their first reports were somewhat confusing: revolt was certain to come, eventually, but in 1770 it seemed some years away. They warned that France must avoid giving the impression, if she joined in the war when it came, of seeking to recover Canada, for this would anger the Americans. She must confine herself to assuring the safety of her present possessions, and to promoting American independence.

When the American rebellion broke into the open in 1775, the foreign minister of Louis XVI was Charles Gravier, Comte de Vergennes (1717-82). He had been born in Dijon, and had learned diplomacy under the tutelage of an uncle, M. de Chavigny. Vergennes scored his first success at the Court of Trier in 1750, and was sent to Constantinople as minister, later ambassador, in 1753, where Choiseul found him not quite zealous enough in provoking a desired quarrel between Russia and Turkey.

Vergennes was a man of subtle intelligence, capable of duplicity on behalf of France when necessary, and burning with resentment of England for the peace terms of 1763. Above all he was cautious, methodical, and circumspect, "saving his trumps until late in the game," fearing to commit himself to the American rebel cause prematurely, lest a compromise-minded government should come to power in England. Like Louis XVI himself, Vergennes had pointed out in 1775 that "The spirit of revolt, wherever it appears, is always a dangerous example." He knew also that most Americans shared the common English prejudices against Catholic France and its absolutist king. So he must be positively sure that they were in earnest about independence, that they really meant to turn their insurrection into a full-scale war, and that they would stand firm throughout the long, hard struggle it might demand.

Toward the close of 1775 Vergennes sent additional scouts to America to report, and soon entered into a close partnership with Caron de Beaumarchais to provide the patriots secretly with supplies and munitions. Favorable reports came in from the French agents; and in Madrid the Marquis Grimaldi expressed the hope that aid to the rebels, which he approved, would result in the exhaustion of both England and America. The next step, and not an easy one, was to secure the King's approval of financial backing to Beaumarchais to the extent of one million *livres*.

Louis XVI was no admirer of revolutionists of any description, and feared, in addition, that aid to the rebels might provoke England to a declaration of war upon France. Finance Minister Turgot predicted bankruptcy in any such event. The king would have to be reassured that Beaumarchais' scheme would do great harm to Britain cheaply and secretly. All the fighting would be done by Americans. Vergennes pointed out that if George III succeeded in subduing his American subjects he would almost surely proceed to conquer and absorb the rich French sugar islands in the West Indies, whereas a friendly but weak ally, such as the infant United States, would help to protect them.

This was an argument Louis XVI could understand. The case for self-defense was the decisive factor; a majority of the Cabinet, including Turgot, went along with Vergennes' program of secrecy; and the "sluggish reluctance" of Louis was overcome. Beaumarchais got a million *livres* each from France and Spain, and became Rodrigues Hortalez and Company, merchants. "Thus before any agent of the rebels reached French soil," says Professor J. R. Alden, "and because the Bourbons saw the situation as being capable of being exploited to their own advantage, they determined to offer concealed assistance to the patriots."[7]

It was indeed fortunate that this was so, because in the American colonies, every step toward soliciting or accepting help from "foreign alliances" was stoutly resisted, and finally taken only with the greatest reluctance. Even after Congress weakened to the point of sending commissioners to Paris, aid continued to be secret, and the rebel representatives could not be publicly received. Benjamin Franklin was a tower of strength in creating goodwill toward the patriot cause. But the news of repeated British victories was discouraging. Vergennes had hopes, during

1777, of engineering an alliance of France, Spain, and the thirteen colonies against England, each pledged not to make a separate peace until independence was assured. But Spain was not interested in independence for the Americans. When General Howe took Philadelphia, there was a further cooling off of French enthusiasm; and the watchful waiting by Vergennes continued.

Then there came to Paris, on December 4, 1777, the electrifying news of Burgoyne's surrender. It was the overwhelming argument. Americans could fight, and would fight, against first-class British and German invaders. Ten days after the tidings came, Vergennes, without waiting to see whether Spain would act or not, offered formal recognition to the rebels, which meant a declaration of war with England, asking in return a pledge not to make a separate peace. The treaty of alliance was prepared by Louis XVI and his cabinet on January 7, 1778, and signed on February 6, providing co-operation until American independence was "formally or tacitly assured"; and renouncing any French claims to American territory west of the Mississippi River.

French aid in the form of money and munitions now began to flow openly to American ports. The first French expedition was a naval one. On April 13, 1778, a formidable fleet of twelve ships of the line left Toulon, accompanied by three frigates. The command had been given to the Comte d'Estaing, who had served in the army until the age of thirty-four, and was hardly qualified to command so large a squadron with the rank of vice admiral. His voyage was a series of catastrophes almost from start to finish. His progress was incredibly slow, partly because some of his ships were poor sailers, and partly because he indulged in practice maneuvers en route. It took him thirty-three days to get from Toulon to Gibraltar.

It has been pointed out many times that if D'Estaing had shown a fraction of the resourcefulness displayed by De Grasse later on, he might have engineered a "Yorktown" at New York three years ahead of his fellow admiral. For Clinton was almost defenseless in New York for ten days before D'Estaing reached Delaware Bay on July 8, since Admiral Lord Howe, with only six sixty-fours, was busy embarking the supplies of his brother's army which had just taken Philadelphia. But D'Estaing might have had his troubles in taking even a defenseless New York, since his heavy ships, badly chosen for the expedition, could, in the opinion of a conclave of pilots, only get over the bar when a northeast wind coincided with a strong spring tide.

The Count d'Estaing was to try again at Newport, Rhode Island, where his sudden departure, in Lafayette's words, caused "general consternation . . . much greater than I expected or could have believed." There was "a rising tide of indignation" against the French alliance in many parts of the country, with open violence in Boston and Charleston. For the time being, co-operation between the two nations, especially in amphibious operations, was going very badly indeed.

Early in 1781 Vergennes shared the general pessimism about the allied cause to the point of confiding to his files a secret memorandum outlining a compromise peace conference that would leave the British in possession of the positions held by them in the Carolinas, Georgia, New York, Maine, and points west. This made mockery of the King's promises concerning American independence, just before Louis XVI was personally called upon to honor them by the brash envoy John Laurens.

8

ARCHITECTS OF VICTORY: LAFAYETTE AND ROCHAMBEAU

"He has gone to America with Lafayette."
—Said, incorrectly, of many French noblemen, 1777-81

The true contribution of the Marquis de Lafayette (1757-1834) to American independence has been obscured by so dense a cloud of legend that it is difficult to recover. His Marquis father had been killed at the battle of Minden in 1759, and his mother died in 1770, leaving Lafayette an orphan at thirteen with a very large fortune. At sixteen he married the daughter of the Duc d'Ayen, granddaughter of the Duc de Noailles, thus allying himself with one of the most powerful families of the ancient nobility.

At nineteen Lafayette was a captain in the Guards dragoons, "reserved, awkward, and inexperienced," but with an overpowering *amour de la gloire*. In 1776 he heard of the American declaration of independence. "At the first news of this quarrel," he wrote many years after the event, "my heart was enrolled in it." There were many ingredients which supplied him with motivation: discontent at home, traditional hatred of England, desire to win military renown, and, least of all, some cloudy idealism. In his *Lafayette Comes to America*, Professor Louis Gottschalk has shown conclusively that "it was not because he was already a champion of liberty that he espoused the American cause."[1] It was rather in America that he acquired ideals of liberty and reform.

He did overcome difficulties in reaching American shores, but in making his "romantic escapes" at the age of nineteen

75

he did not have the entire government of France against him, as is sometimes supposed. He had demanded and been given a commission of sorts as major general in the American army by Silas Deane in Paris on December 7, 1776. When he appeared in Philadelphia, speaking little English, he seemed to be just another foreign adventurer in search of fortune as well as fame. The young Marquis quickly changed that picture by offering himself as a volunteer without pay. His tender of help was accepted by a Congressional resolution on July 31, 1777, stating that "in consideration of his zeal, illustrious family and connexions, he is to have the rank and commission of major general." Congress intended the commission to be purely honorary, leaving it to the discretion of General Washington to assign suitable duties to the French nobleman.

Washington was notorious for his personal attitude of dignified reserve in his relations with his officers; but Lafayette turned out to be the exception to the rule. He charmed his way into a life-long intimacy with his fatherly commander-in-chief, who sometimes showed him what amounted to favoritism. Yet Lafayette himself made every effort to deserve the command of a division, which was finally recommended by Washington to Congress on November 1, 1777, because "he is sensible, discreet in his manners, had made great proficiency in our language, and from the disposition he discovered at the battle of Brandywine, possesses a large share of bravery and military ardor." Brandywine had been his first baptism of fire in America, and the occasion of his first battle wound.

Lafayette was a man of many enthusiasms, and his services to the American cause were extremely varied. Not always the ideal *liaison* man between the French and the American top commands, since his rank and standing were higher in the New World than in the Old, he was by far the most effective French advocate of aid to the rebels at the Court of Versailles and before the French public at large. By anticipating the formal treaty of alliance, he had come to symbolize it. One of his most important missions brought him back to France in February, 1779, at a time when French assistance to America had accomplished disappointingly little. On landing he was technically guilty of having defied the King's orders by leaving; but after tendering a profuse letter of apology to Louis XVI, reminding that monarch that "the recent treaty would seem to justify" his having allowed "the emotions of my heart to overcome my reason," he was forgiven. He was lionized in the *salons*, received "the kisses of the ladies," and from Queen Marie Antoinette a promotion to *mestre de camp* (roughly, colonel) in the French army.

Lafayette set to work to induce the King through Vergennes to send an army to America, but about all the cautious minister would say was that "perhaps we shall decide that the great blows should be struck in America rather than Europe." The eager Marquis soon found that his projects conflicted with a vast Franco-Spanish scheme to invade England, which would absorb all the country's military resources, including himself. Furthermore, the Count d'Estaing's fleet had not yet returned from across the Atlantic, and nothing could be undertaken until he made his report.

On February 22, 1779, soon after Lafayette reached France, John Adams had written him a letter in which he spoke of the urgent necessity of more aid for America, particularly naval aid. But the prospects of getting it were darkened by the news at the end of the year of D'Estaing's dismal and costly failure at Savannah. Lafayette feared that it would have "a bad effect upon America," reducing French naval prestige to the zero point. In the middle of the year, Lafayette had told Vergennes that a French expeditionary force would give the allies a military preponderance in America, "*if* [and he underlined these words] *it were well led*." The first naval enterprise, alas, had not been well led, even though Count d'Estaing showed great personal bravery (being twice wounded) at the siege of Savannah.

Yet in January, 1780, the prospects of obtaining a French army for America suddenly brightened. The invasion of England had been abandoned. Choiseul's predictions were about to come true; France and Spain would strike at her colonies instead. After making a far-from-modest bid to head the new expedition himself, Lafayette learned to his chagrin that an older general, the Comte de Rochambeau, had been selected to command six thousand soldiers escorted by Commodore de Ternay with six ships of the line. They were to serve as auxiliaries and under General Washington's orders.

Lafayette swallowed his disappointment, and, as an authority at first hand on American deficiencies in *matériel*, he visited Rochambeau, telling him that he had better take with him such things as a printing press, mortars, flints, flour, biscuits, wool, leather, tenting, tools, and bricks. More importantly, he informed the Count that there could be no success until and unless the allies controlled American waters. Rochambeau sent a digest of this advice on March 1, 1780, to the head of the French navy, M. de Sartine.

Lafayette returned to America in April, 1780, to a tumultuous welcome in Boston, only to find Washington's army reduced to a "very small number . . . almost perishing for want" after a winter worse than the one at Valley Forge. Soon word was to come of Charleston's fall; and in general conditions were so bad that Lafayette hardly dared to write the truth to his friends in France. But when he told Washington of the prospective arrival of Rochambeau, the American commander lost no time in planning an immediate joint attack on New York before Clinton and Arbuthnot could return from their South Carolina success. If Admiral de Guichen could only be induced to bring his fleet from the West Indies so as to assure naval supremacy, the main stronghold of the British in America might be successfully stormed.

This first of Washington's plans to stage an allied descent upon New York collapsed when De Ternay and Rochambeau arrived two months later than expected, after a seventy-day voyage, to learn that Clinton had returned to his New York base. Rochambeau had been handicapped by lack of shipping, and had brought only five thousand men, leaving a "second division" behind in Brest, which he begged the King to send along later. The French forces arrived at Newport on July 11, 1780, and soon learned that Rear Admiral Thomas Graves had joined Arbuthnot in New York two days later, bringing the British squadron to the number of ten ships to De Ternay's six. Mistakenly supposing that the French Commodore had brought twelve ships of the line, Lafayette wanted to go ahead with the New York attack; but Washington wisely held that the allies did not have a decisive naval superiority, which, he said, must be considered "as a fundamental principle, and the basis upon which every hope of success must ultimately depend."²

In the ensuing debate, Lafayette was the only one of the allied leaders who favored the landing of troops on Long Island to attack New York without naval superiority. That notion was soon exploded by the appearance of Arbuthnot's squadron to blockade Rhode Island; while Rochambeau's "second division" remained equally bottled up in Brest. Lafayette felt "personally affronted" by this enforced French idleness, an irritation shared by some of the younger French officers. The root of many of the army's troubles, Lafayette concluded, was lack of money. With enough hard cash "three quarters of our troubles would disappear."

But money, clothing, guns, and powder would not be enough. Rochambeau had finally convinced him that the presence of a French fleet had done some good (it kept Clinton in New York), and would do more good in the future. Hence he struck a new note in his latest plea to Vergennes: "Situated and disposed as America now is, it is essential to the interest as well as the honor of France that our flag reign on these seas, that the campaign be decisive, and that it begin next spring . . . with a corps of ten thousand and an assured naval predominance . . . every year of delay increases the number of vessels, men, and money you will ultimately have to send."

To Madame de Tessé he wrote: "All this is as dull as a European war . . . But without ships we can expect only blows . . ." To Franklin he repeated his plea for maritime supremacy, and lamented the "nack'd, shokingly nack'd" condition of the soldiers, "worse off in that respect than we have ever been." To his wife he wrote: "You may rest assured of the health of your friends in America so long as our maritime inferiority continues. . . . If we had had some vessels, it would have been possible to do more."³

Lafayette's pleading for ships (as well as money and clothing) reached its peak in the letter he addressed to the new French Minister of Marine, the Marquis de Castries in January, 1781, in an effort to reinforce the crucial mission of John Laurens to Paris. With naval superiority, he said, "We can do everything, without it we can do nothing—at least with certainty." The next campaign must be decisive in order to avoid a compromise peace, and only naval preponderance could make it so. Lafayette was by this time a thorough convert to the views of Washington and Rochambeau on the subject of command of the sea. "With a naval inferiority," he told Vergennes, "it is impossible to make war in America. It is that which prevents us from attacking any point that might be carried with two or three thousand men. It is that which reduces us to defensive operations, as dangerous as they are humiliating. The English are conscious of this truth, and all their movements prove how much they desire to retain the empire of the sea." He asked for "a decided naval superiority for the next campaign"; and pointed up the importance of placing not only Rochambeau but any new naval contingent under Washington's orders, without any accompanying secret instructions.[4]

Lafayette wrote such a plethora of letters, capable, as Professor Gottschalk says, "of opening almost every door worth trying in the French capital" for John Laurens that not all of them had been completed by the time the American envoy sailed. So we cannot tell exactly how much Lafayette's tireless "scrawling" to his friends in Paris had to do with the ultimate success of Laurens' mission. That he made a strenuous epistolary effort to win both De Grasse's fleet and much-needed money for the American cause is incontestable.

COUNT DE ROCHAMBEAU

It sometimes happens that a brave man will earn the rewards of fame, but will not reap them because he is relatively inarticulate. One such hero was Jean Baptiste Donatien de Vimeur, Count de Rochambeau (1725-1807), whose pen wrote mainly terse military orders and dispatches. He came from a long line of warriors; but as a second son he was destined for the priesthood. The death of his older brother when Jean was sixteen changed all that, because "he must now serve his country with the same zeal that I might have served God." He entered the army in 1741 as standard-bearer of the Saint-Simon regiment of infantry of which his uncle was captain; and for the next twenty years he was almost continuously at war in some of the most dangerous operations of the era. He was a colonel at twenty-two, and received a severe wound in the forehead at Lawfeld, which brought from the King a pension of two thousand *livres*.

His fortune was greatly increased by the dowry of the wife whom he married in December, 1749. She was Jeanne-Thérèse d'Acosta, daughter of a wholesale merchant in foodstuffs, a *bourgeoise* who brought her husband over three hundred thousand *livres* and an income of twenty thousand a year. The couple might have shone at Court, but the Count's tastes were simple, and he preferred life in his native town of Vendôme.

Rochambeau took part in the Minorcan campaign of 1756, and came out a brigadier general with the Cross of Saint-Louis. In the following year he plunged into the wars in Germany, where he spent the next six winters with his troops, leaving them only twice for short periods. His father could say, in asking for his son's promotion to major general, that he was "madly in love with his work." He had received the colonelcy of the famous regiment of Auvergne; and soon acquired another wound. Fame and the King's favor came soon after the battle of Klostercamp in 1761. He was made a *maréchal de camp*, and one of the four inspectors of infantry. In some ways this was a thankless job, trying to change ingrained military habits. But in co-operation with the Duc de Choiseul, Rochambeau managed to take a significant role in the rebuilding of French military institutions.

When France entered the war with England as an ally of the American insurgents, Rochambeau expected to take part in the Franco-Spanish invasion of England as the commander of the advance guard which was to attack Portsmouth and the Isle of Wight. When that project was given up after months of planning, Rochambeau had just recovered from a bout with rheumatism. He was about to go to Vendôme to settle the estate of his father, who had recently died, when he was called to Versailles.

It was there that he received the orders and instructions to proceed to North America with an army of auxiliaries for the aid of Washington. He knew that the Marquis de Lafayette had been pleading for just such an army and wanted to command it. But Louis XVI and Vergennes desired an older, more experienced, and more stable general than Lafayette. Rochambeau had been a brigadier before Lafayette had been born. He was a tough professional soldier, veteran of many sieges, a man of action primarily, not a man profusely given to words. Yet when Lafayette brashly suggested that Rochambeau might be somewhat lethargic, the latter squelched him superbly in a letter beginning: "Permit me, my dear Marquis, an old father, to reply to you as a tender son whom he esteems highly . . ." The general's watchwords were duty and simplicity. He was a strict disciplinarian in the mode of his century, which would now be considered brutal. A great believer in promptness in meting out both punishments and rewards, his Auvergne regiment was known as one of the best behaved in the French army. In America, he told Washington: "I will maintain as strict discipline as though the army were encamped under the walls of Paris."

His approach to Washington was a model of co-operativeness: "You may do with me what you please." This was not because his army was burning with zeal for American liberty and equality, but because both the lieutenant general and his men were soldiers of the King of France who had been ordered to America to fight his hereditary enemies, the British. The late Professor Gilbert Chinard ventured the opinion that Rochambeau was "more of a true republican in spirit and in conduct than Lafayette himself";[5] but this is debatable. What is much less contestable is the estimate made of Rochambeau, years later, by the Marquis de Ségur: "He seemed to have been purposely created to understand Washington and to be understood by him and to serve with republicans. A friend of order, of laws, of liberty, his example more even than his authority obliged us scrupulously to respect the rights, properties, and customs of our allies."[6]

9

ARCHITECTS OF VICTORY:
DE GRASSE AND WASHINGTON

"Among the architects of victory at Yorktown, De Grasse takes first rank."   —John C. Miller, *Triumph of Freedom*

A French naval officer whose permanent position was that of Commodore (*Chef d'escadre*) was chosen by Louis XVI in March, 1781, to become Lieutenant General of the Naval Army (Rear Admiral) to take "command of the squadrons in the waters of North America," thus outranking any other admiral on this side of the Atlantic. He had been born a member of an ancient family of the Provençal nobility in the feudal castle of Bar at Bar-sur-Loup, Alpes Maritimes, on September 13, 1722, and had been christened François Joseph Paul de Grasse-Rouville with the title of Count de Grasse.

Even as a child, he had unusual size and strength, and showed a fondness for the outdoors. When he made little progress with a tutor, his father enrolled him at the age of eleven in the Séminaire de la Marine at Toulon, conducted by the Jesuits for the purpose of preparing young noblemen to become naval officers. One of the professors at the school, Father Paul Hoste, had published the pioneer volume on naval tactics in 1697. The young De Grasse did not complete his course at the seminary, however, since he was selected to become one of the sixteen pages of the Grand Master of the Knights of St. John at Malta. Admission to that order required four patents of nobility on the father's side and three more on the mother's, and also a vow of celibacy. De Grasse stayed at Malta, regarded as "the great school of war for the French navy," for six years, returning to France at age eighteen.

The early years of his long career in the French navy were spent in a number of frigates and line-ships, until he joined the *Gloire*, 40 guns, as ensign in Admiral La Jonquière's action against Admiral Anson in May, 1747, off Cape Finisterre. The *Gloire* justified her name by fighting Anson's flagship *Prince George*, 90 guns, for three hours, until seventy-five men lay dead on her decks and her captain, the Chevalier de Saliès, had been decapitated by a cannonball. Ensign de Grasse, who was standing beside him at the time, was severely wounded and taken prisoner to England with others from the six surrendered French ships, where he remained for three months. The French earned the praise of Anson for their stubborn gallantry, which cost them over seven hundred casualties and a reputed three hundred thousand pounds of treasure. It is curious to note that both De Grasse's first and last major actions at sea were extremely hard-fought and sanguinary, were with noted British admirals, and ended in captivity in England.

In 1754 the young Count became a lieutenant; and in 1762, just before the end of the Seven Years' War, he was promoted to the rank of captain. In 1764 he fell deeply in love, at the age of forty-two, with the beautiful Antoinette Accaron, daughter of the principal *valet de chambre* to Louis XV, but hardly De Grasse's equal in social position. Breaking his youthful vow of celibacy, he married her in January, 1765, in the presence of the King and Queen, and shortly afterwards he purchased the Chateau of Tilly, receiving the additional title of Marquis de Tilly from Louis XVI. After bearing him seven children: two sons and five daughters, of whom one son and four daughters survived, his wife died in 1773.

Count de Grasse remarried while serving in the West Indies. His new wife, a wealthy widow, Catherine de Pien, had been married three times. She was of noble birth and had large estates in San Domingo from her most recent husband, Count de Villeneuve-Tourettes. The marriage was a happy one until her death in 1780. In 1786 the admiral married for the third time, his bride Christine Marie Delphine Lazare de Gibon, daughter of the secretary of the French embassy at Malta, a union which was not as successful as his second. There were no children by these later marriages.

In 1772 De Grasse was assigned to an experimental unit called *l'escadre d'évolutions*, commanded by Sieur d'Orvilliers. Its purpose was to give ship captains experience in fleet movements at sea. Consisting of three ships of the line, six frigates and three corvettes, the squadron embarked upon a cruise for "war-like maneuvers" lasting for nearly four months. At the end of this advanced training, d'Orvilliers made the following comments regarding De Grasse as a commanding officer. "He was the best skilled captain in the squadron. Although his vessel was very inferior in quality [it was the corvette *Isis*], he nevertheless gave to the evolutions all the precision and brilliance possible. His frequent collisions with other ships during the cruise seems to demand something more perfect in his estimate of a situation at a glance, but they show his confidence in approaching vessels; and whenever the King may confide a squadron to me, I shall always choose the captains who prefer to risk a collision rather than abandon their position with the certainty of failing to execute a movement. De Grasse is a captain of the first distinction, made for a general officer and to conduct the squadrons and fleets of the King."[1]

Under the same admiral, De Grasse in the *Robuste*, 74 guns, had command of the second division of the French fleet in the battle off Ushant on July 27, 1778, in which twenty-seven French ships opposed thirty of the British under Admiral Keppel. The result of the indecisive engagement was a victory for d'Orvilliers, then sixty-eight years of age, in the sense that it failed to establish that degree of naval supremacy that would have enabled the British to confine the French to their seaports, thereby rendering aid to America impossible. It also provoked a violent controversy between Admirals Keppel and Palliser, whose respective courts-martial split the Royal Navy into political factions for years to come. At Ushant, the *Robuste* was the eighth ship in the French battle line. De Grasse received no special mention in dispatches after the engagement, possibly because of the poor handling of the van ships by the Duc de Chartres.

In January, 1779, De Grasse was ordered to take a squadron of four ships of the line to Martinique to reinforce Count d'Estaing, who had just failed to recapture the island of St. Lucia from the British. The *Robuste* took part in the action of July 6 against Admiral "Foulweather Jack" Byron off Grenada, in which Byron was forced to retreat, damaged but not annihilated. De Grasse had fought in two battles in which the French had had the upper hand, but did not gain noticeable advantages. D'Estaing's next venture, his attempt to retake Savannah in cooperation with the American land forces, met with dismal defeat. On October 9, 1779, the allies were repulsed with very heavy losses.

De Grasse with his division of four line ships and four frigates was ordered to take the troops back to the Antilles. His comments on Savannah were bitter: "Great God! It would have been necessary to have seen it to believe it, and, in not saying the half, we would be thought to exaggerate and be partial. But nothing is so true, and I should not wish to repeat the experience for a million of revenue. The navy suffered a long time the fruits of that campaign."[2] Count de Bougainville was equally disgusted by this "barren American campaign," and wrote at its close: "The squadron which might have destroyed Byron is dispersed, overwhelmed by sickness and misfortune, tortured by hunger and thirst, and the troops raised for the defense of our colonies have been reduced to the merest handful."[3]

D'Estaing's return to France left De Grasse with six ships of the line as the senior naval officer in the West Indies until the Count de Guichen arrived in March, 1780, with sixteen of the line, four frigates, and a convoy of eighty-three merchantmen. In the series of battles with Admiral Rodney which followed, De Grasse commanded the blue squadron or rear division of seven ships in his flagship the *Robuste*. It was in the first of these engagements, on April 17, 1780, that Admiral Rodney claimed that his veteran captains had let him down by failing to comprehend his signals or to obey them. In terms of damages to ships (three of the British vessels were "near to sinking") it was a French victory; but since they had been thwarted in their plan to attack Barbados, it was something of a defeat. De Grasse commanded the rear division in two more brushes with Rodney, with much the same result in shattered English ships but no territorial gains for the French. In the three engagements the total losses were very nearly the same: the British had one hundred and eighty-eight killed, the French one hundred and ninety. There were five hundred and sixty-seven British wounded, and five hundred of the French.

When De Guichen returned to France instead of going to the North American coast at the urging of Lafayette and Luzerne, De Grasse had been supposed to take over the command of the nine remaining line ships; but he was ill, and it went to Baron de Monteil. Rodney completely misjudged De Guichen's intentions, and dashed for New York to oppose him. De Grasse sailed with De Guichen on August 16, and arrived on October 23 at the principal port of their new Spanish ally, Cadiz. Being on leave to recuperate from his illness, De Grasse went to Paris and to Versailles, where he was well received. It was said that the Queen singled out the handsome officer by offering her arm to him while they were walking through the palace galleries, and her act may have given credence to the charge that he received his new command in the West Indies by means of Court intrigue. There is ample evidence that De Grasse tried to have another officer appointed, but that the King insisted that he return to the Antilles, and at once.

The verdicts on his performance as admiral are confusingly contradictory. On the one hand he has been praised as a bold and enterprising commander, "the French Rodney"; while on the other he has been called "over-cautious" and "a timid tactician." Tornquist called him "a good seaman and known for his bravery, but besides, somewhat too careful." Merlant notes that "he did not seem to have the power of making himself beloved." This may have been because of the characteristics depicted by Guérin in his *Histoire Maritime de France*. "Obedience galled him, and as a result he brought to command a biting *hauteur marqué*, and disposition that never stooped to conciliate . . ."[4] It is certain that De Grasse possessed a formidable temper. When, after the battle of September 5, his fleet remained in the Chesapeake and was called upon for every conceivable kind of supplies by the allied armies on shore, a request for thirty pounds of candles for the artillery was refused with a "Damn it! You have stretched the blanket too tight!" A few days later, however, he wrote to Rochambeau: "I am a Provençal, and a sailor, which is enough to entitle me to a quick temper, and I acknowledge my fault and trust in your friendship."[5]

Admiral de Grasse was unusually tall in stature, standing six feet, two inches, and, as someone remarked: "six feet, six inches on days of battle." Combined with a tendency to corpulence which led some to say he was "more sheath than sword," his imposing figure may have inclined Tornquist to the comment that "his brutal character agreed with his grim appearance." In his attitude of severity toward his ship captains, there is no doubt that he bore a considerable resemblance to his opponent Rodney.

GENERAL GEORGE WASHINGTON

The career of George Washington (1732-99) to the year 1780 is so familiar that it hardly needs even a brief recounting. He had already had a quarter of a century of military experience, beginning with frontier activity in the French and Indian War in his early twenties. He had distinguished himself against "the public enemies" of England, the French, at the engagement known as Braddock's Defeat in 1755, and at the capture of Fort Duquesne (now Pittsburgh) in 1759. He had become a large landowner in 1752 by inheriting the estate of Mount Vernon from his half-brother Lawrence; and in 1759 he married Martha Dandridge Custis. In that same year he was elected to the Virginia House of Burgesses, where he became a leader in the movement for independence, and later represented Virginia as a delegate to the First and Second Continental Congresses.

In those days a man might be prominent in one colony and yet quite unknown outside it; and this was true to some extent of Washington when he was chosen on June 15, 1775, to command the Continental Army. He lost no time in assuming that office at Cambridge, Massachusetts, on July 3. But not until the following March 17, 1776, could the British be forced to evacuate Boston. Washington then moved his army to New York in the hope of being able to defend that city, but inferiority in numbers forced him to move northward to avoid entrapment in lower Manhattan. Seeking always to preserve his army, the general moved across New Jersey and the Delaware, scoring brilliant *coups* at Trenton in December, 1776, and at Princeton soon afterwards. Defeats late in 1777 at Brandywine and Germantown led to the loss of Philadelphia and the harrowing winter at Valley Forge. That historic ordeal was followed by the attack on Clinton's army, after the latter had been ordered to give up Philadelphia, at Monmouth Court House on June 28, 1778, when Washington's appearance checked General Charles Lee's retreat and halted the British counterattacks. In July of that year, Washington resumed his former station at White Plains on the Hudson above New York City, where his position was too strong for Clinton to attack, without being strong enough to justify the Americans in besieging New York without additional help.

Washington held the title of supreme commander of the rebel armies, but it was extremely difficult for him to exercise his authority directly over such great distances with agonizingly slow means of communication. At times his army could not even use the best methods of sending messages that were available for sheer lack of funds. Hence the area commanders, such as Gates at Saratoga and Camden, and Greene in the Carolinas, exercised a considerable amount of independent authority. But it was Washington who held the whole army together as time after time it threatened to disintegrate. It has even been said that "he held the Revolution together by the force of his character." It was he who saw, more clearly than anyone else, that, for all intents and purposes, the Continental Army *was* the Revolution. If it could be destroyed the British might indeed be able to subdue the rebellion for a long time to come. But as long as Washington and his army were in the field and not dispersed or annihilated the core of the independence movement lived and endured; and no amount of British victories in detail could add up to a winning of the war.

Thus in a very real sense there could never have been a Yorktown campaign without the indefatigable tenacity of General George Washington. His true genius as a national leader lay in the universal respect which he commanded and the fact that he could not be dispirited or discouraged by adversity. This does not, however, settle the question of his disputed role as one of the architects of the "Grand Design" which brought victory at Yorktown. The case for Washington as a "naval genius" has been put forward by Captain Dudley W. Knox, U.S.N.[6] The core of his argument holds that Washington the army general showed "naval genius" in perceiving the immense advantage possessed by the British through their command of the sea. They had "the bewildering mobility of sea power," which they could match against his much slower capacity to move his army about by land. All American seaports were vulnerable, for at any moment a British fleet carrying troops might appear, and the task of defending all the coastal cities simultaneously was an impossible one. Boston, Newport, New York, Philadelphia, and Savannah had each had their turn at being attacked, and Charleston was about to follow.

As long as the Royal Navy provided the King's army with such freedom of movement, Washington's problem of achieving a lasting American victory on land appeared to be insoluble. If the British foolishly campaigned in the interior, they could be defeated, but they could be dislodged from the coast cities only with the greatest difficulty. What was needed for victory was seapower. The colonists could not hope to build ships of the line themselves which would match the "heavies" of the King. The American navy of the Revolution was a handful of frigates assisted by hundreds of highly effective privateers. But lightly armed ships were no match for British seventy-fours and nineties, as Charleston (where half the American navy was captured) was to show.

Within two months of assuming command of the army, Washington learned something about the state of mind of the coastal settlements in face of British naval mobility, as pleas for garrisons poured in. He also saw that supplying defense detachments to all of them would mean that he would have no field army left. The question: Where will the British strike next? would continue to haunt coastal communities for several years to come. The fleet of another naval power, if strong enough, would make all the difference in the world. Everyone knew that both France and Spain had been quietly building up their navies. If France could be induced to enter the war, Spain might join her, and a combination of the two might challenge British rule of the waves.

Such thoughts began to take on substance with Louis XVI's

signing of the French alliance on February 6, 1778, followed by the departure of D'Estaing's fleet from Toulon for America in April. Washington was to have his first demonstration of what seapower could accomplish. It was a most disappointing one, since D'Estaing arrived too late to attack Admiral Howe's weak fleet engaged in evacuating German regiments from Philadelphia; and could not induce any pilots to risk trying to take his heavy warships over the bar at Sandy Hook. Combined sea and land attacks on Savannah and Newport by French and Americans did not succeed. Perhaps, after all, the French navy was not the answer? Washington told Benjamin Franklin on December 20, 1780, that he was "disappointed . . . especially in the expected naval superiority, which was the pivot upon which everything turned. We have been compelled to spend an inactive campaign, after flattering prospects at the opening of it."[7]

D'Estaing had failed, but he had aroused hopes which Washington put into words for the first time in replying to the Council of Massachusetts in September, 1779. They had asked him to request that a few ships be detached from D'Estaing's fleet for the protection of their northern commerce along the New England coast. Washington replied: "If Count d'Estaing could spare a detachment superior to the enemy's naval force upon this continent . . . the measure would have a high probability of effecting many important and perhaps decisive advantages . . . that, in the present or future circumstances should permit him to concert a combined operation with the troops of these States, I should be ready to promote the measure to the utmost of our resources, and should have the highest hopes of success."[8]

A full two years before the siege of Yorktown, then, Washington must be credited with having grasped the main outlines of the formula of victory. He had not lost faith in French naval power because of its meagre accomplishments in its first campaign. As soon as possible, he wanted a fleet to return, for he was now fully convinced, as he wrote to Count de Rochambeau by way of Lafayette on July 15, 1780: "In any operation and under all circumstances, a decisive naval superiority is to be considered as a fundamental principle, and the basis upon which every hope of success must ultimately depend."[9]

Lacking naval superiority, Washington and Rochambeau

could do little in 1779-80, although both of them were eager to take the offensive. They stayed in their camps because they were so sure that they could accomplish nothing of lasting worth without a fleet. This was not a conviction shared by the Marquis de Lafayette, who (as already pointed out) reported to Washington on July 31, 1780 that "Both the French general and admiral were of the opinion that nothing could be undertaken unless we had naval superiority, as I know it is your opinion also (though it is not mine). . . ." It is Knox's contention that "the major elements of the Yorktown strategy had reached maturity in Washington's mind before the Hartford conference [with Rochambeau on September 20, 1780], and had been strongly advocated by him much before then."[10]

All this can be granted without crediting Washington with planning to utilize a French fleet, if one could be obtained, in the vicinity of the Chesapeake. At the time of the Hartford conference and for many months thereafter, Washington gave every evidence of a strong conviction that New York was the place where naval superiority should be brought to bear. But, and it is one of those "buts" which make all the difference, no matter how firm and dogmatic Washington might be about the necessity of maritime dominance as a principle, his mind and will were flexible and open to rational argument in the light of circumstances when it came to place and time of its application. It was this willingness on his part to adapt the grand design in accordance with events which were largely determined by others, to improvise and execute both daringly and efficiently, which constitute his best claim to "naval genius." If it is true that genius in general consists of the infinite capacity for taking pains, then Washington and Greene possessed it in full measure.

10

THE ACTION: ENGLAND'S
UNSOLVED PROBLEM

"The ultimate reason for British failure in the southernmost states was their failure to place a sufficiently large force in the field to overcome the odds that Nature and man placed against them."
—Edward Channing, *A History of the United States*

How could England quell a rebellion in her thirteen American colonies three thousand miles away? The initial stage of any move from across the ocean would have to be naval, even though the aim was to carry out a police action on land in that hot-bed of the revolt, Boston, Massachusetts. It soon became evident, however, that more than one section of the country was defying the authority of the Crown. But during the first phase of the struggle, from April, 1775, to March, 1778, the British sought primarily to seize and occupy the principal seaboard cities of Boston, Newport, New York, and Philadelphia, in the confident expectation that the independence movement would soon collapse for lack of trade and of directing centers. The theory of the planners in London seems to have been that the hinterland of America was virtually uninhabited; and that the lifeblood of her overseas commerce was regarded by Americans as absolutely essential. By taking possession of the coastal cities, it was believed that they would automatically become rallying-points for loyalists and radiating centers of renewed allegiance to George III.

It is easy for us to see that the British should have fought the rebellion, right from the start, as a maritime affair. England had absolute naval control of the North Atlantic, if she cared to exercise it. There was no American navy; and there was small chance of creating one that could challenge the mighty ships of the line of the Royal Navy. Yet English accounts of the first few years of the war are full of regrets about lost naval opportunities. Whatever the strategic doctrine in Whitehall, the forces sent to the North Atlantic station, and their commanders, were totally inadequate. "Three successive admirals: Samuel Graves, Shuldham, and Howe, were unable to carry out essential operations," says Captain William M. James, R.N. He believes that if a strong force had been on hand, it might have sealed the ports and controlled the whole seaboard, thereby supporting the colonial governors and giving "a very different turn to the course of events."[1]

One reason for this has already been mentioned: the warships of England were occupied elsewhere, specifically in the rich sugar islands of the West Indies. They came to regard voyages northward as mere side trips to be made in the late-summer hurricane season, diversions from their more important missions in the south. Thus England and France alike, says Shea, "wasted their strength on the reduction of petty islands, when a continent was at stake."

Having missed the opportunity to fight and win a maritime war, the alternative was a series of territorial campaigns to "reduce" the northern and central colonies to obedience by seizing key areas. This despite the warning of the elder Pitt, who told Parliament in 1777: "You may ravage, you cannot conquer. It is impossible. You cannot conquer the Americans. I might as well talk of driving them before me with this crutch."[2] And so it proved. The British armies won many battles, but they could not win campaigns. The army of the American Fabius, George Washington, had a way of eluding pitched battles and striking by surprise. Other *ad hoc* armies sprang up hundreds of miles from where they might have been expected to appear. It was all very frustrating to generals accustomed to formal combat.

The first deep shock to London's complacency came with the news of Burgoyne's surrender at Saratoga in September, 1777. Thanks to a series of blunders on the part of Germain, Howe, and Burgoyne himself, and plenty of hard fighting by Arnold and Morgan on the lakes and on land, the British attempt to seize the Hudson-Champlain line came to naught. Clinton soon found that his large garrison in New York was neutralized; that state was no longer an avenue of conquest. One more try was to be made to grab West Point through Benedict Arnold's treason. When that was thwarted in September, 1780, there was little that the British army could hope to gain in the northern states.

Washington's army was just as incapable of dealing the enemy a decisive blow. The American commander-in-chief labored under innumerable handicaps, the greatest of which was naval inferiority. That meant that, until the entry of the French, he could do nothing about the inestimable military advantage enjoyed by the British: mobility. Toward the end of 1779, then, the war seemed headed for that worst of possible conclusions, a permanent stalemate and a shaky compromise peace. Both sides were becoming war-weary; for no other end seemed to be in sight.

Yet the true situation had been drastically altered by France's entry into the war (followed by Spain and Holland). Saratoga was the war's first great turning point; and Yorktown was indeed to become the child of Saratoga, and of Charleston. "After the French came in," says Nickerson, "the British government was no longer in a position to try to crush the rebellion by force of arms."[3] A few Englishmen sensed this; but George III was as adamant as ever. He could not see that England had failed to use her maritime supremacy to the full while she possessed it. Quantities of pre-alliance French aid had reached the rebels, some assisting in the Saratoga victory. Now the Royal Navy was without the means to compel a decision. For the only way it could have won the war after March, 1778, was by preventing French aid from reaching the rebels. That could be done only by a tight blockade of the ports of America or those of France, or both. The long American coastline made the first alternative impracticable; the second was adopted too late.

Lord Sandwich made the fateful choice of a "let out and then follow" policy in regard to the Toulon and Brest battle fleets, in spite of the warnings of Germain. He believed that he did not have enough line ships to secure the Channel against invasion, guard Gibraltar, and preserve the King's possessions in both the West Indies and America. So he waited until first D'Estaing and then De Ternay were known to have sailed for America, and then sent Byron and Graves in vain pursuit.

His choice placed the British armies in America in mortal danger, for no amount of victories achieved by them, no quantity of territory conquered, could possibly change their fundamental insecurity. As long as formidable French fleets were at large, and the total British force in America was divided and incapable of mutual support among its parts, the Royal Navy was its sole salvation. Territorial conquests without command of the sea were bound to be disastrous exhibitions of bravado in chasing will-o'-the-wisps. Clinton and Cornwallis were just about to embark upon such a futile adventure, at first glowing with all the colors of victory, as they shifted the center of gravity of the war from the Hudson River to Chesapeake Bay.

11

HOW CORNWALLIS GOT TO YORKTOWN—BRITISH VICTORIES IN THE SOUTH: CHARLESTON AND CAMDEN

"From a military point of view, the campaigns of 1780 and 1781 in the Carolinas are the most interesting of the whole war." —John A. Doyle

How was it possible for the battle of the Chesapeake to result in the capture of an army in what Professor Coupland calls "the most damaging and humiliating defeat in all our [British] records"? First of all it is necessary to get rid of the common delusion that General Earl Cornwallis at Yorktown had been lured into an artfully devised trap on a peninsula which any schoolboy could see might easily be sealed off by a land army. It is true that the general's presence in Virginia was a blunder, but he was not stupid in finally coming to the sea instead of pursuing Generals Greene and Lafayette into the interior.

On the contrary, in establishing himself in the port of Yorktown, Cornwallis was returning at last to his true base of operations, his link with Clinton in New York, with Rawdon in Charleston, and with Germain in England. Instead of endangering his seven-thousand-man army, he believed that he was insuring its safety. For Lord Cornwallis persisted in the one assumption that was characteristic of all the British commanders in America, with the single exception of Sir Henry Clinton. It was that the Royal Navy never allowed the command of the sea to slip from its grasp; hence any of the King's armies could embark

97

or disembark at its pleasure. Yorktown was to restore Cornwallis's mobility, not to terminate it. Had it not been chosen because it was deemed a safe place to accommodate a large fleet of line-of-battle ships?

In coming to Virginia in the first place, however, Cornwallis had made a serious strategic miscalculation, which had its roots both in his temperament and in his experiences at Charleston and Camden. The siege of the former city provided, as the first step on the road to ultimate disaster, the greatest British military victory of the war. It was a triumph achieved by a rare combination of sea and land superiority during a brief era of good feeling between the army and navy commanders. The victors were Sir Henry Clinton and Vice Admiral Marriott Arbuthnot, who proceeded forthwith to quarrel furiously and for many months afterwards. But upon this one occasion they managed to conduct the most successful British combined operation of the war.

The accomplishment was preceded by a period of intense gloom at Clinton's New York headquarters. During the summer of 1779, said that general, "My spirits, already pressed down by many adverse incidents, began to sink under the additional weights of new disappointments."[1] The latter were the manifold failures of promised reinforcements to reach him, and the incessant demands of Lord George Germain that detachments from his garrison be sent to Canada, Georgia, Florida, and the West Indies. "For God's sake, my Lord," he burst out in a letter to Germain on May 22, 1779, "if you wish me to do anything, leave me to myself, and let me adapt my efforts to the hourly circumstances." On July 3 he was still in despair as he wrote to General "Flintlock" Grey: ". . . not a word from Europe this month, not a farthing of money, no information, no army. Good God!"[2]

On July 21, 1779, Lord Cornwallis arrived in New York to be second in command, with a "dormant" commission as Clinton's eventual successor under certain circumstances. Much has been made of this document as a cause of ill will on Clinton's part, since he was well aware that the Earl was Germain's favorite general. Actually the commission was a form of insurance against the possibility that a high-ranking German officer might inherit the supreme command. Before Cornwallis had left England, he

CHESAPEAKE BAY

GLOUCESTER

TARLETON'S RAID
CHARLOTTESVILLE
YORK RIVER
WILLIAMSBURG
Virginia RICHMOND
YORKTOWN
PHILLIPS
PETERSBURG
LYNNHAVEN BAY
RIVER DAN
PORTSMOUTH

HILLSBORO
GUILFORD
North Carolina
CAPE FEAR RIVER
RAMSOUR'S MILLS
SALISBURY
COWPENS
CHARLOTTE TOWN
GREAT PEEDEE RIVER
BLACK RIVER
WINNSBOROUGH
HOBKIRKS HILL
CAMDEN
WILMINGTON
NINETY SIX
South Carolina
ORANGEBURG
GEORGETOWN
SANTEE R.
Atlantic Ocean
EUTAW SPRINGS
EDISTO R.
ASHLEY R.
COOPER R.
CHARLESTON
LESLIE
SAVANNAH RIVER
SAVANNAH
PORT ROYAL SOUND
Georgia

Cornwallis Route 1781

0 25 50 100 150
MILES

METZIG

had written reassuringly to Clinton: "I come to share fortunes with you, but I will not let you desert me." Nevertheless Clinton promptly tried to do exactly that, making one more of his periodic requests imploring "His Majesty's leave to resign both my commissions into His Lordship's hands . . . to be relieved from a burden which I found myself unequal to. . . ." One gathers the impression that, at this juncture, neither general was filled with joy at the prospects of his American assignment.

When Clinton's latest offer to resign was refused by the King like all the others, he set about making preparations for his descent upon Charleston with what forces he could muster. On October 7 he ordered the evacuation of the garrison at Newport, Rhode Island, a move that was to infuriate Admiral Rodney later, but which added a precious three thousand men to the New York army. The reinforcements from England finally came in on August 25 with Vice Admiral Arbuthnot, who was taking over the naval command. But they consisted, Clinton maintained, of only about three thousand young recruits instead of the six thousand six hundred seasoned soldiers he had been led to expect. "Even of these the numbers fit for duty were few, and they brought with them a malignant jail fever, which soon spread itself among the rest of my army and sent above six thousand of my best troops to the hospital."[3]

In London, of course, the statistics of the army in America conveyed a very different impression, for Clinton appeared to be doing very little with his formidable army of over twenty-seven thousand men, including ten thousand hired Germans and four thousand loyalists. As a consequence, the ministerial pressure for some bold offensive move in some direction on Clinton's part was unrelenting. To Germain the obvious stalemate in the North pointed unerringly toward the South as Britain's military promised land. The air of optimistic expectancy at Whitehall was heightened in October, 1779, by the surprisingly successful defense of Savannah by General Augustine Prevost against the combined Franco-American forces of Count d'Estaing and General Lincoln, resulting in over eight hundred casualties to the attackers at a cost of about one-sixth as many to the outnumbered defenders. This avoidance of defeat was hailed as better than most British victories, for it meant the frustration of the boasted naval assistance of France to the rebel cause. As a result, the province of Georgia was believed to have been restored "to a state of perfect security and peace"; and this encouraged Clinton to lose no time in seeking a similar pacification of its neighboring province of South Carolina.

It was his announced object "to obtain possession of the opulent province of South Carolina, and its operations were to begin with the siege of Charleston." This was not a new strategic idea: the region's largest city, "the New York of the South," had long been coveted by the British. Both Clinton and Cornwallis would be paying it a return visit, since they, with Admiral Sir Peter Parker, had tried in vain on June 28, 1776, to capture what General Lincoln called "the only Mart and ye Magazine of the State." Clinton had hopes not only of thoroughly subduing the spirit of rebellion in the two Carolinas, but also "that such a hold be afterward taken of the Chesapeake as should prove at least a barrier between them and the northern states." Looking at the long and difficult land route from the Middle Atlantic states to the South, he saw, says Professor Willcox, that "the Chesapeake, in short, was the place to clamp a torniquet on the artery of American supplies." Thus British preoccupation with the Chesapeake was not something which began suddenly in 1781. As early as the spring of 1779, Clinton had had dreams of setting up "a commodious post in Virginia [with about two thousand of his troops] for the purpose of co-operating with the Southern army in the reduction of North Carolina, should circumstances at the time encourage such an effort."[4] Soon afterward his attention had been drawn for the first time to the possibility of locating such a post in the sleepy tobacco-shipping port called Yorktown. This came about because three of Admiral d'Estaing's ships, the *Fendant* and two frigates on their way back to the West Indies after their bloody repulse before Savannah, were forced by a storm to take refuge in the York River and to winter there. Some land fortifications had been built for their protection, and although deserted later, they remained a reminder that the French might some day return.

But it was not Yorktown but Charleston which pointed to the Chesapeake as the scene of the war's decisive battle. This was because once the Carolinas became the focus of British strategy, her generals and admirals had to think of victory or defeat in terms of possible American assistance coming from the North around or across the Chesapeake. From that moment on, it became almost inevitable that there would be a battle for the control of that bay, and that it might well decide the entire conflict.

The city of Charleston, then inhabited by about nine thousand whites and five thousand Negro slaves, had been free from the threat of hot war for nearly four years. That state of affairs had not impelled its citizens, busy with its thriving commerce, to strengthen or even to maintain its defenses. When Brigadier General Benjamin Lincoln of Rhode Island was sent there by Congress to take command in December, 1778, he found the forts on the islands in ruins, and the needed works across the Neck unfinished. At first he had only fifteen hundred soldiers, but this number finally rose to four thousand, of whom twenty-five hundred were militia, with promises of more to come. But his powers as military commander were extremely limited by local political considerations. In those days the sentiment for state's rights was overwhelming; and Lincoln found that he must beg the Assembly of the state for men and materials. Not nearly enough of either were forthcoming.

On his second try at the conquest of Charleston, Sir Henry Clinton was taking no chances whatever. As soon as he had made absolutely sure that Admiral Count d'Estaing and his fleet had returned to Europe, he left Major General Knyphausen in New York with a force equal to Washington's dwindling army across the Hudson, and after a delay of one day for the proper celebration of Christmas, set sail from Sandy Hook on December 26, 1779. His armada of ninety-four ships was escorted by Arbuthnot's five ships of the line, one fifty, and two frigates. Clinton was taking all the troops he could spare from the New York garrison to the number of seventy-six hundred, and sixteen hundred horses. The fleet promptly ran into a Cape Hatteras winter storm (one transport with Hessian troops was blown clear back across the Atlantic), "a long series of blustering, disagreeable weather," which obliged most of the ships to throw overboard all but three hundred of the horses, and sank an ordnance store ship "with the chief part of our artillery and ammunition."[5]

It was not until February 11, 1780, that Clinton was able

cautiously to disembark his troops on Johns Island thirty miles south of Charleston, and to commence his leisurely and methodical approach to the city. So rough was the going that it wrung from one Hessian officer the cry: "What a land to wage war in!" Not until March 30 was Clinton ready to cross the Ashley river and encamp about three thousand yards from the American lines, thus beginning the investment of the city.

By April 7, General Lincoln had received fifteen hundred more Continentals from North Carolina and Virginia, but of the promised thousands of South Carolina militia, only about three hundred appeared. After the Savannah fiasco, discouragement was rife in the patriot ranks, and some pleaded the fear of smallpox in Charleston. Spain had entered the war in alliance with France on June 21, 1779, and Lincoln even applied to Havana for the help of a fleet and an army, promising in return to send two thousand men to aid a Spanish attack upon St. Augustine, but all in vain. By hindsight it is only too apparent that the American general should never have attempted to defend a three-mile perimeter on both the landward and seaward sides of the city with a garrison of only fifty-five hundred men, some of them armed "citizens not used to warfare," and a squadron of nine small frigates under Commodore Whipple. Lincoln may possibly have believed that he could duplicate the stubborn defense of Savannah by the enemy general Prevost, and he may have been further deceived by the tortoise-like approach of Clinton's forces. It is more likely, however, that his downfall came about because he counted too heavily upon the arrival of additional reinforcements.

Neither Whipple's lightly armed vessels nor the harbor forts could prevent the British battleships from crossing the bar on March 20. On April 8 thirteen of their fleet ran the batteries of the forts into the lower bay during a heavy rainstorm, and began to bombard the city. Toward the end of April Clinton was reinforced to the tune of three thousand more soldiers from New York under Lord Francis Rawdon, and now had about fourteen thousand men available for the siege, which he proposed to conduct strictly "in form."

In action, there was co-operation among the British, but behind the façade of interservice harmony two serious cracks began to open during the siege. Because of the loss of the ordnance ship, Clinton's army found itself short of ammunition. Admiral Arbuthnot, he was convinced, had both powder and shot to spare, but would offer him only powder, and that reluctantly. So Clinton recorded in his *Journal of the Siege:* "I must ever be on my guard with this man, who . . . will study to dog me." Shortly thereafter Clinton tried to get Arbuthnot to occupy the Cooper River with some of his ships, and got only promises. Whereupon he confided this to paper: "In appearance we were the best of friends. But I am sure he is false as hell, and shall behave in consequence." These experiences left Sir Henry, over a year before he managed to have Arbuthnot recalled, "determined never to serve with such an old woman."[6]

A rift also opened at Charleston between Clinton and his second in command and nominal successor, Lord Cornwallis. It was the beginning of a violent controversy that reached its peak after Yorktown. Clinton first became enraged when he was accused of ignoring a royal order about the provincial corps, and said in his *Journal:* "I ought to have seen through him [Cornwallis] when he betrayed my private conversation to Sir William Howe in 1776. All since is of a piece . . . 'Tis not time for altercations, but I can never be cordial with such a man." Germain had told Clinton in a letter received at Charleston on March 19, 1780, that he was to retain his supreme command. When Cornwallis, who had expected to succeed his chief before the end of the campaign, learned about the letter, according to Clinton, "his carriage toward me immediately changed . . . from this period he was pleased to withdraw his counsels and to confine himself to his routine of duty in the line, without honoring headquarters with his presence oftener than that required."[7] Before leaving Charleston, Clinton noted: "I am sure [Cornwallis's conduct] was not friendly, though his professions are still so."

For the unhappy General Lincoln at Charleston there was still one escape route by way of Monk's Corner on the Cooper River. In Washington's judgment Lincoln should, once the bar had been crossed, have saved his army and "relinquished the city." But the American general listened too long to the entreaties mixed with threats of the Charlestonians, and hung on. Caught between an overwhelmingly superior army and navy, and a mercurial populace clinging to state supremacy (and in-action), Lincoln had only a choice of evils. The issue of possible escape was settled for him by twenty-six-year-old Lieutenant Colonel Banastre Tarleton and his legion, about half cavalry and half infantry, recruited in America and clad in green uniforms. They made a surprise night attack which routed General Isaac Huger's force of about six hundred cavalry at Monk's Corner on April 14. Lord Cornwallis quickly seized the ground between the Cooper River and the sea, and the iron ring around Charleston and its garrison was closed by both sea and land.

A small sortie was attempted on April 24; but it did not interfere with the inexorable approach of the three British parallels and their batteries equipped with sixty large cannon, none less than twenty-four-pounders. On April 26 Brigadier General Louis Duportail found his way into the city from Philadelphia, inspected the fortifications and declared them untenable. When the citizens learned that an evacuation of the Continental troops was even being considered, "Some of them declared to General Lincoln," says General William Moultrie in his *Journal*, "that if he attempted to withdraw the troops and leave the citizens, they would cut up his boats and open the gates to the enemy. This put a stop of all thoughts of an evacuation of the troops, and nothing was left for us but to make the best terms we could."[8] Still playing for time in the hope of being reinforced, Lincoln tried to arrange with Clinton a "convention" similar to the bargain struck between Burgoyne and Gates at Saratoga, which would allow his army to leave the city in exchange for its surrender, but the British leader would have none of it.

The immensely strong-walled but thinly defended Fort Moultrie fell bloodlessly on May 8. On May 9 "all night there was a most tremendous Cannonade ever heard . . . carcases [red-hot shot] thrown into the town, and shells with an incessant fire of artillery . . . It appeared as if the stars were tumbling down . . . It was a dreadful night."[9] When the residents of Charleston saw some twenty of their houses crumbling and burning under the shelling, they experienced a sudden change of heart, and now petitioned General Lincoln to capitulate at once in order to spare further destruction of their city. As Lincoln explained his surrender in a letter to Washington: "The Citizens in general discouraged, the militia of the town having thrown down their arms, the Enemy being within twenty yards of our lines and preparing for a general assault by sea & land—many of our cannon dismounted and others silenced for the want of shot, a retreat being judged impracticable and every hope of timely succor cut off," there was nothing to do but accept Clinton's terms.

It had been a deliberate, obstinate siege in the ancient military tradition, lasting for forty-two days. But thanks to the extreme caution displayed by both sides, neither one making a sally in force against the other, it had not been a bloody one. In spite of "the amazing number of shells thrown . . . the rebels," said a Scottish officer, "throw shells better than we do, they did no harm," and "a great deal of very severe firing at times," the Americans lost only ninety-two killed and one hundred and forty-six wounded, while the British army casualties amounted to seventy-six killed and one hundred and eighty-nine wounded.

On May 11 General Lincoln surrendered without the honors of war usually accorded to a brave garrison. Their colors must be cased and a British march must not be played as they marched out. A British observer said that "Lincoln limp'd out at the head of the most ragged rabble I ever beheld . . . The Militia, *poor creatures*, could not be prevailed upon to come out. They began to creep out of their holes the next day . . . they are to be allowed to go home and plough the ground. There *only* can they be useful."[10] (Italics his.) On the following day Major General Leslie "took possession of Charleston, seven General officers, a Commodore, ten Continental regiments and three battalions of artillery, together with the town and country militia, French, and seamen, making in all about six thousand men in arms. The titular Governor, Council and civil officers were made prisoner.[11] In his report to Germain, Clinton boasted that "there were few men left in South Carolina who are not our prisoners or in arms with us." The private soldiers among the captured were ultimately "crowded into prison ships and other loathsome quarters, where more than eight hundred, or one-third of their number, died within the thirteen months of their captivity."[12]

In addition to the loss of an army and a fleet, the patriot leadership of Charleston was effectively extinguished by the trans-

porting of seventy-eight of its citizens, including Lieutenant
Governor Christopher Gadsden, to St. Augustine, Florida. Two
hundred and ten Charlestonians signed an address of loyalty to
Clinton and Arbuthnot, congratuating them on their triumph,
but claiming later that this had been done merely to save their
estates, and was "at no time the language of their hearts." According to many British reports in the following months, the
populace was eager to change sides. Clinton wrote to William
Eden on May 30, 1780: "All the rebel grandees are come in . . ."
Others said: "Between two and three thousand men have come
in from the country, sworn allegiance, got certificates and returned . . . Since the 12th of May, rebellion has disappeared in
this province . . . Not a rebel dares to show his nose . . . North
Carolina must fall of course . . . Everything now has the finest
prospect."[13]

The fall of Charleston was a shattering blow to the rebel cause
in the South, the "largest single American loss of the war." In
faraway Versailles, Minister de Vergennes wrote anxiously to
Lafayette in the belief, based on British reports, that the contending armies were equal in numbers, wondering whether the
city might have been lost through treachery to the principle of
independence, and declaring that more zeal and unity needed to
be displayed by the Americans and their agents in France. To the
patriots who were present at the surrender it was "a mortifying
scene . . . as the thirteen stripes were levelled in the dust." British
spectators were correspondingly elated. Said one of them: "I believe the Congress has not felt so severe a stroke since the com-
mencement of the rebellion."[14] Saratoga had been avenged; the
infamous "Burgoynade" had been wiped out by the "Lincoln-
ade," of which there would, the British sympathizers believed,
be many more to come. On the triumphal return of "Our Conquering Heroes" to New York on June 21, 1780, Clinton and
Arbuthnot were hailed by *Rivington's Royal Gazette* as "coming
from the Conquest and Complete Reduction of the Province of
South Carolina; His Excellency having restored Peace and perfect Decorum amongst the inhabitants of that opulent, populous
and very important Colony."[15] A versifier in the same publication, speaking on behalf of "a goddess," proclaimed:

'Father Time, I've one HERO to add to your store;
Brave CLINTON has conquered; Rebellion's no more!'
Well pleased, in his Annals, Time wrote down the Name
Made the record authentic, and gave it to FAME.

What Clinton and Arbuthnot had really demonstrated was
their joint mastery of the essentially European art of conducting
a well-planned, long-drawn-out formal siege with a numerical
superiority of at least two to one. What linked their exploit to
Yorktown was its impact in England, where it confounded the
Opposition, saved Lord North's government, and strongly confirmed the blind optimism of George III and Germain. Dispatches announcing "the joyful event" were carried to the King
by the Earl of Lincoln and to the Lords of Admiralty by Sir
Andrew Snape Hamond. "When Lord Lincoln arrived at Buck-
ingham House with his private dispatches, His Majesty George
the Third was out on horseback, attended by the Prince of
Wales and the Bishop of Osnabrück (his second son Prince Frederick Augustus), but on his return gave him a most gracious reception. Immediately on receipt of the important news, the
whole Line, consisting of four thousand men, was drawn out in
front of their encampment in Hyde Park, and fired a *feu de joie*,
accompanied by a triple discharge of the Artillery . . . Never was
national joy so universal, as that expressed on the public annunci-
ation of the surrender of Charleston. The Republicans and Patriots are always excepted in these public Rejoicings, for they, as
usual, mourned the Event in sackcloth and ashes, and for this
pious reason, because 'Success only served to procrastinate the
war.'" The House of Commons voted its thanks to Clinton and
Arbuthnot "for the eminent and very important service per-
formed by them . . . in the reduction of Charleston."[16]
In New York James Rivington assured his readers that "Clinton's conquest of Charleston, and of course of the whole Province
of South Carolina, is a decisive stroke that must bring the Rebellion to a speedy conclusion." In London Germain was sure
that his previous optimism had been completely vindicated, and
wrote to Clinton on July 4, 1780: "I trust you will still find an
opportunity of prosecuting your plan of operations in the Chesapeake, from the success of which (added to the reduction of

Carolina) I am sanguine enough to expect the recovery of the whole of the Southern provinces in the course of the campaign."[17] It is to Clinton's credit that he did not entertain such roseate dreams without significant qualifying clauses. On May 30, 1780, before leaving Charleston, he wrote to William Eden in London: "In short if a French or Spanish fleet does not interfere, I think a few works if properly reinforced, will give us all between this and Hudson's river . . . I leave Lord Cornwallis here in sufficient force to keep it against the world, without a superior fleet shows itself, in which case I despair of ever seeing peace restored to this miserable country."[18]

On May 10 came the news from Germain, written on March 15, 1780, that "a superior fleet" was indeed on its way from Brest, which impelled Clinton and Arbuthnot to sail away to New York early in June with about one-third of the victorious army. Lord Cornwallis was left in Charleston with one Hessian, six British, and six provincial regiments, about eight thousand men in all. What was more important, before leaving for New York Clinton had acquiesced in an arrangement for direct communication between Cornwallis and Germain. He remained as commander-in-chief, and believed that he had made his orders to Cornwallis absolutely clear: "To regard the safety of Charleston and the tranquillity of South Carolina as the principal and indispensable objects of his attention." Only when those goals had been reached, and "in a proper season of the year," was "His Lordship at liberty, if he judged proper, to make a *solid* move into North Carolina." (Italics his.)[19]

Britain now had two distinct armies in the colonies, and soon had two virtually independent commands, linked only by the Royal Navy's supposed command of the sea along the North American coast. Clinton's army was in fact locked up in New York; but Cornwallis's troops seemed to be endowed with complete freedom of movement. Before leaving Charleston, Clinton had received assurances from his subordinate that organized resistance, after "Bloody" Tarleton's atrocious massacre of Colonel Buford's Virginians at Waxhaw Creek on May 29, 1780, was at an end. It seemed to be, for the British met little or no resistance in swiftly setting up ten garrison posts along the rivers and the seacoast. This had the effect of still further dividing Cornwallis's army. That general's severely military methods of compelling allegiance, his disregard of civil rights, and the plunderings and confiscations by his officers, soon alienated many of those who might otherwise have rallied to his cause.

Furthermore, the reaction of the patriot party to the loss of Charleston was very different from what the British had expected. Edmund Burke, writing as an opposition leader, pointed out in his contribution to the *Annual Register* for 1781 that "the loss of Charleston produced a directly contrary effect to that which might have been expected. For instead of depressing and sinking the minds of the people, to seek for security by any means, and to sue for peace upon any terms, the loss being now come home to every man's feelings, and the danger to his door, they were at once awakened to a vigor of exertion, scarcely to be expected in the circumstances."[20] Small rebel bands soon made their appearance, and although they could not attack major posts or meet Cornwallis's army in the field, they could and did carry out a whole series of hit-and-run raids under such gifted guerrilla fighters as Francis Marion, Thomas Sumter, and Andrew Pickens. All three were officers in Governor John Rutledge's militia, who kept up an active and effective resistance for three years "practically without a government, and without pay."

This partisan warfare was savage and merciless on both sides, as only the blood-feuds of a civil war could be. Some of the participants were "desperate characters who would fight on any side for plunder." As Marion said in one of his letters: "Many of my people have left me and gone over to the enemy." But Cornwallis was also troubled by desertions; and so effective were the harassing tactics of the enemy that in four short months after the fall of Charleston he was singing a most unhappy tune. On August 6, 1780, he wrote to Clinton that the whole country between the Pee Dee and Santee Rivers was in "an absolute state of rebellion, every friend of government has been carried off, and his plantation destroyed."

The reaction of Congress to the Charleston disaster was also different from what some had expected. The fainthearted had predicted that Georgia and the Carolinas would be given up as lost, and that the new nation would consist of only ten states. But on June 13, 1780, the Congress appointed a man whom its

members regarded as a more energetic and experienced commander of the Southern Department than General Lincoln had
proved himself to be. He was General Horatio Gates, the victor
at Saratoga, once a major in the British army, who enjoyed in
some Congressional quarters a military reputation greater than
Washington's. The supreme commander had not even been consulted about the choice, Washington's own strong preference
being for his Quartermaster General Nathanael Greene. Charles
Lee said prophetically to Gates: "Take care lest your Northern
laurels turn into Southern willows."

Gates left his farm in Virginia in late July, 1780, and took
command of about fourteen hundred veteran Continentals from
Delaware and Maryland under Major General Johann de Kalb
at Coxe's Mill, North Carolina. They were some of the most
reliable troops in Washington's army, whom he had originally
sent south to lessen the pressure on Lincoln at Charleston. Gates
was soon joined by enough local militia to bring his effectives up
to three thousand men, but nearly a thousand of them had never
been in battle. He believed that he was prepared to surprise Lord
Rawdon and his thirteen-hundred-man garrison at Camden. This
in spite of his own earlier estimate that he was taking over "an
army without strength, a military chest without money, a department deficient in public spirit, and a climate that increases
despondency."

General de Kalb had already made plans for a circuitous approach to Camden by way of Salisbury and Charlotte, where
both food and recruits might be obtained, but Gates was in a
hurry to show results, and decided to save fifty miles by taking a
more direct and barren route through territory infested with
Tories. His greatest weakness was in the commissary department, notoriously insufficient as far as the militia were concerned, and almost nonexistent for the Continentals. Beginning
his march south in the heat of midsummer on July 27, Gates's
men were soon barely subsisting on a diet of half-ripe corn,
green apples, and green peaches, which left them weaker by the
hour.

Gates had hoped to catch Rawdon before he could be reinforced by Cornwallis from Charleston, but the latter was alerted
on August 9, and hastened to Camden with about nine hundred

men. Both commanders had literally hundreds of sick and half-
sick soldiers in their ranks. Cornwallis believed himself and Rawdon to be outnumbered by at least two to one, for Gates had
boasted of having an army of seven thousand men. Only three
thousand fifty-two of them, however, were reported as fit for
duty on the day of battle. In the absence of the usual rum ration,
Gates had ordered the issue of a gill of molasses per man. Combined with half-cooked meat and cornmeal, this last-minute diet
nearly wrecked his troops.

Both generals, because of the daytime heat, undertook night
marches which brought their forces into collision in the darkness.
Each hesitated, awaiting daylight. Gates could have drawn back
at the last moment, but he made the fatal error of playing Cornwallis's own game of attack. Tradition has him boasting: "I will
breakfast tomorrow at Camden with Lord Cornwallis at my
table." As General Greene said later in Gates's defense, his principal mistake at Camden was in fighting at all. He was facing an
aggressive general who wanted above all else to bring his enemy
into action. Cornwallis was later to show himself deficient
enough in strategic wisdom, but at Camden (and elsewhere) he
proved himself a brilliant and daring field-tactician.

As luck would have it, each general placed his best troops opposite to the enemy's weakest. Gates's limited experience at Saratoga led him to place far too much confidence in his militia.
Facing the crack regiment of regulars under Lieutenant Colonel
Webster, they began what looked like an attack. In a very few
minutes, said the American Colonel Otho Williams: "The im-
petuosity with which the British advanced, firing and huzzaing,
threw the whole body of the militia into such a panic that they
threw down their *loaded* guns and fled in utmost consternation."
(Italics his.) The stampede carried away all but De Kalb and his
tried-and-true Continentals, who even managed repeatedly to
drive Rawdon back. But they could not hold off Cornwallis's
whole army. Fighting fiercely to the end, the massive De Kalb
fell with his eleventh and mortal wound. Tarleton's dragoons,
attacking from the rear, commenced a rout in the course of
which some Americans were chased twenty miles. In the words
of John Marshall: "Never was a victory more complete, or a
defeat more total." The American casualties were never accu-

rately determined. Cornwallis probably overestimated them at eight to nine hundred killed and one thousand captured. He reported sixty-eight of his own men killed and one hundred and forty-five wounded.

Gates had incurred "the most disgraceful defeat of the war," and lost the last shreds of his military reputation by racing one hundred and eighty miles to Hillsboro, North Carolina, in three and one half days. All that remained of the Southern army finally assembled there: about seven hundred Continentals. Just before the Camden catastrophe Gates had unwisely detached four hundred of his regulars to join Thomas Sumter in search of a British supply train. In another of his lightning-like cavalry dashes, Tarleton and his legion wiped out this force at Fishing Creek, South Carolina, killing one hundred and fifty and capturing three hundred.

At last Cornwallis could write to Clinton with some assurance that "the internal commotions and insurrections in the province will now subside." Once more the rebellion in the South seemed to have been extinguished for good. In London, Lord North's government began to feel a new security, and Earl Cornwallis received the thanks of Parliament for Camden. Would he be content to rest upon his new laurels, or would he go in search of additional easy victories?

12

CORNWALLIS *VERSUS* GREENE: COWPENS AND GUILFORD COURT HOUSE

"Amongst timid friends and adjoining inveterate rebels . . ."
—General Earl Cornwallis (after Guilford)

In four months the American patriots had seen two of their armies, each as large as Burgoyne's, ignominiously annihilated. Yet the very completeness of the British victories served to hasten the eventual downfall of Cornwallis. This was because the comparatively simple and costless triumphs of Charleston and Camden helped to buttress the illusions which still filled the minds of the majority of Englishmen at home about the probable recovery of the South and its effect upon the final outcome of the war. Among these congenial myths, which had managed to survive nearly six years of harsh experience, was the firm conviction that raw, undisciplined American settlers turned amateur soldiers could not possibly stand up to attacks by well-drilled British or German regiments, nor could they be expected to withstand professionally directed sieges. Furthermore, the South was supposed to be teeming with suppressed loyalist sentiments, and the number of substantial residents who had hastened to pledge allegiance to the Crown appeared to be fully as large as the Government optimists had expected it to be. It would take about a year more of energetic campaigning by Cornwallis to discredit both of these comforting falsities.

But in the autumn of 1780, nothing seemed to stand in the way of a rapid reconquest of the unredeemed colonies toward the North. This would be accomplished by the irresistible might of

Cornwallis, perhaps "a modern Hannibal," as his adversary General Greene once called him. The noble Lord would roll back the rebels, first to the Dan, then the Potomac, the Delaware, the Hudson, the Connecticut, the Charles, and the Penobscot. Cornwallis himself, being on the spot, did not share all these rosy dreams. But there can be no doubt that, under the influence of his Carolina successes, he developed an overall conception of British strategy which was quite different from that of Clinton, his commander-in-chief. It was, moreover, a plan which had no little appeal to his superiors in London. For Cornwallis had taken over the role of conductor of the adventurously offensive movements in America, while Clinton found himself cast once more as the timid champion of the stationary defensive.

Clinton had assigned to his subordinate the task of "restoring tranquillity to every part of South Carolina," and always maintained that Cornwallis would have succeeded "had he attended to that alone." But the Earl was not, temperamentally, the sort of general who could remain sitting on his hands in the unhealthy miasmas of Charleston. His vigorous efforts to occupy all the centers of population in the province had dispersed his forces, leaving him with no large army of maneuver. But with no organized enemy in the field that did not seem to matter.

What did eventually matter a great deal was the degree to which he was to be successful or unsuccessful in truly pacifying the back country. His problem was to recruit enough loyalist militia to man his many outlying posts, so that his regulars could be withdrawn for further conquests to the northward. Before leaving, Sir Henry Clinton had issued a proclamation calling upon all the inhabitants of the province to take an active part in restoring royal government; and Cornwallis said that he expected the great body of the citizens to do so. He thought this would be especially true in the interior, where many of the settlers were originally from the highlands of Scotland. On July 4, 1780, he wrote confidently to his brother William: "The people of the back country seem most sincerely happy at returning to their union with Great Britain, and execrate the tyranny of their late rulers."[1]

Yet recruiting in the interior went badly. In one place Cornwallis called upon all the inhabitants to join him, and not a single man responded. Those who did sign were not reliable, especially when serving in a unit by themselves. One whole corps changed sides and joined Sumter, giving up their officers as prisoners. Lord Rawdon said the Carolina loyalists were very little help, even in providing dependable information. By the following April 18, Cornwallis himself had reluctantly come to the conclusion that "Our experience has shown us that their numbers are not so great as has been represented, and that their friendship was only passive . . . When a storm threatens, our friends disappear!" His response was increased severity of treatment: he proclaimed the death penalty for any American who joined the King's militia and then took up arms for the rebels, and quarrelled with Clinton over the issuance of pardons to those who had taken the oath of allegiance. Yet in London Lord George Germain, the incorrigible optimist in such matters, says his biographer Alan Valentine, "preferred to accept other and more favorable reports that were still coming to him from Tory merchants and planters in and about Charleston, and from British officers in his special confidence."

The war in the South had now become a matter of bitter raiding and "bush fighting" by small bands of rebels who seemed to have no chance of disputing Cornwallis's occupation forces. Even before his sweeping victory at Camden, the Earl had had in mind a full-scale invasion of interior North Carolina, for the double purpose of supporting the Tories there, and of cutting off aid to the patriots from that quarter. This could be construed as merely a means of safeguarding his South Carolina conquests, and hence in accord with his orders from Clinton, which permitted "solid" operations in North Carolina.

Three weeks after Camden, on September 8, 1780, Cornwallis pushed a column toward Charlotte, North Carolina, hoping as usual to pick up loyalist assistance. While there, however, he received a shocking piece of news. A flanking body of about eleven hundred Tory militia under Major Patrick Ferguson, sometimes called "the British Marion," who had been sent into Tryon County, had been cornered by over a thousand hastily assembled mountain riflemen under Colonels Shelby and Campbell on the top of King's Mountain. On October 7 they had all been either killed (like Ferguson himself) or captured by the enemy, along with a large stand of arms. The Americans, who had quickly dispersed after the battle, had lost twenty-eight killed and sixty-two wounded.

Cornwallis's first probing toward the North had turned out badly, and he retired to Winnsboro, South Carolina, a somewhat chastened commander. There he became ill for a time, and Lord Rawdon took over the command. Clinton commented later that King's Mountain, "though in itself confessedly trifling, overset in a moment all the happy effects of our successes at Charleston and Camden," and "unhappily proved to be the first link in a chain of evils that followed each other in regular succession until they at last ended in the total loss of America."[2] Yet the troops so thoroughly beaten there were, after all, only militiamen; and Cornwallis himself had doubted, in a letter to Clinton on August 29, 1780, Major Ferguson's claim that they would "do their duty and fight well" without the presence of regulars. When more than two thousand first-rate reinforcements under General Alexander Leslie joined him in December, Cornwallis's martial spirits revived to the point of resuming his invasion of North Carolina with his mobile army of about four thousand men.

In that same month of December, 1780, the Southern Department of the American army received a new commander, Washington's original choice for the post, General Nathanael Greene of Rhode Island. Brought up a Quaker, but found to be possessed of "worldly propensities," Greene was enough of a renegade from pacifism to become a first-rate fighting man. He was then thirty-nine years old, a veteran of Trenton and Monmouth, and an omnivorous reader of books. Unlike Gates, his unhappy predecessor, Greene could honestly stand comparison with Washington in terms of military sagacity. His response to adversity was: "We fight, get beat, rise and fight again." Even though he was fated never to win a major victory by driving his opponent from the field, many of his apparent defeats were Pyrrhic victories for the British, and he contributed mightily to the outcome of the war.

"I think I am giving you a general," wrote Washington to the Congress, "but what can a general do without men, without arms, without clothing, without stores, without provisions?" After the rout at Camden, Greene could count on a Southern army of from fifteen to twenty-five hundred men, about one thousand of them veteran Continentals, and all of them desperately short of everything Washington had mentioned, plus the matter of pay. Outnumbered by more than three to two, Greene adopted the Fabian tactics of his commander-in-chief, and refused to play Cornwallis's game of pitched battles if they could possibly be avoided. He hoped rather to keep the British leader off balance by fanning the latter's hopes for a general engagement, while thwarting them. Greene's first move appeared to Cornwallis to be a supreme act of military folly. For the American divided his already tiny army, sending Brigadier General Daniel Morgan off toward the southwest with one-third of his forces "to spirit up the people" and to "hold Cornwallis in doubt as to his own line of conduct," while he and General Huger proceeded to the southeast.

Cornwallis imagined that it would be simplicity itself to dispose of these "two trifling corps" separately, for they were almost one hundred and fifty miles apart. He sent the redoubtable Tarleton with eleven hundred men to destroy Morgan. Both Greene and Morgan hoped to use speed of movement and knowledge of the country and its rivers to avoid any large-scale action, although Morgan confessed to Greene that "it is beyond the art of man to keep the militia from straggling." Tarleton chased Morgan up the Broad River valley far into the interior until, on January 16, 1781, the American master rifleman decided that he and his less than a thousand men had run far enough. He stopped at an abandoned drovers' camp on the Old Cherokee trail called Hannah's Cowpens, saying "I'll whip them here, or lay down my bones." It was a good position in which to force his militia to fight, since the Broad River in his rear was too high for fording. "A retreat," he commented later, "was the very thing I wished to cut off all hope of."[3]

Morgan made an unorthodox but masterly arrangement of his slender forces in three lines. At the foot of the sloping ground nearest the enemy he placed a thin screen of raw militia; at one hundred and fifty yards up the rise, the Carolina and Georgia militia under Andrew Pickens; and at the top his core of about three hundred Continentals and some experienced Virginians. Over the crest of the hill were concealed over a hundred mounted troopers under Lieutenant Colonel William Washington.

Tarleton came on with about two hundred and fifty British regulars in addition to his legion, for a total of about eleven hundred men and two cannon. He liked the looks of the battle-field that Morgan had chosen, especially because the situation of the enemy would be desperate in case of defeat. After the first rank of the American militiamen had taken their toll and retreated, but without panic, the British came forward steadily in (as one American soldier said) "the most beautiful line I ever saw." As Morgan had anticipated, the second line of militia did not hold for long, and the British cavalry dashed in expecting to start a rout. But William Washington's troopers chose just the right moment to charge on their own account, and "were as hard to stop as a drove of wild steers going to a Pennsylvania market."[4] Tarleton had expended most of his cavalry and had committed all but his last mounted reserves; yet the main body of Americans was still to be dislodged. Hard pressed on one flank, the Continental line sagged but did not break.

Scenting victory, the British were coming on "like a mob," when something quite unprecedented occurred. Lieutenant Colonel John Eager Howard of the same Maryland regiment which had refused to succumb to the rout at Camden, ordered his men to make a bayonet charge, "which order was obeyed with great alacrity." At about the same moment, William Washington's troopers closed in on one flank, and Pickens's militia, which by now had re-formed in the rear, charged in from the other for a beautifully executed double envelopment. No one present, least of all Colonel Tarleton, could recall ever witnessing Americans charging British regulars with the bayonet in an open engagement. Said Tarleton in his report: "An unexpected fire at this instant from the Americans, who came about as they were retreating, stopped the British, and threw them into confusion. Exertions to make them advance were useless . . . An unaccountable panic extended itself along the whole line. The Americans, who before thought they had lost the action, . . . advanced upon the British troops, and augmented their astonishment. A general flight ensued."[5]

Tarleton salvaged less than two hundred of his mounted

men in his precipitate retreat from Cowpens. He tried to minimize his losses, but one hundred and ten bodies were counted on the battlefield, and of the seven hundred and two British captives, some two hundred were wounded. Morgan had lost twelve killed and sixty wounded in the single hour of fighting, and had captured eight hundred muskets, one hundred dragoon horses, and "all their music." He had given Tarleton "the devil of a whipping" in the most brilliant tactical exploit of the land war, discouraging the loyalists and raising the morale of the patriots. But the real question posed by Cowpens was: how much would Cornwallis and Clinton learn from it?

Fearing for his military reputation, Tarleton had demanded from Cornwallis either an expression of confidence in writing, or a court-martial. His chief gave him the former, blaming the Cowpens defeat on "the total misbehavior of the troops." He wrote to Germain that "the unfortunate affair of the 17th of January was a very unexpected and severe blow." Clinton blamed it on the "loose, flimsy order of two deep in line" on entering action, "ever too much the practice in America," although Clinton himself had done nothing to change the rules.[6] Neither British general seems to have perceived the folly of operating in the backwoods of the Carolinas with military tactics designed for use in Europe.

General Greene was not deceived by the outcomes of the King's Mountain and Cowpens engagements. "Our prospects are gloomy," he said, "notwithstanding these flashes of success." To General Huger, however, he expressed his long-run confidence in the coming campaign: "I am not without hopes of ruining Lord Cornwallis, if he persists in his mad scheme of pushing through the country . . . Here is a fine field and great glory ahead." Lord Cornwallis had reacted to the news of Cowpens with a furious resolve to punish Morgan and recover the British prisoners, including twenty-nine of his commissioned officers. But Morgan sped northward to the Yadkin River for his junction with Greene, leaving Cornwallis always one lap behind, thanks to Greene's foresight in providing boats for each of the major river crossings. Washington deserves some of the credit for Greene's sagacity, since on dispatching him southward he had written: "Pay direct particular attention to the Boats."[7]

COWPENS AND GUILFORD COURT HOUSE

At Ramsour's Mill on January 24, 1781, Cornwallis in a desperate hope to speed up his army's movements made a huge bonfire of his baggage, supplies, tents, spare clothing, and even his rum. It was said later that Cornwallis's was "the only army that ever marched two hundred miles without a bottle of wine or a pint of brandy."[8] All his troops were now light brigades, but the supplies they could carry on their backs were not to be enough. The British general had no real plan of campaign except to get between Greene and Virginia, or at least to chase him out of the Carolinas. Actually he was allowing Greene to lure him into rugged forest country farther and farther from his base.

When Greene and Morgan joined forces at Guilford Court House on February 9, they considered the possibility of making a stand, but decided instead to cross the Dan River into Virginia. The American militia had been melting away through the expiration of enlistments. Neither army had tents; Greene's men had one blanket for each three soldiers; and both armies were hungry. There would be food in Virginia, and also reinforcements. Cornwallis found himself thwarted once more in his chase of Greene by the latter's monopoly of river boats. The British fell back to Hillsboro, a loyalist center, which was then the capital of North Carolina, and plundered it for supplies.

Having received some militia reinforcements, Greene recrossed the Dan on February 23, and began a series of lightning moves to confuse the enemy. His decision to return to North Carolina was a timely one, for it turned the tide of Tory sentiment which had risen on Cornwallis's approach. On March 10 he explained in a letter to Governor Thomas Jefferson of Virginia: "I have been obliged to practice that by finesse which I dared not attempt by force . . . Nothing shall hurry me into a measure not suggested by prudence." Greene now had over four thousand men in arms to face Cornwallis's two thousand, although relatively few of the Americans were veterans of actual fighting. The temptation to use this preponderance in quantity, though not in quality, proved to be irresistible. "An American army," writes Burke Davis, "had at last come to look upon the enemy without fear because it was no longer awed by superior reputation, by allegedly superior arms, training, tactics, uniforms, and a long tradition of military superiority."[9] For his part

Cornwallis as usual was only too eager to oblige by attacking, since he had become convinced that only a pitched battle with Greene could solve his problems. As long as that elusive American general kept the field Virginia was safe and the Carolinas, in his estimation, could never be regarded as secure.

On March 14, 1781, Greene took up his position at Guilford Court House (now Greensboro, North Carolina), then a small clearing in the wilderness near the Salisbury road, and awaited the British advance. He adopted Daniel Morgan's Cowpens battle plan of three lines, with about fourteen hundred North Carolina militia screening the front "to fire two rounds and then retire." His second line consisted of Virginia militia sprinkled with veterans; and the third was made up of Maryland and Virginia Continentals. Unlike Cowpens, however, the Guilford position had a line open for escape to the rear; and Greene's three formations proved to have been placed too far apart.

The cool and deliberate advance of the British infantry terrified the screening militia, who broke into flight after firing only one volley, and before any of them had been shot at. Once in panicky motion, they did not, as at Cowpens, re-form their ranks in the rear. Greene believed that their swift exodus was what cost him the victory. The clash of the British and German regulars and the second and third lines of Americans was a very different story. As Greene himself said: "The fighting was long, obstinate, and bloody." Fortune seemed inclined to give the palm of victory first to one side and then to the other. The performance of the Virginia militia varied; as St. George Tucker said: "Some were undoubtedly entitled to General Greene's thanks for their conduct, while others ought to blush." The same was true of the third line, where the First Maryland regiment fought magnificently, driving back Webster's Guards; but the newly recruited Second Maryland fell apart completely, streaming away through the woods to the rear in a panic which Greene himself could not stop.

So great was the pressure of the First Maryland and William Washington's dragoons that Cornwallis, against the protests of some of his own officers, cold-bloodedly ordered his artillery to "open fire upon friends as well as foes . . . though every ball levelled at the enemy must pass through the flying Guards."[10]

The tide of battle was turned. Both commanders had used up their choicest units with the exception of a few mounted reserves. Greene hesitated to commit the last of these, which if employed might have driven Cornwallis into acknowledged defeat. The American general, knowing that his was the only army protecting Virginia, gave the order to disengage, allowing the British to take his four cannon and thus claim victory by possessing the field.

Cornwallis boasted a complete triumph, which was duly celebrated in Charleston and New York. As a matter of fact he retired with his decimated army as rapidly as if he had been defeated. It was a triumph in name only, for in winning it, Cornwallis had lost something far more valuable: his confidence in the invincible superiority of his own soldiers. "The Americans," he said, "fought like demons." His losses were reported as ninety-three dead, four hundred and thirteen wounded, and twenty-six missing, or about 28 percent of his command, as against seventy-eight Americans killed and one hundred and eighty-three wounded. Before the battle Greene had written Jefferson that he hoped "at least to dispose of Cornwallis's army in such a manner as to encumber him with a number of wounded men";[11] and that was exactly what he had done.

General "Lighthorse Harry" Lee came closer to summarizing Cornwallis's real accomplishments at Guilford: "Nearly a third of his force slaughtered, many of his best officers killed or wounded, and that victory for which he had so long toiled, and at last gained, bringing in its trail not one military benefit."[12] As Cornwallis himself admitted: "The unexpected failure of our friends rendered the victory at Guilford of little value," because they were smart enough to perceive that it was not a victory. In London, Horace Walpole commented: "Lord Cornwallis has conquered his troops out of shoes and provisions, and himself out of troops"; and Charles James Fox declared: "Another such victory would be the ruin of the British army."

Abandoning seventy of his sick and wounded to the enemy, Cornwallis began a rapid one-hundred-and-seventy-five mile withdrawal to the sea at Cape Fear at Wilmington, North Carolina. This time it was Greene who could not move fast enough to catch him. There he could once more be in touch with New

York and Charleston. Clinton later made a sarcastic summary of Cornwallis's achievements to that point: "After forcing the passage of several great rivers, fighting a bloody battle, and running eight hundred and twenty miles over almost every part of the invaded province at the expense of above three thousand men, he accomplished no other purpose but having exposed by an unnecessary retreat to Wilmington, the two valuable colonies behind him to be overrun and conquered by that very army which he boasts to have completely routed but a week or two before."[13]

13

CORNWALLIS AND LAFAYETTE
IN VIRGINIA

"These English are mad; they march through a country and think they have conquered it. . . ." —Marquis de Lafayette

Lord Cornwallis installed himself and his staff in comfortable quarters in Wilmington's largest mansion, where they had the services of plenty of slaves. The respite gave him a chance to rest his exhausted army and to reflect concerning his future plans. Upon his decision, little as he suspected it at the time, was to rest the outcome of the war.

"From Camden to Guilford," he said, "we have been precluded from all communication with the rest of the world, as though in the deserts of Arabia . . ." This meant, of course, that he had been out of touch with Sir Henry Clinton, and during those three months he had come to treat his commander-in-chief with something close to indifference. In this attitude he had been powerfully encouraged by the man who directed them both, Lord George Germain in London, with whom he had been permitted to correspond directly. To Germain the aggressive Cornwallis seemed to be conquering thousands of square miles of territory in the Carolinas with trifling losses, while the cautious Clinton, with three or four times as many troops, remained cooped up in New York.

Cornwallis felt increasingly that he was acting directly under orders from Germain, and that he did not even need to notify Clinton of his plans. He had no clear conception of Clinton's own program for Virginia, and no urge to find out what it was.

He assumed that when Clinton sent troops to that province they were, like General Leslie's, intended to be reinforcements for himself. The sad truth of the matter, from the British point of view, was that henceforth Clinton and Cornwallis were fighting two different wars, with each commander regarding the other as failing to give proper support to *his* campaign.

Since it had been partly lack of supplies which had forced Cornwallis to abandon the ground at Guilford Court House which he believed he had won, one might have supposed that he would, by this time, have been keenly aware of his dependence upon British domination of the sea, which was his only reliable source of provisions. But both Cornwallis and Germain continued to take the Royal Navy's accustomed control of the ocean for granted. Only Clinton seemed to grasp the underlying facts and some of their implications. Late in 1780 when his naval associate and nemesis, Vice Admiral Arbuthnot, proposed to send Rear Admiral Thomas Graves and six line ships, that is, the bulk of his forces, to winter in the Leeward Islands, Clinton wrote him a vigorous letter of protest, explaining that such a move would concede naval superiority to the French, enabling them to transport an army to the Carolinas "without leaving me power to render Lord Cornwallis any assistance against them." Fortunately at that time Arbuthnot listened to Clinton's advice, so prophetic of what was to happen only nine months later.

If Cornwallis at Wilmington had adhered faithfully to Clinton's orders to safeguard his conquests in South Carolina above all else, he would have taken his army back to Charleston, there to resume his primary task of consolidating British rule. But that course of action smacked too much of defeat to be adopted by a conqueror who had marched so many hundreds of miles, he claimed, "with uniform success." And besides, it would mean the abandonment of the North Carolina loyalists whose hopes he had just aroused. His second alternative was to return, after restoring the health and spirits of his army, to the attempt to drive Greene back into Virginia. But after the revelation of American fighting spirit at Guilford, the notion of a return engagement was one for which he had little relish.

There was a third possibility, which seems gradually to have assumed the proportions of an obsession in Cornwallis's mind.

It was based upon his conviction that the Carolinas could not possibly be secured as long as the rebels in those provinces were supplied from the storehouses of Virginia. All the evils he had encountered seemed to him to be traceable to that "center of insurrection" in the North. If Virginia, known to be lightly defended, could only be crushed, he reasoned, then all the provinces to the south would be forced to submit from lack of resources. It was even easy for Cornwallis to convince himself that Clinton also believed that a strong position must be established and a decisive blow struck in the vicinity of the Chesapeake. Had Clinton not sent the traitor Benedict Arnold, now a British brigadier general, with fifteen hundred provincials to make raids in the James River valley from Portsmouth in December? And in addition, word came in March that Major General William Phillips had just landed another two thousand men from ships in Chesapeake bay. To an ambitious, fighting general, neither Charleston nor upland North Carolina seemed to hold out any comparable attractions.

On April 10, 1781, three days after his arrival in Wilmington, Cornwallis set down his thoughts about British strategy in a letter to Phillips. In it he expounded his conception of the central role of the Chesapeake, rather than New York, in future British plans of conquest. He wrote as if he had full confidence in his complete independence of Clinton as well as in the ultimate approval of Germain. "I assure you," he said, "that I am quite tired of marching about the country in quest of adventure. If we mean an offensive war in America we must abandon New York and bring our whole force into Virginia, then we have a state to fight for, and a successful battle may give us America."[1] On the same day he wrote to Clinton in much the same vein, which must have caused Sir Henry no little astonishment: "I cannot help expressing my wishes that the Chesapeake may become the seat of war—even, if necessary, at the expense of abandoning New York. Until Virginia is in a manner subdued, our hold on the Carolinas must be difficult if not precarious."[2] He repeated the same idea, with less emphasis upon quitting New York, in a letter to Germain written eight days later.

To Clinton, of course, this was all complete nonsense. His private comment was: "If the Chesapeake had become the seat of war and New York evacuated to enable us to carry it there, it would certainly be the speediest way to finish the war. For the whole army could probably have been annihilated in one campaign, commencing in July."[3] It was not that Clinton had no plans of his own for the Chesapeake. On his way to Charleston a year earlier, he had wanted to establish a post there for the purpose of "obstructing the march" of any reinforcements Washington might send to the Carolinas. More recently he had had his eyes on the peninsula between the Chesapeake and the Delaware as the location of one arm of a pincers movement aimed at Philadelphia. But Generals Arnold and Phillips had been sent there merely as raiders bent upon destroying Virginia's stores of arms and tobacco.

As he read Cornwallis's letter from Wilmington, Clinton could find no hint in it that his subordinate was himself seriously making plans to invade Virginia. On the contrary, Cornwallis spoke only of refreshing his troops and receiving reinforcements that would enable him "to act offensively or even to maintain himself in the upper country, where alone he could hope to escape the fatal sickness which had so nearly ruined his army last autumn." In his later attempts to explain his fatal resolve to move northward, Cornwallis stuck to the theme that "the amount of sickness among all ranks of the army was positively alarming," and that he hoped to improve their health by moving to Virginia, which Clinton called "the graveyard of armies." But nowhere did Cornwallis offer any proof of the superior sanitary advantages of fever-ridden Virginia over the "upper country" of the Carolinas. Clinton made a marginal note on Cornwallis's letter of April 10: "Does not this letter distinctly imply that His Lordship had not the least idea of coming northward, but of retiring to the back country to avoid sickness of last year?"[4]

Viewing the British military situation as a whole, with its three scattered armies, the only way to make any strategic sense out of Cornwallis's action is by supposing that Clinton would evacuate New York and join him in Virginia, a most unlikely move on Clinton's part. As a health measure, Cornwallis's plan was absurd. As a major stroke against the patriots' supply bases, it had some merit, but it neglected completely the general's own logistic problem, which the French fleet's arrival quickly made insoluble. Worst of all, it involved the complete "desertion" of the Carolinas, which were to be completely pacified *before* he made any conquests to the north.

In South Carolina, Lord Rawdon was left with about eight thousand men dispersed in ten posts, a large proportion of them Tory militia of doubtful military value. Cornwallis frankly admitted his fear that "Rawdon's posts will be so distant from each other, and his troops so scattered, as to put him into the greatest danger of being beat in detail, and that the worst of consequences may happen to most of the troops out of Charleston." The accuracy of this prophecy makes all the more incredible the cynicism of the action which followed it.

The abandonment of the North Carolina loyalists, which Cornwallis had sworn to defend, was bound to have a deadly effect upon the morale of British sympathizers everywhere. Fighting in the South had been marked by manifold desertions on both sides as first one and then the other seemed to offer the maximum security for those without strong convictions either way. Nothing discouraged loyalist recruiting more than the departure of the ever-victorious soldiers of the King. As one of Cornwallis's officers said: "Our march through this country may be compared to the passage of a ship through the waves which give way on the least impulse, but immediately close when the body has passed."[5]

On April 25, 1781, Cornwallis made the first key decision of the Yorktown campaign when he marched his army out of Wilmington to join Generals Phillips and Arnold at Petersburg, Virginia, without giving Clinton notice in time for the latter to countermand the move. From that moment on, he was "in touch with his fate." When Clinton received the stunning news he told Cornwallis quite frankly that if he had had any intimation of the probability of his intention, he would certainly have tried to stop him. General Greene had turned south to make life miserable for Rawdon, believing that Cornwallis would surely follow him. To his amazement, he was unpursued; and just eight months after the debacle at Camden his Continentals stood before that town. Word was sent to Marion, Sumter, and Pickens to harry the British outposts without fear of much resistance. Lord

Rawdon was about to be "beat in detail," as had been predicted.

On entering Virginia Cornwallis found himself facing a general for whom he had little respect, and whose army seemed even less formidable than Greene's. Clinton described Lafayette's soldiers as "a small body of peasantry, full as spiritless as the militia of the southern provinces, and without any service." As for the Marquis de Lafayette himself, his age, twenty-four, filled the forty-two-year-old Earl with disdain for "the boy," as he called him. He would teach the impulsive and enthusiastic young volunteer, ridiculously given the office of major general, a few elementary lessons in the military arts.

The young Frenchman's presence in Virginia as the commander of the American forces requires some explanation, especially since one phase of it foreshadowed Cornwallis's predicament at Yorktown. Many historians have fastened upon Benedict Arnold's treasonable attempt to deliver West Point to Clinton in September, 1780, as the nadir of American fortunes during the war. Only three months later, now a British general, Arnold was given the command of a raiding expedition in Virginia. Acting with his usual vigor, against almost no opposition, he swept from Portsmouth through the valley of the James up to Richmond, destroying, looting, and terrifying the unprepared populace. When he finally drew back to his base before Steuben and the Virginia militia, Washington saw a chance of trapping him between a French fleet and a patriot army. This "bag Arnold" enterprise can almost be regarded as a dress rehearsal for the Yorktown campaign later in the year.

On February 20, 1781, Washington instructed Lafayette to go by land to the Head of Elk, then down Chesapeake Bay to Hampton Roads in search of Arnold, and, if the traitor should fall into his hands, "to execute the punishment due his treason and desertion in the most summary way." Lafayette had been picked for the task both for his military talents and his diplomatic qualities of tact and persuasiveness. Nothing could be accomplished in Virginia, Washington knew, without the wholehearted aid of the State authorities, with whom Steuben had clashed repeatedly. Lafayette had twelve hundred New England and New Jersey Continentals, but "not a sou of money."

There seemed to be a chance of surrounding Arnold by both

land and sea, since Admiral Arbuthnot's British squadron, which had kept De Ternay bottled up in Newport, had been temporarily crippled by a winter storm. Thus Chevalier Destouches, who had succeeded De Ternay in the middle of December, 1780, sailed out for the Chesapeake. But Arbuthnot managed to repair his ships in time. He met Destouches off the Virginia Capes on March 6, and although the French commander showed greater skill in the engagement, he could not consolidate the command of the sea, and was obliged to return to Rhode Island.

Lacking the indispensable element of a French naval blockade, Lafayette had to retire to Annapolis, Maryland, his mission to capture Arnold a failure. He wanted to rejoin Washington for the projected attack on New York; but on April 6 he was ordered back south again to operate under General Greene. He was not happy, he wrote in confidence to Alexander Hamilton, at "being removed from the North just at the moment that French troops were about to fight." As a good soldier, he obeyed orders, although, as he told La Luzerne: "We have neither money, nor clothes, nor shoes, nor shirts and in a few days we shall be reduced to green peaches."[6] He was plagued by desertions among the New England men who had fully expected, after chasing Arnold, to return to their homes.

Leaving baggage and artillery behind, Lafayette raced to Richmond, Virginia, just in time to save that city from Phillips and Arnold. With many fewer soldiers, some of them "poor fellows, almost naked," and no boats or wagons, he could act only defensively, and then only by dint of rapid marches. Phillips and Arnold mysteriously headed to Petersburg; and Lafayette learned that Cornwallis, instead of following Greene back into South Carolina, was coming north to join them there. Lafayette was now in grave danger of being caught between two armies, each of them superior to his own motley array. He sent an urgent plea to his only possible source of reinforcements, Major General Anthony Wayne of the Pennsylvania Line, to hasten to his relief. For soon he had to pit against the crack cavalry of Tarleton and Simcoe militia dragoons "who cut a ridiculous figure without pistols, swords, saddles, bridles, or boots."

Like General Greene himself, Lafayette was an indefatigable

beggar in his approach to the civil authorities on behalf of his needy battalions. He bombarded Governor Thomas Jefferson of Virginia with appeals for food and clothing and horses and boats and militia. Sometimes he got only oxen and scows and polite expressions of regret. For Jefferson accurately described his constituents as "an unprepared people, who have now the war for the first time seriously fixed in their country . . ." As the governor of a democratic state, it was not in his power to do anything more than represent to the General Assembly what needed to be done. Jefferson repeatedly "demanded troops from the counties in vain; the men would not respond."[7] As Lafayette described the situation to General Weedon on May 15, 1781: "With the handful of men I have, there is no chance of resisting the combined armies unless I am speedily and powerfully reinforced . . . There is more militia going off than there is militia coming in."[8] When their enlistments expired, he said, there was no stopping them, "you might as well stop the flood tide from flowing."

Nevertheless he received one piece of good news. Thanks to Greene's belief that he was now able to cope with Rawdon before Camden, Lafayette was told that he might devote his undivided attention to Virginia, giving him an independent, if a sorely ill-supplied command. The effect was sobering; "I become timid," he wrote to Greene, "in the same proportion as I become independent." Fate was also kind to him. Just before Cornwallis arrived at Petersburg, General Phillips died from some variety of fever, and the command reverted to Arnold, on May 20, 1781. A few days later, seventeen hundred German reinforcements arrived from New York, sent by Clinton when he heard of Cornwallis's "retreat" to Wilmington and intended, not for the invasion of Virginia, but for the reconquest of North Carolina. Lafayette was now even more heavily outnumbered, and wrote to La Luzerne that after Wayne's arrival: "We shall be in a position to be beaten more decently, but at present we can only run away."

Clinton had clung as long as possible to the hope that Cornwallis had gone back to Charleston, and was fairly stunned when he was obliged to face the truth of his presence in Virginia. Speaking later with hindsight and on his own behalf, he said:

"How great was my disappointment and astonishment when, instead of hearing that His Lordship's army was, upon being refitted, marched back into the country to protect friends (as he promised to do) or for the purpose of occupying some healthy and defensible position for the security of at least South Carolina (as His Lordship had also before promised, and as his letter of the 10th intimated was then his intention) I found he had come to the fatal resolution of abandoning both Carolinas to their fate and flying into Virginia, to save the corps immediately under himself, as he says, from being hemmed in and cut off by General Greene's army, should it return upon him after proceeding against Lord Rawdon!"[9]

Mystified as he was concerning Cornwallis's true motives in coming into Virginia, Clinton came forward with two plans based upon his belief that Washington and Rochambeau would soon make a major attack. Clinton would either move southward through Pennsylvania to meet Cornwallis coming northward; or Cornwallis might establish and garrison a base on the Chesapeake, shipping the rest of his army to reinforce New York. The trouble was that these plans were only suggestions, not orders, and Cornwallis rejected both of them. Clinton simply did not dare to tell him to go back to Charleston, protect the Carolinas, and try conclusions with Greene. It may have been a failure of command nerve on Clinton's part, or it may have been the result of a growing awareness that Cornwallis had Germain's support, and that he did not. Confirmation of the latter view was soon to reach him, for on June 6, 1781, Germain wrote him that he was now "well pleased to find Lord Cornwallis's opinion entirely coincides with mine of the great importance of pushing the war on the side of Virginia with all the force that can be spared until that province is reduced."[10]

Cornwallis's own plan was to establish a naval base in the Chesapeake with his whole army to defend it, using it as the center of his campaign to reduce the province of Virginia to impotence. He and Clinton spent a good part of the summer in a long series of arguments over two moot points: where to locate and fortify the naval base; and how many of Cornwallis's men could be sent back to New York. Knowing that Clinton might summon a part of his force at any moment, Cornwallis could not stray too far from the seacoast. On the other hand, he was, in order to justify his presence in Virginia, committed to destroy the province's storehouses and factories. That could be done only by the smashing of their vulnerable shield, the ragged army of Lafayette.

Cornwallis now had over seven thousand men to Lafayette's three thousand or less, since harvest time was approaching and the American militia could not long be kept in the field. Toward the end of May, Cornwallis wrote to Clinton: "I shall now proceed to dislodge Lafayette from Richmond, and with my light troops destroy any magazines or stores in the neighborhood . . ." He would then proceed to Williamsburg to await Clinton's orders. Lafayette's task was to conceal the real weakness of his army by swift movements and to elude a major action, always keeping to the higher ground between Cornwallis and Philadelphia. As the British general advanced, he retreated "from river to river," trying to protect as many magazines as possible. Cornwallis had hoped to prevent Lafayette and Wayne from joining forces, but was obliged to give up that idea. He sent Tarleton to the temporary state capital at Charlottesville, where he captured seven members of the Assembly and missed snaring Governor Jefferson by the narrowest of margins.

Wayne finally joined Lafayette on June 10, 1781, and as Cornwallis turned back toward Williamsburg, they followed him southward. Numerically the American forces now amounted to nearly five thousand men, still incapable of a pitched battle with Cornwallis, but able to defend important storehouses. Lafayette knew very well that he was not forcing Cornwallis to recoil before him, but the Frenchman was enough of a politician in uniform "to try to give his opponent's movements the appearance of a retreat . . . which will look well in a gazette."[11] This was a pretense that was both effective in raising patriot morale at the time, and, later on, in giving the Marquis the credit for having "driven" Cornwallis down into Yorktown. When Steuben joined him on June 19, 1781, the total of his Continental regulars rose to nearly two thousand, with more than three thousand militia available until the harvest got under

way. Among the reinforcements were about six hundred mountain riflemen, "agile as cats."

The Marquis de Lafayette, always avid for glory, began to
feel the same urge for open battle that had stirred in General
Greene at Guilford. It seemed as if an engagement between his
forces and Cornwallis's "retreating" army now impended.

14

CORNWALLIS
GOES TO YORKTOWN

"I never saw this post [Yorktown] in a favorable light."
—Earl Cornwallis to Sir Henry Clinton, October 20, 1781

It was an intercepted letter which changed the situation in Virginia. Somewhere between New Windsor and Morristown, New Jersey, on June 5, 1781, a public courier carrying letters from Washington to Lafayette was held up by a young loyalist named John Moody. The dispatches were sent to Clinton in New York, who paid two hundred guineas for the haul. In the more personal of the letters, Washington revealed to Lafayette that he had conferred with Rochambeau and Commodore de Barras at Wethersfield, Connecticut, on May 21, 1781, about their joint plans for the coming campaign. Washington had strongly favored, as he had all along, a large-scale combined attack upon New York, maintaining that it would oblige the British to recall their armies from the South. But the two French leaders had argued for going directly to the assistance of Lafayette and Greene. Washington made it clear that the final verdict had gone in his favor and that the French had acquiesced.

At the time, it seemed to the patriots a great calamity that so vital a strategic decision had become known to the enemy. In the long run, however, the theft contributed powerfully to Cornwallis's downfall. For Clinton, always apprehensive about his position in New York, took fresh alarm at the prospect of an assault by Washington, Rochambeau, and whatever French fleet might appear. Two more purloined letters from other French and American officers said about the same thing. Could this be a widespread plot to deceive him? He could not believe so. He had already weakened his garrison, seriously, he thought, by sending some of his best men to reinforce Cornwallis, who now had, according to his figures, at least seventy-five hundred soldiers. Lafayette could not possibly be facing him with more than half as many creditable troops. So, on June 8, 11, 15, and 19 Clinton fired off a whole series of letters to Cornwallis ordering him to take the defensive, and, as soon as he had completed "the operations then in train," to send just as many men as he could spare —Clinton listed units numbering about two thousand—to reinforce the threatened garrison in New York.

Now it was Cornwallis's turn to be shocked by the sudden ending of his virtually independent command, and the complete frustration of his plan for reducing all of Viriginia. It was some time, however, before he received this bad news as he made his way toward Williamsburg. He believed that he had, as he originally intended, struck heavy blows against the rebel stores in Virginia. He reckoned his toll of destruction at five thousand stands of arms, six hundred barrels of powder, two thousand hogsheads of tobacco, and hundreds of other items.

As harvest time approached Lafayette's ranks began to shrink; and even at its peak in numbers, his army never matched the British in either quantity or quality. Yet it was Cornwallis who presented the sorrier figure of the two as he made his way toward the coast in order to comply with Clinton's urgent demand for reinforcements. In the public eye, the noble lord presented the spectacle of a powerful army giving way before a weaker opponent. The overeager Anthony Wayne was lured into a trap at Green Spring, which cost the Americans about one hundred and forty casualties and two guns, a sharp reminder of British power and skill. When Cornwallis arrived at Portsmouth, the province north of the James River was at last free from marauders; and Lafayette could hardly escape receiving public credit for having engineered the British withdrawal.

Momentarily the war in the province seemed, in Lafayette's words, "in a state of languor," since both sides appeared to have their eyes fastened on New York. Lafayette's militia had shrunk to about fifteen hundred men, and all signs indicated that Cornwallis was about to embark some of his army at Portsmouth. On July 26 Lafayette warned both Washington and the Congress that such a move might be under way, and even tried to send word to Count de Grasse suggesting that the admiral might intercept Cornwallis's transports at sea. It also occurred to Lafayette that Portsmouth, where he and Destouches had narrowly failed to trap Arnold in March, might prove to be the place to bag Cornwallis, provided that this time a French fleet would furnish the vital blockade by sea. The Marquis made some dispositions of his forces that would be useful in case Portsmouth could be besieged. But no French fleet appeared.

Meanwhile Cornwallis had proposed to Clinton that when reinforcements had been sent to New York as ordered, the rest of his army should return with him to Charleston, in effect abandoning the Chesapeake-base project entirely. The news from South Carolina, as both of them had feared, had been anything but good, even though Rawdon had beaten Greene again at Hobkirk's Hill north of Camden on April 25, and a month-long siege of the British post at Ninety-Six had failed in June. Other weaker posts had fallen to the rebels, and Rawdon held firm control of hardly more than Charleston and Savannah. It was now Clinton who would have none of Cornwallis's Carolina proposal, maintaining that both he and Rear Admiral Thomas Graves, who had succeeded Arbuthnot, agreed upon the absolute necessity of a winter naval base in the Chesapeake suitable for the accommodation of a large fleet of line ships.

Finally, in mid-July, Cornwallis was given an order cancelling the shipment of troops to New York and assuring him that he was to retain his entire army in Virginia. "It was Germain," says Captain W. M. James, R.N., "who caused this *volte face*, for Clinton had just received definite commands from him that no troops were to be withdrawn from Virginia and that the main operation was to be an advance through that colony."[1] This meant that Cornwallis's army was now being manipulated by three different commanders: Germain, Clinton, and himself.

After a survey by his engineers, Cornwallis found Old Point Comfort unsuitable for the protection of a large fleet by shore batteries, and settled instead upon the combination of the ports of Yorktown and Gloucester on opposite banks of the York

River. Whether, as he claimed, he was specifically ordered by Clinton to do this became a matter of dispute. But on July 26, 1781, Cornwallis wrote to Graves in this vein: "The Commander-in-chief having signified to me in his letter of the 11th instant, that he thought a secure harbor for line of battle ships of so much importance in the Chesapeake, that he wished me to possess one, even if it should occupy all the force at present in Virginia . . ." Certainly the general felt himself urged by both Clinton and Graves to establish such a post, and his reasons for rejecting Old Point Comfort for the purpose were valid ones.

Cornwallis arrived at Yorktown on August 1, 1781. His movement in that direction puzzled Lafayette, but it also served to heighten the latter's hopes that he might be, after all, the one to entrap the Earl and his army. On July 31, he wrote to Washington: "Should a French fleet now come to Hampton Roads, the British army would, I think, be ours." A week later, on August 6, he repeated the same idea: "Should a fleet come in at this moment, our affairs would take a very happy turn."[2] But Lafayette was to have some time to wait.

General Washington now found himself in something of a quandary, the possessor of a secret too valuable to be entrusted to paper. Too many American written messages had already fallen into British hands, a few of them intentionally no doubt, but others unintentionally and harmfully. He dared not to write to Lafayette in so many words of the trap that was being prepared, or even that he must not under any circumstances allow Cornwallis to slip away by land for the very good reason that a French fleet and a Franco-American army were about to converge upon the Chesapeake.

By the end of July, however, Washington began the cautious unfolding of his secret by broad hints that Lafayette should stay in Virginia, because New York, after all, might not be the place where the most military glory was to be won. To make sure that the Marquis read between the lines, Washington said: "Your penetration will point out my meaning." Lafayette showed that he was very much in tune with his patron's thinking. He replied that he was staying in Virginia all right, and added: "I have pretty well understood you, my dear general."

At this stage Lafayette displayed ample respect for the talents of his opponent. He wrote to General Knox that Cornwallis's "abilities are to me more alarming than his superiority of forces. I ever had a great opinion of him. Our papers call him a mad man, but was ever any advantage taken of him when he commanded in person? To speak plain English, I am devilish afraid of him."[3] In his letters to friends in France, Lafayette did very little boasting about his driving Cornwallis to the sea. To Vergennes on August 24, 1781, his language was: "When you have Cornwallis ahead of you, Monsieur le Comte, and when you are running after him through the sands of Virginia . . ." To Maurepas he had said: "You will be alarmed at the role they have given my youth. Five hundred miles from any other troops, they have wished to oppose me to the fortunes of Lord Cornwallis . . ."[4]

It was only much later that Lafayette "remembered" that it was he who pushed Cornwallis into Yorktown; and, as he explained in his *Commentaires*, his principal object in Virginia had been "to force him between the rivers in such a way that he would have no means of retreat." In point of fact, whatever Lafayette's hopes and dreams he never had the power to conduct any such premeditated campaign of pressure on Cornwallis. This is not to detract from his fine combination of prudence, audacity, and sheer doggedness in covering those movements of the British general of which others were the cause. The end result, in Lafayette's own words, came about "as if by enchantment." It is no wonder that the glory-hungry Marquis came to believe that it was he who had cast the magic spell.

By the middle of August, 1781, Washington dared to make it plain that aid was coming "from this quarter," and that Lafayette must hem Cornwallis in until it and the indispensable French fleet arrived in the Chesapeake. The young general replied almost ecstatically: "I heartily thank you for having ordered me to remain in Virginia and to your goodness to me I am owing the most beautiful prospect I may ever behold." His army had expanded again to about five thousand men, a force he was afraid he might not be able to feed. To the new Governor Thomas Nelson, Jr., he painted a frightening picture of his situation on the verge of victory: "Few men in the field; not a sixth part of what is called for—a greater number without arms, the greatest

part of whom live from day to day upon food which is injurious
to their health, without six cartridges per man, and the poor
Continentals that will soon be our only dependence falling off
for want of spirits and flour . . . Should it be known to Lord
Cornwallis, he may ruin us at one stroke, and defeat every project that may have been made for the protection of this state."[5]

But in spite of all such handicaps, and the August weather
which had given "almost all his people a fever," Lafayette moved
his men closer and closer to the Yorktown peninsula. He was
most afraid that Cornwallis would make a break for North
Carolina, but the Earl had no such intention. According to
Tarleton, Cornwallis was confidently expecting the arrival of
the British West Indies fleet. When Brigadier General Duportail
of the engineers reached Lafayette, the full scope of the grand
design for Yorktown was finally revealed to him. Not only was
De Grasse expected in force from the Antilles; De Barras might
also bring the Rhode Island squadron to the Chesapeake; and
both Washington and Rochambeau were on the way with the
cream of their armies.

Lafayette redoubled his efforts to rally enough militia to
frustrate any move which Cornwallis might make. "I expect
every minute that our prey is escaping," he wrote to Governor
Nelson on August 30. On that very day, and sooner than he had
been expected, Admiral de Grasse's fleet had been sighted off
the Chesapeake by a British dispatch boat. Lafayette, who had
sent Colonel Gimat to Cape Henry to meet him, did not hear
of the arrival of a fleet until the following day, and did not
know at first whether it was British or French. Shortly it appeared that French naval superiority had indeed been achieved,
although Duportail had told Lafayette that De Grasse could stay
for only about three weeks in American waters.

Admiral de Grasse proved to be anxious to do his part; and
the Marquis de Saint-Simon, who commanded the land contingent, went out of his way to be accommodating. Saint-Simon
held a rank in the French army that was certainly equal to, if
not superior to Lafayette's in the American. Yet he expressed his
complete willingness to serve under the orders of a general
seventeen years younger than himself. He told the Americans
that he had thirty-one hundred soldiers and eight cannon which

could be landed immediately; and De Grasse added that he could spare eighteen hundred sailors for land duty if Lafayette wanted to attack at once. Here indeed was a temptation to glory of the most alluring sort: nearly five thousand well-equipped men from the French fleet plus the nearly five thousand with Lafayette might defeat Cornwallis's seven thousand and monopolize the credit for winning the war!

But on second thought, Lafayette realized that a frontal assault upon prepared fortifications would be very costly in lives, especially without the aid of siege artillery, and might possibly be a failure. Ten thousand men against eight or nine thousand (because Cornwallis could also use sailors from the British ships) would hardly be margin enough for safety. By waiting for Washington and Rochambeau, who had held on tenaciously for years and months respectively, Lafayette would not only share the glory with them, he would also raise the ratio of attackers to defenders to more than two to one. If Saint-Simon's corps could be landed and deployed quickly, Lafayette believed that the land ring around Cornwallis could be made strong enough to hold until the main allied forces came up.

When Cornwallis heard of the landing of Saint-Simon's regiments, he assured his own men that "Saint-Simon's raw and sickly troops were nothing better than undisciplined vagabonds, collected in the West Indies, enervated by a hot climate, and would soon be conquered, were it only by the first attacks of cold weather prevalent in these countries."[6] The British general's first mistake at Yorktown was in allowing the "undisciplined vagabonds" to land at Jamestown unmolested. "It was a pleasant surprise for our troops," wrote Lieutenant Tornquist, "that on landing Cornwallis did not move in the least to hinder them, since indeed a single cannon shot could have caused much damage in the narrow and in many places winding river." The "zeal and celerity" with which Saint-Simon took advantage of this enemy blunder won the praise of Washington in an order of the day on September 15. It was far from easy going; "painful labor," Tornquist called it, "the cannon and their mounts had to be dragged by main strength to the mouth of the swamp."

As for the appearance of the French troops, in spite of the ancient American prejudice against Frenchmen as "light, brittle, queer-shaped mechanisms, only busy frizzing their hair and painting their faces" discovered by the Abbé Robin in his travels, these soldiers aroused general admiration. They were "all very tall men of a fine soldierly appearance . . . in splendid uniforms of white faced with blue . . . never," said Lieutenant William Feltman, "did I behold a more beautiful sight." "The finest body of troops," averred General Wayne, "that he had ever seen."[7] A nameless correspondent from Lafayette's army said: "Let me make you acquainted with Major General the Marquis of Saint-Simon, and the French army. You have seen the British troops and the troops of other nations, but you have not seen troops so universally well-made, so robust, or of such an appearance as those General Saint-Simon has brought to our assistance. I do not pretend to know the secrets of our commander, or I would tell you what is to be done; I pretend, however, to see a great general in the Marquis of Saint-Simon, an affectionate politeness in his officers toward ours, and a general impatience in the French Army to complete the Gordian knot in which our second Fabius, Lafayette, has been entangling his Lordship."[8]

By contrast, the motley and ragged appearance of many of his own troops embarrassed Lafayette. The Virginia regiment was so unclothed that he said: "I shall endeavor to keep it a little out of sight." To relieve their sartorial distress, the Americans, despite the poverty of their own stores, gave the French all the flour they could spare, getting along themselves on cornmeal. Lafayette was to remember for many years the generous role his troops played without grumbling, although "all the preferences were for the French."

By failing to oppose the landing of Saint-Simon's troops, as Saint-Simon himself believed he ought to have done, Cornwallis permitted himself to be hemmed in by land. He had one remaining hope of escape—by sea. If Admirals Rodney or Hood or Graves appeared off the Chesapeake in sufficient strength to drive away De Grasse, all might still be well. His army could then be transported to Charleston or New York.

15

DE GRASSE AND
SAINT-SIMON DECIDE
TO COME NORTH

"The coming of the Marquis de Saint-Simon's troops gave Washington such confidence and such delight that he is described by the Count des Deux-Ponts as 'playing the boy and swinging his chapeau in ecstasy.'"
—Robert C. Winthrop

The Bourbon monarchies of France and Spain were bound together by the Family Compact of 1733, which had been tested in their disastrous Seven Years' War with England. It had held firm until the Falkland Islands crisis in 1770, when France's refusal to make war produced a lack of harmony which removed Choiseul from office. Since both countries thirsted for revenge against Great Britain, the American war brought Charles III of Spain and his uncle Louis XVI of France together again, though without their earlier enthusiasm for co-operation. Both wanted to tear up the Treaty of 1763 and to harm England as much as possible, but Spain opposed the creation of a strong and independent United States as a threat to her colonies. Her Court refused to receive American agents, although she did send some aid, independently, to America through New Orleans, and gave a certain amount of financial assistance.

Being displeased at France's open alliance with the Americans, Spain waited for over a year before allowing herself to be induced to honor the terms of the Family Compact. She entered the war in June, 1779, as the ally of France only, and at the price of French promises to aid in recovering Gibraltar, Minorca, and the

Floridas. A combined Franco-Spanish invasion of England was planned for the autumn of 1779. When that move was abandoned early in October, the grand strategy of the Bourbon allies for the year 1780 was outlined by the French Minister for Foreign Affairs to his ambassador in Madrid in these terms: "To blockade Gibraltar, to have sufficient force in America and Asia to resist the British, and to take the offensive in the Antilles."[1]

As part of the French contribution toward the carrying out of this plan, the three regiments of Agenais, Gâtinais, and Touraine embarked at Brest in February, 1780, to reinforce the garrison of Cap Français (now Cap Haitien). That city was then known as "the Paris of the Antilles," where everyone went to know the latest fashions. It was the capital of San Domingo, a colony shared by France and Spain, which "had reached a height of prosperity without parallel in the history of colonial possessions."[2] Luxurious living, danger, and disease went hand in hand in the "soldier's hell of the West Indies," for hurricanes, fevers, and British fleets made life at Cap Français anything but tranquil.

The commander-in-chief of the three French regiments came from one of the oldest houses of the nobility. He was Claude-Anne, Marquis de Saint-Simon (Montbléru). His family had given France the famous memoirist of the court of Louis XIV, the Duc de Saint-Simon, and the Marquis was accompanied to America by his younger brother, the Baron de Saint-Simon as aide-de-camp, and a young cousin, Count Henri de Saint-Simon as commander of the gunners of the regiment of Touraine. It was the latter who, on his return to Europe, was to give his name to the famous cult of Saint-Simonians. The Marquis de Saint-Simon had been colonel of the Touraine regiment at Arras, and had just been promoted to the rank of *maréchal de camp*. On arriving in the West Indies, he was ordered by the Marquis de Bouillé to embark his grenadiers on board De Guichen's flagship *La Couronne* on April 15, 1780, in the hope of delivering the Barbados with its thousand French prisoners of war, or possibly retaking the island of St. Lucia from the British.

What followed was a series of three inconclusive engagements between De Guichen's twenty-two ships of the line and Rodney's twenty-one, requiring forty days of continuous navigation "with the slow-match lighted and ready for the cannon" for about one-third of the time. Rodney himself wrote to his wife that "for fourteen days and nights the fleets were so near each other that neither officers nor men could be said to sleep. Nothing but the goodness of the weather and climate would have enabled us to endure so continual a fatigue. Had it been in Europe, half the people must have sunk under it."[3]

It was the news of this enterprise of De Guichen's which aroused Charles III of Spain to send his Admiral Don Joseph Solano with twelve ships of the line and twelve thousand soldiers under General Don de Maria on eighty-three transports to assist De Guichen in some joint operation in the West Indies. He noted that "he merely hoped that this combined affair would be directed toward the South rather than the North," or, in other words, close to his own colonial interests in Florida. But when Solano, having eluded the British fleet under Rodney, reached De Guichen on June 1, 1781, the latter was to learn why it was said that "it was better to have the Spanish navy for an enemy than an ally." The Spanish troops had been so crowded on board the transports, "that a pestilential distemper broke out amongst them, which increased so much during the voyage, that it became absolutely necessary to land the men in Martinique . . ."[4] This frightfully unsanitary condition of his fleet, costing as many as five thousand lives, caused Don Solano to refuse all co-operation with De Guichen, and even to ask the French admiral for an escort as far as the Bahama Channel on the way to Havana and Puerto Rico, which was provided. The French and Spanish fleets separated; and it was this ignominious failure of the Spanish navy to do its share in the West Indies strategy which was to have a definite influence on the Yorktown campaign. Later on it was to provide De Grasse with a powerful argument for other kinds of help from the Spanish at San Domingo and Havana.

When the news of De Guichen's presence at the eastern end of Cuba reached Newport it aroused false hopes of gaining his assistance still farther north. Both Rochambeau and De Ternay had been authorized to call upon the French commander in the Antilles for reinforcements. Using this power of requisition, De Ternay asked Guichen for four ships of the line for the purpose of breaking Arbuthnot's blockade of Narragansett Bay, which was dooming both his squadron and Rochambeau's army to futility. Rochambeau wrote hopefully to Washington on September 9, 1760: "Can it be that the Spanish are not ready for their expedition?" But all these northern hopes of assistance from the Antilles were dashed on September 25, when the news arrived of De Guichen's having returned to Cadiz in August, leaving ten of the line in the West Indies. He left before De Ternay's requisition arrived, and De Monteil, his successor, could not read the cipher, not having received the key.

So the story of French naval assistance to the Americans continued to be one of disappointment and frustration; but developments more favorable to the allied cause were in the offing. When De Guichen left, the Marquis de Saint-Simon found that his corps had been transferred to the service of Spain to form a part of General de Maria's army. But the Spaniards showed no signs whatever of bestirring themselves in a military way. Thus it came about that on September 6, 1780, a year less one day before the decisive battle of the war, Saint-Simon wrote to his old associate Count de Rochambeau in Newport: "I should be delighted to be under your orders and I should gladly give up the command *en chef* which I have here."[5] This letter arrived at Newport on board the *Gentille* on September 30, 1780, and Rochambeau immediately forwarded it in translation to General Washington, remarking that "two thousand men under the orders of M. de Saint-Simon are at the Cape waiting for their instructions."

As early as the last of September, 1780, then, Washington and Rochambeau knew not only of the Marquis's presence in the Antilles, but also of his eager desire to come to their assistance rather than to retain a higher rank in the service of Spain in Florida or elsewhere. During the winter there was the usual lull in military activity. On January 7, 1781, the Marquis de Saint-Simon wrote again to Rochambeau following the latter's response to his previous letter. What follows is the English translation sent to Washington on February 3, 1781. "I found here, sir, at my arrival, the letter which you have favored me with from Newport on the 27th of September. I directly wrote you to express my gratitude for the friendship and concern you bear to me. I mentioned the fear I was in, lest we should not undertake anything in these seas. Mr. de Maria's army has very much suffered by sickness since his arrival at Cuba; he has lost more than one-third of his men, and my corps whose destination is to serve with them has lost one-fourth. Besides it is divided: there is one-half here and the other at San Domingo. That division had engaged me to go to the Havannah to try to obtain from the Spanish general that it might be reunited, and to have leave from him to embark upon the ships of the Chevalier de Monteil, in expectation of his making some enterprise. . . . But the Spanish general has refused me . . . At Martinique they are making considerable preparations to receive a great number of troops, among which they talk of the regiments of Normandy, Neustrie, Auvergne and Rouergue; it is your second division. I desire very much to have an order to join it."

Saint-Simon repeated his declaration that "he would willingly leave the command in chief that I have here" to serve under Rochambeau. He went on: "I believe your campaign will be warmer than ours. This is the season to act in these climates and we lose it. I am very sorry of it; it is hard to be in a country so exceedingly destructive of men, and to do nothing in a military way."[6] It must be granted that this French aristocrat was not burning with zeal to promote the political ideals of the Founding Fathers. He was simply intent upon reaping the glory which "a warmer campaign" might bring, and striking a blow against England.

Saint-Simon was mistaken about the coming of Rochambeau's second division, which remained blockaded in Brest. Instead, the French king bestowed an outright gift of six million *livres*, to be spent in France under Franklin's direction, and later he underwrote a loan of ten million *livres* from Holland. After much more pleading at Court, a new fleet was to replace De Guichen's in the West Indies under François-Joseph-Paul, Count de Grasse, given the temporary rank of lieutenant general on March 22, 1781. He was to raise his flag over the finest warship in existence, the *Ville de Paris*, 110 guns, gift of the City of Paris to the French nation.

In the words of Vergennes, "The Count de Grasse has been ordered to conduct, sometime toward the approach of next winter, a part of his fleet to the coast of North America, or to detach a portion of it to sweep the coast and to co-operate in any undertaking which may be projected by the French and American generals, or to form a part of it if they are unable to co-operate. The number of ships to be sent to the North will depend upon the need which the Spanish have of our assistance . . . If they have made preparations for some great enterprise, we shall have to lend them a hand; for if a serious blow is struck at the common enemy and it is successful, the advantage will be equally great for all the allies."[7]

It is obvious that De Grasse, if he was to follow his instructions, must first meet all Spanish requirements in the West Indies, and would then be authorized to come North with only a part of his fleet. In getting ready to sail from Brest, he displayed great energy; and he made a remarkably swift passage of the Atlantic, by towing some of his slower ships, in thirty-eight days from his departure on March 22, 1781. On April 5, while at sea, the admiral detached the 50-gun *Sagittaire* and a convoy of thirty ships for Newport with six hundred and sixty replacements for Rochambeau's first division. Also on this ship was a letter from De Grasse to Rochambeau which was to have resounding consequences. In the letter De Grasse said: "His Majesty has intrusted me with the command of the naval force destined for the protection of his possessions in southern America, and those of his allies in North America. The force which I command is sufficient to fulfill the offensive plans, which it is in the interest of the Allied powers to execute, that they may secure an honorable peace. If the men-of-war are necessary for fulfilling the projects which you have in view . . . It will not be until the 15th of July, at the soonest, that I shall be on the coast of North America."[8]

On April 28, 1781, De Grasse's fleet and convoy came in sight of Martinique with the prospect of an encounter with the combined forces of Rodney and Hood. Fortunately for the French Rodney was still preoccupied with the disposition of the loot at St. Eustatius, and mainly concerned that Hood should protect the process by blockading the four line ships of the Chevalier de Monteil in Fort Royal harbor. In spite of Hood's protests Rodney had obstinately refused permission for his second-in-command to cruise to the windward of Martinique in order to be sure of intercepting De Grasse. Hood had only seventeen ships of the line and five frigates, but all of them were copper bottomed, against about half of De Grasse's twenty, a compensating advantage. It is true that the Admiralty showed great laxity in failing to send a faster ship to Rodney with the news of De Grasse's departure. The dispatch was entrusted to the cutter *Swallow*, rather than to a frigate, and it arrived on May 17, or three weeks too late.

In his hopeless leeward position, Hood tried his best to keep De Grasse from reaching his destination, but in vain. "Never," he said, "was a squadron so unmeaningly stationed . . . Never was more powder and shot thrown away in one day before." When the two van divisions got within range, however, six of Hood's ships were considerably damaged. De Grasse blamed his captains for failing to obey signals and keep in better order, but the principal reason why he did not inflict a greater defeat upon Hood's inferior force was his own extreme caution. This may be excused by pointing out that, after all, his mission was to get his convoy and fleet safely into harbor at Martinique.

Although Rodney was soon jolted out of his complacency at St. Eustatius to join Hood on May 11, De Grasse and De Monteil had temporary naval superiority in the Antilles, and quickly took advantage of it to capture the island of Tobago, about half the size of Martinique, and famous for its indigo. Rodney had at least one chance for a major engagement with the French on June 5, 1781, but refused on the ground that it would have been within the power of the enemy "to entangle his Majesty's fleet among the Grenadines, to decoy them into the channel between Grenada and the Spanish Main, where the currents are so rapid that the fleet might be driven to leeward . . ."[9]

De Grasse came back to Martinique on June 18, having secured one hundred head of cattle at Grenada, together with wood and water for the coming campaign. He sent frigates to the various French islands to collect the convoys for the autumn trade to France, amounting finally to over one hundred and fifty vessels, which he escorted to Cap Français on July 16. Important mail was awaiting him there. It had been brought by the frigate *Concorde*, which had left Boston on June 20 and arrived on July 8, eluding all the British men-of-war along her route. She also carried twenty-five American pilots for De Grasse's fleet.

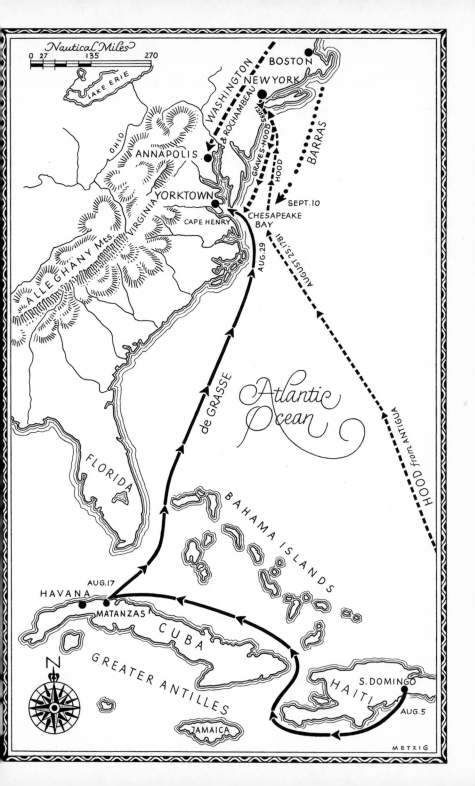

There were three letters from the Count de Rochambeau, written on May 28 (with a postscript on May 31), June 6 and June 11. The first told of Cornwallis's invasion of Virginia, Washington's desire to attack New York, and the presence of Rear Admiral Graves's fleet of seven line ships in New York. It summed up in these terms: "That is the state of affairs and the very grave crisis in which America, and especially the states of the South, finds herself at this particular time. The arrival of M. le Comte de Grasse would save this situation, all the means in our hands are not enough without his joint action and the sea superiority which he is able to command." Rochambeau then left, as we shall see, the choice between New York and the Chesapeake as his destination in the hands of De Grasse. The postscript reiterated the need of bringing men: "It is needless to write you the important service you will render if you are able to bring here a body of troops and your ships. Washington's army and my troops before New York will be weak and though the garrison of that place at present may not be more than eight thousand men, ours will hardly be more than a third more; five or six thousand more new men would give us the means of making certain the operations."[10]

Rochambeau's second letter was an appeal for money to pay his troops beyond August 2, pointing out to De Grasse that "it would be to the greatest advantage for the interest of the King" if he would "have the goodness to use for the security of the service of the army the influence of his credit and call for the help of the navy in the Antilles, up to the amount of one million two hundred thousand *livres* in specie. . . ." Otherwise the French war chests would soon be empty.

The general's final plea told of Washington's four letters to him urging the bringing of his corps to the Hudson, a course which he had decided to follow, and there "attempt, by menacing New York with him, to make a diversion in favor of Virginia. I must not conceal from you, Monsieur," he told De Grasse, "that the Americans are at the end of their resources, that Washington will not have half of the troops he is reckoned to have, and that I believe, though he is silent on that, that at present he does not have six thousand men; that M. de Lafayette does not have a thousand regulars with militia to defend Virginia, and nearly as many on the march to join him; that General Greene has pushed a small force far in advance of Camden, where he was repulsed, and that I do not know how and when he will rejoin M. de Lafayette; that it is therefore of the greatest consequence that you will take on board as many troops as possible; that four or five thousand men will not be too many, whether you aid us to destroy the works at Portsmouth, Virginia, near Hampton Roads, where up to now they have always kept fifteen hundred men while the others operate in the country, and all their flotillas with which they have tormented the poor Marquis de Lafayette on the rivers in a very evil manner; whether then to force the Hook in seizing Sandy-Hook for your land troops, which ought to facilitate the entrance of your squadron over that bar . . . finally to aid us afterwards to lay siege to Brooklyn . . . There, Monsieur, are the different objects that you may have in view, and the actual and sad picture of the affairs of this country. I am quite persuaded that you will bring us naval superiority, but I cannot too often repeat to you to bring also the troops and the money . . ."[11]

These three letters of Rochambeau's unquestionably made him, at that point, the person chiefly responsible for the direction taken by the subsequent course of events. For in spite of his agreement to accept Washington's scheme to attack New York, in advising his countryman De Grasse he placed the Chesapeake first, and that is where De Grasse decided to come. There is little indication that Rochambeau was the architect in detail of the Yorktown campaign, but he does deserve the credit for insisting all along upon the importance of naval superiority somewhere, and there is no question but what his choice of the Chesapeake prevailed.

Washington, who preferred not to write directly to De Grasse, expressed his wishes through the French minister to the American Colonies, the Chevalier de la Luzerne, as well as through Rochambeau. The American commander was still thinking in terms of a merging of the fleets of De Grasse and De Barras at Sandy Hook "to shut in, or cut off Admiral Arbuthnot." He too stressed the need of "a respectable corps of troops from the West Indies." Thus, he believed, "by one great, decisive stroke, the enemy might be expelled from the continent, and the independence of America established." On the same day he urged Rochambeau to press this matter of bringing troops upon De Grasse, "especially as I am very dubious whether our force can be drawn together by the time he proposes to be here." He mentioned the figure of "four or five thousand men" as adequate to the carrying of "our object," which in his mind was still New York.[12]

Admiral de Grasse thus found himself implored by all the French and American commanders in the most pressing manner to bring three things to their assistance, all of them difficult to come by and full of risks to be taken upon his own responsibility. A less resolute man might have hidden behind a wall of handy excuses. First there must be a fleet sufficiently powerful to insure the command of the sea on the North American coast against any force that Rodney and Graves could assemble. The second requirement was a body of regular troops formidable enough to make up for Rochambeau's missing second division and to fill the alarming gaps in Washington's depleted army. And finally, a very large sum of money in the form of specie was needed to replenish the allied war chests and thereby raise the morale of men whose pay, in the American army at least, had been too long sadly in arrears.

As for the place where he should appear, De Grasse made the choice of the Chesapeake (in his letter of July 28 which the *Concorde* brought back to Newport on August 12) as "the point which appears to me to be indicated by you, Monsieur Comte de Rochambeau, and by Messieurs Washington, De la Luzerne, and De Barras, as the one from which the advantage you propose may be most certainly attained."

Too much praise can never be given to the magnificent audacity, the remarkable energy, and the political tact displayed by De Grasse as he rose to his three great occasions. His actions evidenced a breadth of view beyond anything his previous record could have foretold. His strategic vision was remarkable, for he grasped and exemplified in the highest degree one of the great principles of victory in war—achieving a concentration superior to that of the enemy at the right time and place.

Of the three vital undertakings the securing of the needed troops appeared to be the easiest to accomplish, perhaps because he knew that the Marquis de Saint-Simon was already eager for "a warmer campaign" than General de Maria's. De Grasse made application to the new acting governor of San Domingo, Count de Lillancourt, for the temporary loan of the three French regiments in the Spanish service "under an express promise to restore them to him by the month of November."

It is to the journals of two officers in De Grasse's fleet that we owe our knowledge of the intricacies of the more difficult task of raising one million two hundred thousand *livres* in cash. One of them was a young Swedish lieutenant serving with the French navy, Carl Gustav Tornquist, who had come to Paris in search of experience, glory, and prize-money. He was assigned to the *Vaillant*, 74 guns, known as one of the poorer sailers in De Grasse's fleet. He tells how the admiral and Chevalier de Charitte, captain of the *Bourgogne*, 74 guns, first tried to raise three hundred thousand *piastres* in San Domingo. As another journal explains: "The merchants of the Cape would give it only on two conditions: first, that some men-of-war should be detached to escort their trade convoy to Europe; second, that security should be given for the reimbursement. The admiral refused the first article, because he did not wish to enfeeble his fleet; for the second, he offered to pledge his own plantation in the island and his chateau of Tilly in France. M. de Charitte also offered his; they were accepted, but the money was not forthcoming and time was lost."[13] Tornquist adds that "although the properties of these gentlemen greatly surpassed the sum in value, the proposition was not accepted, about which Count De Grasse had reason to be dissatisfied." Vaugirard called the business "a scandalous refusal."

Recourse was then had to a Spanish director general of the customs, Señor de Salavedra, who pointed out that the galleons had sailed to Europe. "The admiral urged him so much, that he agreed to go to Havana, with his letters to the Governor, and to do his best to assist the public treasury by the purses of individuals." The frigate *Aigrette* was sent off to the Cuban capital; and "it must be said to the honor of the colonists there, that all were eager to do so, ladies, even, offering their diamonds."[14] Other accounts maintain that the Havana request for money was addressed to Don Solano, admiral of the diseased and inactive

Spanish fleet, who, not having access to any such sum, appealed to the generosity of the inhabitants of Havana, who raised the money in less than six hours, "the sum serving as an excuse for the seventeen Spanish men-of-war not to accompany De Grasse." A bitter Frenchman added: "Is it not a shame for these vessels to lie rotting two years in a port? It is only a nation as cowardly as the Spaniard that can wallow so in inaction, leaving its allies to bear the brunt of the war."

Admiral de Grasse's greatest decision of all concerned the number of ships of the line he would take north. His orders mentioned only a part of his fleet as available for service off the North American coast, and then only if the Spaniards did not have prior need of them. His first obligation, of which Washington was not fully aware, was to provide for the security of the French and Spanish interests in the West Indies. Fortunately "there happened to be at San Domingo a Spanish commissary from the island of Cuba; it was agreed with him that a Spanish squadron should protect the coasts and commerce . . ."[15] Spain would not lift a finger to come north, but it would stand guard over the Antilles, thereby releasing De Grasse. No wonder Lafayette wrote to Luzerne after the French fleet arrived in the Chesapeake: "The Spanish have behaved like little angels." De Grasse was now free to take his entire fleet, on his own responsibility, to the aid of the Americans. It was a magnificent gamble on the part of De Grasse. "If the British Government had sanctioned or a British admiral had adopted such a measure, however necessary to carry an important political operation, the one would have been turned out," said Captain Thomas White, R.N., "and the other would have been hung. No wonder that they succeeded and we failed."[16]

Before De Grasse's departure, he had both gains and losses in terms of ships. When he arrived at Cap Français he found not only six line ships which had been left there by De Guichen, but also four of De Monteil's squadron just returned from a campaign with the Spaniards against Pensacola. The admiral was, however, to lose two of his vessels, one of the line and one a frigate, through almost identical accidents of a peculiar nature. On July 23, a ship's clerk on the *Intrepide*, 74 guns, went down into the cockpit to draw the sailors' rations of *tafia*, the brandy that was the French breakfast equivalent of the British tot of rum, with wine being issued at the other two meals. Careless handling of the lantern started a fire which spread rapidly over the whole ship. Lieutenant Tornquist, who witnessed the event in the crowded harbor at the Cap, said that finally "the stern sprang into the air with a majestic rumble, but a horrible sight . . . People in the city were injured, and houses and several of the ships were damaged."[17]

At nearly the same time the frigate *Inconstante*, 40 guns, fell a victim to the very same sort of mishap several miles off the San Domingo coast. About twenty sailors of the *Intrepide* had been lost by drowning when they jumped into the sea; but the casualties on the *Inconstante* were far greater: only about eighty of her complement of two hundred surviving by clinging to masts and spars. As a result of these twin catastrophes the admiral issued an order that an officer must henceforth always be present when the distribution of brandy was to take place. De Grasse had been obliged to leave eighteen hundred men sick at Martinique, and feared that he might have to leave as many more at San Domingo.

Saint-Simon's troops could be accommodated on the ships of the line, but in order to transport their equipment and ten pieces of field artillery, De Grasse found that he would need a convoy of fifteen merchant ships escorted by frigates. "To charter them," says Lieutenant de Loture, "De Grasse did not hesitate to spend his personal fortune, a detail which has been too much ignored." The three French regiments of infantry, with one hundred dragoons and three hundred and fifty artillerymen, boarded the vessels on August 3; and on August 5 the fleet of twenty-six ships of the line, divided into three squadrons commanded by De Monteil, De Grasse, and De Bougainville in that order, set sail toward Cuba. According to the Chevalier de Vaugirard: "Nine of De Grasse's ships had been in the West Indies for a long time, and did not appear to be in condition to follow him, but the pressing needs of the Americans did not permit him to hesitate for a moment."[18] Two more of his seventy-fours, the *Bourgogne* and the *Hector*, whose sailings had been delayed, joined the others on August 7.

"To reach North America," says a journal of the voyage, "the

fleet took an extraordinary route, the sense of which we afterwards saw. There was dread, no doubt, lest the frigate sent to
Havana for money would be taken or not arrive soon enough.
Moreover, had the fleet gone by the ordinary channels, the
enemy might have been informed of its course and got to the
Chesapeake ahead of it."[19] The enemy, incidentally, did get to
the Chesapeake ahead of it, but was not informed of its whereabouts or its course. "The fleet followed the old [Bahama] channel, the dreaded channel, where no French fleet had ever passed."
That passage had the reputation of being tedious and difficult,
the abode of "storms with rain and severe thunder in constant
alternation."[20] In passing between Cuba and the Bahamas there
were three days of contrary winds and threatening reefs. The
Northumberland, 74 guns, was nearly lost when its wheel was
given a wrong turn by the helmsman and she ran into breakers.
On August 9 Spanish coastal pilots were picked up at the small
port of Baracoa on the western tip of Cuba.

On August 17, at Matanzas, the *Aigrette* rejoined the admiral
on schedule from Havana with its cargo of money, which was
divided among the ships of the fleet; and on August 19 the Spanish pilots were sent back to Cuba. Lieutenant Tornquist gives a
highly graphic but unscientifically geographic account of their
northward progress aided by the Gulf Stream. "On the night of
August 17 we were in the channel between Florida and the Bahama Islands, whose greatest width is ten German miles. The
constant current which always flows northward with great speed
brings it about that, although the wind may be contrary, one
does not consider it remarkable to find oneself in twenty-four
hours from twenty to thirty German miles more northerly than
the most careful calculations would indicate. Presumably the
river Mississippi which falls into the sea in the neighborhood together with the bends of the land which break against the northern archipelago [his word is "skerries"] are the causes of this
current which then favored us, so that on August 22 we were
already out of the channel, that is to say that the current had
taken us ninety leagues farther than our calculations indicated,
during three-and-a-half days of sailing."

Tornquist relates that "the day after when we were at 32°
37′ latitude and 87° 5′ longitude west of Paris, in strong thunder

and storm, three sails were sighted which, after four hours' pursuit during nicer weather, were captured. They were the *Corp Morrant*, 24 guns, *Queen Charlotte*, 18 guns, covered below the water with tin plate, and a little yacht from Charleston. A few days later the ship *Sandwich* was also captured. It carried twelve eighteen-pounders on the second tier, and on the upper deck twenty-two nine-pounders. It had been detached from Admiral Rodney's fleet on account of a bad leak, one hundred and twenty miles north of the Leeward Islands, to seek harbor in Charleston. On August 24, being off Charleston, the cutter *La Mouche* was sent off to Europe with dispatches."[21] Captured on the *Sandwich* was Lord Rawdon, on his way to England, but now obliged to witness Cornwallis's downfall.

Late in the evening of August 29 in calm weather, "the fleet anchored on the banks outside of Chesapeake Bay five leagues from land. Early the following morning the whole fleet weighed and steered into the bay and anchored again in the roadstead of Lynnhaven within the Horseshoe bank in three columns, the van farthest out in eight to ten fathoms, the bottom being sand mixed with shells. The British frigate *Loyalist*, 26 guns, was captured by the *Glorieux*, 74 guns, which pursued it into the bay. The other enemy frigate *Guadaloupe*, 28 guns, escaped to Yorktown under the protection of its batteries." Since the British had the *Charon*, 44 guns, two smaller frigates, and six armed sloops in York River, De Grasse sent the *Vaillant* and *Triton* to join the *Glorieux* in blocking any sortie which they might attempt. He dispatched the *Experiment*, 50 guns, with the frigates *Andromaque*, 32 guns, and *Diligente*, 26 guns, to the James River to see to it that Lord Cornwallis did not make his way to North Carolina.

It is quite apparent that Lieutenant Tornquist took part in the landing operations, for he tells of his first impressions of that part of Virginia, including an atrocity story which must have impressed him at the time. "On a beautiful estate two miles from Hampton," he writes, "a pregnant woman was found murdered in her bed through several bayonet stabs; the barbarians had opened both her breasts and written above the bed canopy: 'Thou shalt never give birth to a rebel!' In another room was just as horrible a sight, five cut-off heads, arranged on a cupboard in place of plaster-cast figures, which lay broken to pieces on the floor." Dumb animals had been similarly mistreated. "The pastures were in many places covered with dead horses, oxen and cows. A storehouse of tobacco, which had been collected from Virginia, Maryland, and the Carolinas during many years, containing ten thousand hogsheads of tobacco, was laid in ashes. Such," concludes Tornquist, "was our first sight on landing in this unfortunate country. We did not find a single trace of inhabitants, for those who had been unable to flee lay on the ground, as a token of the godless behavior of their enemies."[22]

16

RODNEY DALLIES
AT SAINT EUSTATIUS

"Admiral Rodney lost all his powers the moment he made the capture of St. Eustatius." —George III

With Cornwallis's only hope of escape from Yorktown resting on the British naval commander in the West Indies, nothing could be more crucial in deciding the outcome of the war than that officer's conduct during the spring of 1781. Now begins the strange story of the fascination of an island for an admiral. The admiral was Sir George Brydges Rodney, and the island was St. Eustatius, often called Statia for short. It is a small, rocky, volcanic bit of land, about eight square miles in area, located at the northeast corner of the Leeward Islands chain. Its agricultural output was negligible, hardly more than six hundred barrels of sugar a year. But in the 1770's its commercial importance as an international trading center was phenomenal.

For St. Eustatius belonged to Holland, which meant neutrality and unbounded free trade in the near neighborhood of other rich and productive islands ruled by Great Britain, France, Denmark and Spain. In an age of mercantilism, each of these powers automatically sought to monopolize the trade of its own colonies; and when war came those belonging to the belligerents were strictly forbidden to trade with the enemy. But they managed to do so, all the same, through the convenient medium of St. Eustatius. They also made use of the island to store goods which might otherwise be lost in the seizures of territory that were constantly occurring as British, French, and Spanish admirals roamed the Caribbean.

In addition, St. Eustatius became an ideal mart of exchange for the American patriots, both as a source of American goods, including such contraband as gunpowder at fancy prices, and as an outlet for exports of tobacco, cotton, hemp, lumber, and indigo. Some idea of the extent of this trade may be gained from the statement of the Dutch Rear Admiral Count van Bylant that during his thirteen months' stay at the island in 1778-79, the number of ships sailing from the port was three thousand one hundred and eighty-two. Business adventurers flocked to St. Eustatius from many countries of both continents, and some of them took the precaution of becoming Dutch citizens.

The single landing place on the island was soon lined with a "lower town" consisting of over a mile of warehouses, renting for the scarcely believable total of 1,200,000 pounds a year. Even these storehouses could not hold all of the goods in the process of transshipment, so that the very beach itself was lined with bales of cotton and hogsheads of tobacco. St. Eustatius was in truth "one vast magazine . . . for its bigness," said Rodney, "the richest island in the world."

The one thing which nobody bothered about was any measure for the defense of all this wealth. As Tornquist observed, "The inhabitants scarcely knew that a general war had been declared in Europe." Although the island could easily have been fortified, there were no works of any consequence, a garrison of only fifty or sixty Dutch soldiers, and no attempt to bring the inhabitants under military discipline. Worse still, there was only a very scanty and irregular amount of naval protection. It seemed as though everybody thought that it was so obviously to everyone's interest to maintain the neutral status quo, that nobody would think of upsetting it. Thus the whole idea of defense was simply irrelevant.

But St. Eustatius had long been a thorn in the side of the British in their attempt to subdue their American colonies. Too many ships from Europe, and even from English ports, were "clearing for Africa and sailing to St. Eustatius" with contraband for the rebels. What had really stirred Englishmen to wrath, however, was an incident in November, 1776, when the small American naval vessel *Andrew Doria* entered the island's harbor, fired a salute of eleven guns, and received a salute of nine guns in return. This was the first recorded instance in which the American flag (then the Grand Union ensign retaining the Union Jack in one corner with the thirteen stripes) received official recognition in a foreign port. England made a violent protest, calling upon the Dutch to disavow the honor paid to the Congress flag, and to recall Governor Johannes de Graaf, who pointed out that he had replied with only nine guns to a salute of eleven.

There had long been a state of cold war between Great Britain and Holland, for the Dutch commonwealth was a prominent member of the League of Armed Neutrality which had been formed by Empress Catherine of Russia to protect non-belligerent ships from British search and seizure. The influence of the French faction at the court of William V had been increasing for some time. A pretext for beginning overt hostilities was found in the capture by the frigate *Vestal* of the rebel packet *Mercury* carrying Henry Laurens, envoy of Congress in September, 1780, on his way to Holland to negotiate both a loan and a treaty of commerce. Laurens managed to destroy most of his papers, and threw a bag containing the draft of the proposed treaty, which had not been weighted, into the sea, whence it was retrieved by British sailors. The document was believed to justify an immediate attack upon Dutch shipping without a declaration of war, which did not follow until December 20, 1780. The British promptly helped themselves to two hundred Dutch vessels with cargoes worth five million pounds sterling.

On the suggestion of Sir Joseph Yorke, George III's ambassador to The Hague, Lord Sandwich sent secret orders for the capture of St. Eustatius to Admiral Rodney and General Vaughan in the West Indies. Rodney received the orders on January 27, 1781, and sailed from St. Lucia on January 30 with fifteen ships of the line carrying three thousand of Vaughan's troops. Even so, said Captain Charles Middleton (later Lord Barham), "Three days were lost in preparing scaling ladders, towing useless bombs and fireships, to attack a place that might have been taken by two frigates . . ."[1] Seldom has a military expedition enjoyed such a ridiculous preponderance of force.

When Rodney arrived off St. Eustatius on February 3, and demanded its instantaneous and unconditional surrender, the blow "was as sudden as a clap of thunder . . . as tremendous as it was rapid." To oppose his fifteen big battleships there was one Dutch frigate, the *Mars*, 38 guns, and five smaller American vessels of from 12 to 26 guns. The *Mars* had arrived only two days before, and had brought no news of any hostilities. There was nothing for the Dutch to do but submit.

It is important to note the violent state of temper in which Admiral Rodney approached his easy conquest. His delight on receiving the secret orders was ill concealed. In his mind, "This rock of only six miles in length and three miles in width has done England more harm than all the arms of her most potent enemies, and alone supported the infamous American rebellion." He charged that the Statians had been "supplying the united enemies of Britain . . . . with naval and warlike stores," and that "this perfidious assistance had enabled the enemy to take the offensive—otherwise he would have had to act defensively only." He declared further that this "nest of vipers, which has preyed upon the vitals of Great Britain" must be destroyed, and spoke of "leaving the island a mere desert, only known by report." He added that "my happiness is in having been the instrument of my country in bringing this nest of villains to condign punishment. They deserve scourging, and they shall be scourged."[2]

Rodney reserved his special venom for "the English merchants who were base enough, from lucrative motives, to support the enemies of Great Britain," and who, "for their treason, will merit their own ruin . . . the just revenge of Britain is slow, but sure." The admiral had convinced himself that it was "those calling themselves British merchants" who had prevented the American war from being terminated, which was, of course, a gross exaggeration of their influence. They had, he believed, debased and forfeited the name of Englishmen when they had made themselves into Dutch burghers; and "Providence has ordained their just punishment for the crimes they have committed against their country." Such "perfidious people, wearing the mask of friendship, traitors to their country and rebels to their King, deserve no consideration or favor, and none shall they ever meet with at my hands."[3]

Rodney had a more personal reason for his wrath, for he discovered "many hundred tons of cordage" in the island's store-

houses, plainly intended for England's enemies, when he had been
assured earlier that they had none in stock which could be purchased to supply his own fleet. In contrast to this treatment, he
believed that St. Eustatius had supplied the enemy admiral
De Guichen with both cordage and carpenters after the battle of
April 17, 1780, thus enabling the French to keep eight damaged
ships in condition for combat. There was also the fact that when
Rear Admiral Hood with his convoy was approaching the West
Indies twelve merchant ships disappeared one night, which were
later found at St. Eustatius, "busily employed in landing their
cargoes to the agents of the British merchants."[4]

In the harbor of St. Eustatius Rodney captured over a hundred
sail of merchant ships, many of them "deeply laden and very
rich." Hearing that a convoy of twenty-six more carrying sugar
had sailed thirty-six hours before his arrival, convoyed by only
one Dutch ship of sixty guns, he sent Captain Francis Reynolds
after them with the *Monarch*, *Panther*, and *Sybil*. There was a
brief cannonade which killed the Dutch Rear Admiral Krull;
and then the convoy was brought back to be added to the spoils.
Following the usual practice of keeping the Dutch flag flying
over the island for a month after its capture, Rodney decoyed
seventeen unsuspecting trading vessels into the port to be added
to his plunder.

For plunder it was in addition to confiscation. "The English,"
said the Dutch secretary of the island, "acted like robbers, search-
ing, digging, confiscating." Rodney's flag captain, Walter
Young, said that even if the British traders' properties should be
returned to them, "they must lose considerably by plunder,
which it is not in our power to prevent, for want of discipline.
It is almost general, both by sea and land; I am sorry to see
it. . . ."[5] Sober authorities have placed the total value of the loot
at three million pounds sterling, not counting the captured
shipping. It was wealth so prodigious in amount that it astonished
its captors.

Rodney's next problem was: how to dispose of this vast
fortune. On March 17, 1781, the *Caribbean Gazette* contained
an advertisement of a gigantic auction of sugars, tobacco, and
other merchandise captured at St. Eustatius, from which the
original owners of the merchandise would be excluded. This

brought a strong remonstrance from the merchants of the nearby British island of St. Kitts, to which Rodney paid no attention. "An immense concourse of people assembled to attend the sales," says Beatson, "but though there were many bidders, the goods were supposed to be sold greatly below their value."[6] As a consequence Rodney and Vaughan were accused in Parliament by the opposition speakers of lessening the value of their conquest to the Crown.

All the inhabitants of St. Eustatius and all the sailors on the captured ships were declared prisoners of war. Some two thousand of them were rounded up including many Americans. But Rodney's greatest blunder was in declaring all the property on the island as belonging henceforth to George III. Edmund Burke called it "a general confiscation of all the property found upon the island, public and private, Dutch and British; without discrimination, without regard to friend or foe, to the subjects of neutral powers, or to the subjects of our own state; the wealth of the opulent, the goods of the merchant, the utensils of the artisan, the necessaries of the poor, were seized on, and a sentence of general beggary pronounced in one moment upon a whole people."[7]

Rodney seems to have taken peculiar delight in rounding up one hundred and ten Jewish merchants who, he said, "will do anything for money . . . and had been deeply concerned in supplying the enemy with provisions."[8] They were confined, guarded, and stripped while the linings of their garments were searched and eight thousand pounds of notes recovered, then banished on one day's notice without their wives and children.

In Rodney's eyes all this was righteous vengeance, but unfortunately it was wreaked in complete disregard of both international law and a number of specific acts of Parliament. Said Burke: "It was not extraordinary that a man sitting on a great gun in a ship's cabin should hold language like that of Admiral Rodney, for however much he respected his naval character, his judgment as a lawyer could not be expected to have any consequence." When the victors returned to England, they found themselves facing no less than sixty-four damage suits brought against them by indignant merchants, whose claims totalled "far more than the whole value of the captured property."[9] Six years later, only thirteen of the suits had been settled, and in nine of them the verdict had been for restitution.

If Providence had dropped prodigious riches into the laps of Rodney and Vaughan, it was shortly to snatch most of the wealth back again. Rodney was still in debt, and deeply concerned about providing for his children. "Until my debts are paid," he had written to his wife, "I shall be miserable." His insistence upon receiving every farthing of his share of all prize money was notorious. Hence it is somewhat surprising to learn that upon the day after landing at St. Eustatius he wrote to Lady Rodney: "It is a vast capture; the whole I have seized for the King and the State, and I hope will go to the public revenue of my country. I do not look upon myself as entitled to one sixpence . . ."[10]

But it is plain that this self-sacrificing mood did not endure, for only three days later we find him addressing the Admiralty in a somewhat different vein, hinting that *if* the King decided to allot any of the spoils to the services, they should be divided equally between the army and the navy. George III obligingly decreed that all the lawful booty (that is, not belonging to any of his subjects) except the provisions, arms, ammunition, and military stores needed for the defense of the island, should be shared equally among the services. This entitled Rodney and Vaughan to receive one-sixteenth share each in the profits of their extremely lucrative venture. "Seldom," remarks Professor John C. Miller, "has a man been presented with a more tempting opportunity of doing his duty and filling his pockets at the same time."[11]

Rodney's personal pecuniary troubles seemed to be a thing of the past, but the riches that were to pay his debts and endow his children became "frittered down to a mere trifle" some time after he left St. Eustatius. The most valuable portions of the loot were loaded upon a convoy of thirty-four merchant ships guarded by Commodore Hotham with two of the line and three frigates. Rodney assured his wife: "If my great convoy of prizes arrive safe in England, exclusive of satisfying all debts, something will be left for my dear children." George III himself expressed the hope that "the great convoy from St. Eustatius will be brought safe. No event could give more reasonable dissatisfaction than if it should fall into the hands of the enemy; consequently every nerve must be strained to send sufficient intelligence that it may escape."[12]

But when Hotham's fleet was only twenty leagues from the Scilly Islands and safety it was met by the French admiral La Motte-Picquet with six ships of the line and some frigates. Twenty of the English vessels were captured. The *London Chronicle* of May 15, 1781, estimated that Rodney and Vaughan suffered personal losses of three hundred thousand pounds sterling by this disaster. Concerning the loss of this "richest convoy ever sent to England," Charles James Fox observed to Parliament that "as to the riches that were on board of it, when he considered how they had been acquired, they were riches, the loss of which, of all others, he should least regret . . ."[13]

General Vaughan asserted that he had not made a shilling from St. Eustatius; and Rodney found the litigation that ensued "a drain which left him a poor man for the rest of his life." Part of the admiral's legal woes came from "the greatest suppressed scandal of the war." It throws some light on the way Lord Germain's American Department operated, for it stemmed from the mysterious disappearance of a mass of papers relating to England's part in the contraband trade on St. Eustatius. Rodney had sent the mass of documentary evidence back to London with his two most important prisoners: Samuel Curzon, agent of Congress, and his partner Isaac Gouverneur. Both were clapped into the Tower to be tried for treason. The trial, prudently held within the confines of Germain's department, was held in July, and the captives were sent back to prison. They were still there in March, 1782, when Germain was on his way out, and William Knox, his subordinate, who had handled the affair, was afraid that he would be blamed for their thirteen months' imprisonment. "Knox accordingly appropriated the part of their correspondence which he felt proved their term in jail quite justified, and what happened to these papers later on, nobody could discover." Thanks to this disappearance of so much of his evidence, Rodney found himself hard pressed to prove in court that a great number of British merchants on St. Eustatius had been trading with the enemy.[14]

But that was not the end of Rodney's misfortunes. He had left his private funds at St. Eustatius in charge of agents who were supposed to send them to London by way of New York. By some oversight the money remained upon the island when it was presently retaken by the French, who were said to have found about a quarter of a million pounds sterling, a large portion of it, no doubt, constituting the proceeds of Rodney's grand auction. There was added irony in the fact that this latest loss arose from the easy reconquest of St. Eustatius. Rodney and Vaughan had listed as high among "the great and important concerns which absolutely require our attendance at this island . . . the utmost attention to prevent its falling into the enemy's hands." On April 23, 1781, the admiral wrote to his wife that "the island is put in a state almost impregnable," and that he had given "the most positive orders that the island should never have less than three frigates stationed at it."[15] Yet in the following November, the energetic Marquis de Bouillé, in "one of the most romantic of military exploits," surprised and retook the island with a mere handful of men, and restored it to Dutch rule.

No one has summed up Rodney's adult delinquency at St. Eustatius better than his biographer David Hannay: "At a time when a great hostile force was approaching the station committed to his care, the proper place for an English admiral was at sea and at the head of his fleet. He should not have remained on shore with the auctioneer's hammer in his hand superintending the sale of his booty amid surroundings redolent of the redoubted Sir Henry Morgan . . . On the whole, one has to come back to the view that Rodney's eyes had been dazzled and his better nature corrupted for the time being by the fairy gold poured out before him . . ."[16]

17

HOOD, NOT RODNEY,
TO THE RESCUE

"News was then literally worth its weight in gold."
—Dorothy Hood, *The Admirals Hood*

The decisions which had the most to do with the British failure at Yorktown were made by Admiral Sir George Rodney. It was a double lapse, because two things which should have been done were not done, and for each of them the English naval commander of the Leeward Islands station was primarily responsible. If De Grasse was to be countered at the Chesapeake, the chief of the North American station at New York, Vice Admiral Arbuthnot and later Rear Admiral Graves, must be promptly informed concerning the movements of the French fleet. This having been done, Rodney's second duty was to send north adequate reinforcements in time to cope with the advancing enemy. Neither of these needs was properly attended to, although it is true that various misfortunes overtook the attempts Rodney actually made to notify his fellow admirals.

The first hint of fresh French forces headed for the West Indies came to Rodney on February 13, 1781, only ten days after his seizure of the fabulous riches of St. Eustatius. It arrived in the form of an express from Captain John Linzee of the frigate *Santa Monica* that he had sighted "a squadron of eight or ten of the line and a convoy . . . about fifty-four leagues' distance from Cape Finisterre, and sailing a west-southwest course." Rodney's flag captain Walter Young, writing to Charles Middleton in London on that date, said he was "exceedingly happy"

that Rodney had already sent Sir Samuel Hood to cruise off
Martinique to intercept the French fleet. The squadron Captain
Linzee reported was not that of De Grasse but of Suffren on his
way to the East Indies. The fact that Rodney was alerted in
regard to the possible coming of an enemy formation so soon
after his involvement at St. Eustatius is, however, important for
another reason.

Originally Admiral Rodney and General Vaughan had been
expected to go on from St. Eustatius to take the Dutch colonies
of Curaçao and Surinam, but they failed to do so for reasons
about which Rodney and Hood sharply disagreed. Middleton
remarked at the time that "Curaçao ought to have been taken
the same day, for which service Sir Samuel Hood offered himself, but it remains still to be taken, though they were not informed of the war for six weeks after the capture of St. Eustatius."[1] Rodney's explanation of this omission, written to Lord
Sandwich on April 27, 1781, just two days before De Grasse's
arrival off Martinique routed him out of his Aladdin's cave at
St. Eustatius, was that he had not sent Hood to take Curaçao
because of Linzee's warning in February. "Had not Captain
Linzee of the *Santa Monica* been rather too hasty in sending me
an express of the enemy's fleet being in sight of him and steering
for the West Indies," he claimed, "I had determined in a very
few days to have sent Sir Samuel Hood with a squadron to have
taken Curaçao . . . This unlucky express prevented that attack
from me."[2]

In one of his confidential letters to Mr. Jackson at the Admiralty, Sir Samuel fairly ridicules this theory that "an attack
upon Curaçao was prevented by the intelligence sent by Captain
J. Linzee." Hood tells of being "pressed very strongly" by
General Vaughan to ask Rodney for ships to make the attack,
and then, when he had done so, being coldly snubbed by
Vaughan, who "turned away and addressed himself to someone
else." Hood maintained that "The truth is, I believe, that he
could not bear the thoughts of leaving St. Eustatius, where
he fancied there were three millions of riches . . . I dare say he
would have been there to this hour had not the arrival of De
Grasse obliged him to decamp."[3] The picture which Hood paints

of Rodney's and Vaughan's "bewitchment . . . not to be with-stood by flesh and blood" is not a pretty one.

On the very day, May 3, 1781, that Rodney finally tore him-self away from St. Eustatius to hasten to the assistance of the misplaced Hood off Martinique, he wrote to Arbuthnot in New York by the *Garland* that "A very considerable French squadron having arrived at Martinique from Europe on the 29th of last month, I think it my duty to give you information thereof, that you may be on your guard should they visit the continent of America, in which case I shall send you every reinforcement in my power." This letter reached New York on June 19, about two weeks before Arbuthnot returned to England.

Rodney and Hood joined forces between Montserrat and Antigua on May 9, and went to the latter island to repair the damages Hood's ships had sustained in the brush with De Grasse on April 29. De Grasse and De Bouillé took advantage of their erstwhile naval superiority in the Antilles by making an attempt to retake St. Lucia, which failed, and to capture Tobago, which succeeded. Rodney twice guessed wrong about their movements; and, as already noted, refused his one opportunity to bring the French to battle off the Grenadines, believing that "the French had it in their power, night coming on, to entangle his Majesty's fleet . . ." and as he wrote to Sandwich, he was "not such a Don Quixote as wantonly to run his Majesty's fleet into improper danger."[4] Hood, as usual, strongly dissented.

On July 2, 1781, Vice Admiral Arbuthnot having sailed at last for Europe, the command of the New York station devolved temporarily upon Rear Admiral Thomas Graves, pending the arrival of Rear Admiral Robert Digby. On July 4, Graves wrote to Rodney by the brig *Active*, stating that intercepted dispatches "will show you the apprehension of a considerable force, ex-pected from the French commander-in-chief in the West Indies, in concert with whom M. de Barras seems to act, and will demon-strate how much the fate of this country must depend upon the early intelligence and detachments which may be sent by you hither, upon the first movement of the enemy."[5] Graves's mind, at least, was clear on the subject of his complete dependence upon Rodney both for "early intelligence" and "reinforcements." As he wrote to Lord Sandwich on the same day: "Our preservation must turn upon the succors we may receive."

By the same sailing of the *Active*, Clinton strongly urged Rodney to come north again, either to merge his fleet with Arbuthnot's to "settle the campaign in one battle," or to assist the army against "the same tempting object" with which he was already familiar, Rhode Island. The only trouble was that the *Active* reached the British fleet in the West Indies on August 3, 1781, and Rodney had sailed for England two days earlier. Actually the abortive warnings from New York would have been no news to Rodney, who had learned from the frigate *Nymphe* that she had sighted De Grasse and his convoy leaving Martinique on July 5, and had captured the small schooner *Adelaide*. From prisoners taken, Captain Ford of the *Nymphe* had learned the size and probable destination (in the West Indies) of the French fleet, which he reported at once to Rodney. As Professor Miller remarks, De Grasse's coming to the North American coast "during the summer of 1781 was no military secret, in fact, it was one of the best advertised maneuvers of the war."[6] What *was* secret was the size of the fleet he would bring.

On July 7 Rodney wrote the following to Graves in New York: "As the enemy has at this time a fleet of twenty-eight sail of the line at Martinique, a part of which is reported to be destined for North America, I have dispatched His Majesty's sloop *Swallow* to acquaint you therewith, and inform you that I shall keep as good a look out as possible on their motions, by which my own shall be regulated. In case of my sending a squadron to America I shall order it to make the coast of Virginia, and proceed along the coast to the Capes of the Delaware, and from thence to Sandy Hook, unless the intelligence it may receive from you should induce it to act otherwise. You will please to order cruisers to look out for it, off the first-mentioned Capes . . . [Rodney then supplies recognition signals]. The enemy's squadron destined for America will sail I am informed in a short time, but whether they call at Cap Français, I cannot learn, however, you may depend upon the squadron in America being reinforced, should the enemy bend their forces that way."[7]

The operative words in this letter, to be reiterated by Rodney and others until it was too late, were "*a part of which* is reported to be destined for North America." (Italics mine.) Rodney was thoroughly convinced that De Grasse must necessarily divide his forces, sending about half of his twenty-eight line ships to France with the plunder of Tobago and the autumn sugar trade, and bringing only the balance of his fleet (from twelve to fifteen) to the North American coast. Those in fact were precisely De Grasse's instructions. If Rodney (or Hood) went north with a similar number, French and British squadrons would still be equally matched, and there would be nothing to fear. This erroneous strategic arithmetic of Rodney's was a major contribution to the Yorktown debacle.

On the same day Rodney sent an order to Rear Admiral Sir Samuel Hood stating that since he had received intelligence "that a very considerable squadron of the enemy's line of battle ships are intended to reinforce the French squadron in America," he was "to proceed without loss of time" with seven ships to Antigua to fit them "with masts, cordage and sails for a foreign voyage."[8] Rodney himself had promised to watch the enemy "like a lynx," but his watching turned out to be anything but lynx-like.

His health continued to deteriorate, with prostate trouble apparently added to his gout. He could not make up his mind whether to go to New York himself, or to take advantage of the King's permission to return to England. Hood said of him at this time: "It is quite impossible from the unsteadiness of the commander-in-chief to know what he means three days together; one hour he says his complaints are of such a nature that he cannot possibly remain in this country, and is determined to leave the command with me; the next he says he has no thought of going home . . . If he stays much longer, his laurels may be subject to wither."[9] Two vital weeks passed without any action. Lord Sandwich pleaded with him to remain, but Rodney declared that he needed the services of a British surgeon and the waters of Bath. Perhaps if the letters on the *Active* had reached him he might have been provoked into coming to New York. In that event he would have been in command at the battle of the Chesapeake; and Hood firmly maintained that with Rodney in the place of Graves, the results would have been very different from what they were.

Just one year earlier Rodney had rushed to New York on the merest supposition that De Guichen might be going there. But this time he left on a northerly course for England, putting off the final decision about the state of his health until opposite the American coast. He turned over his command to Sir Samuel Hood, instructing him to take fifteen line ships, five frigates and two armed merchant ships, first to escort the Jamaica trade fleet through the Windward Passage, and then "to make his way toward the coast of North America . . . for the purpose of supporting His Majesty's loyal subjects and annoying his rebellious ones, and counteracting such schemes as it may be reasonable to conclude as forward for the junction of the French fleet from Cap Français with that already there, or with the forces of the rebels in America."[10]

At New York on July 19, Rear Admiral Graves received from the Admiralty the news that a very valuable convoy of money, clothing, and military stores obtained by John Laurens was soon to leave, or had already left, France for Boston. Its capture, said the secret instructions, would be "decisive of the state of America and the war." This was a palpable piece of hyperbole: one more example of the folly of directing British strategy from Whitehall. Graves decided to take his whole squadron of six line ships to "Boston Bay" to intercept the prospective prizes. One of his ships, the *Royal Oak*, 74 guns, had become leaky from having run aground on the *chevaux de frise* near the North Battery in New York harbor in April, and was absent in Halifax heaving down.

To Sandwich he explained that "As the convoy for Quebec expected with so much anxiety was about to sail in a day or two, and we had troops moving in transports in the Chesapeake, I concluded that the squadron's being at sea would keep the French in suspense and prevent their attempting anything either by detachment or collectively to disturb our convoys or to intercept the return of the *Royal Oak*, until they knew which way we were gone." One can only suppose that Graves was primarily concerned with the British "army detachments moving upon the coast," and thought of the hurricane season and the coming of De Grasse as some weeks away.

Nevertheless it was an extraordinary decision on Graves's part, since it left the key port of New York entirely unprotected, and if De Grasse had come north a month earlier than he did, he could have sailed into Clinton's stronghold unmolested. Graves voyaged away to the east on July 21, whereupon, as he wrote to Philip Stephens in London: "The intense fog which prevailed without intermission as we approached St. George's Bank deprived us of all possibility of seeing, and soon convinced me how much the squadron would be exposed to accidents, and that the Fog Guns necessary to keep the ships from separation would give notice of our situation, I therefore after having made Cape Ann, determined to withdraw, and we returned to Sandy Hook the 16th of August,"[11] having met the *Royal Oak* en route.

While Graves was groping through the fog in Massachusetts Bay, the *Swallow* arrived in New York on July 27, and was immediately ordered by Commodore Affleck to sail in pursuit of Graves with the dispatches from Rodney, which he did not read. While on his way through Long Island Sound Captain Wells of the *Swallow* sighted a Yankee privateer and set off in hot pursuit. He captured his prize, but was himself attacked by three more rebel privateers, and "pushed on shore upon Long Island, eleven leagues to the eastward" of New York. Captain Wells burnt his prize, "but could not get all his people on shore in time to burn the *Swallow*. . . . The privateers pillaged her . . . the dispatches were destroyed."

Rear Admiral Graves severely reprimanded the *Swallow*'s captain, who pointed out that he had no idea of the tenor or the importance of the messages he was carrying. He had succumbed to the natural impulse of a ship captain to grab a prize whenever and wherever possible. But the result of his zeal was that Graves did not receive a copy of Rodney's July 7 warning until he returned to New York. Even then the news was far from explicit, since it did not say that De Grasse had actually sailed (Rodney did not learn that until July 9), nor did it convey any sure idea of his numbers or their destinations.

There was to be one more attempt, this time by Hood, to get word to Graves about developments in the Leeward Islands station. As previously noted, before Arbuthnot had left for England he had sent the brig *Active* with dispatches for the West Indies, which reached Hood on August 3, two days after Admiral Rodney had departed for home. On August 6, Hood sent the *Active* back to New York with word of his own plans to come there, but without any more exact intelligence about De Grasse. On its way north, the *Active* was captured and taken into Philadelphia, where its commander, Lieutenant Delanne, though a prisoner, managed to get word "privately" to Graves, although not until the day before Hood himself arrived in New York. Hood also sent a copy of his *Active* dispatch to Graves on the frigate *Nymphe*, which Graves received just two hours before Hood's arrival at Sandy Hook on August 28.

The size of the contingent of ships which Hood brought with him had a vital influence upon the outcome of the battle that was to come. Lord Sandwich always insisted that he had sent an ample number of ships of the line across the Atlantic to cope with the French, and that only "a series of unfortunate accidents" could account for the British defeat. According to his Admiralty arithmetic, the New York and West Indies squadrons combined, plus Rear Admiral Digby's small escort on the way, amounted in all to thirty-one ships of the line. The French, he figured, had only eight at Newport under De Barras; and De Grasse, although he might have as many as twenty-eight in the Antilles, had to take care of the summer trade convoy to Europe, and surely would not take more than half of his fleet to reinforce De Barras. Rodney and Hood commanded twenty-one at the Leeward Islands, and in the hurricane season they could be expected to take most of them northward to join Graves's seven plus Digby's three, for a total of twenty-five or more. How, then, could England possibly be expected to lose command of the sea off the American coast?

In the field, however, there was a somewhat different story to tell. The process of subtraction from Sandwich's totals began with the severe damage suffered by the *Russell*, 74 guns, in Hood's vain attempt to keep De Grasse away from Martinique on April 29, 1781. The *Russell* was patched up sufficiently to keep going for a few weeks, and then had to be laid up at Antigua for repairs during the rest of the year. The next casualty was Rodney's own flagship at St. Eustatius, the *Sandwich*, 90 guns, about which the admiral wrote in a letter to the Lord of the same name, dated April 27, 1781: "The poor *Sandwich* has almost done all her duty. I am loath to leave her. . . ." Since he doubted that she could survive a voyage to England, the *Sandwich* was sent to convoy the trade to Jamaica on July 31, there to undergo repairs at Port Royal Yard. What was far more important, however, was Rodney's decision to send both the *Torbay*, 74 guns, and the *Prince William*, 64 guns, to accompany her to strengthen the convoy. He told Vice Admiral Sir Peter Parker, who commanded the Jamaica station, "not to detain them a single moment . . ." and furthermore urged him "to add to their force by sending to North America every line of battle ship you can possibly spare from your station."[12] Because of Parker's apparent failure to take Rodney's pleas seriously, and his own desire to protect Jamaica and its trade, he held the two ships until a convoy was ready, so that they did not reach New York until October 13, 1781, some five weeks after the decisive battle and less than a week before Cornwallis capitulated. This was Admiral Parker's contribution to the disaster: one more illustration of the bedevilment of British strategy by a divided command and a primary concern for the safety of commerce.

It is not surprising that where Sandwich, in London, saw only naval strength, Hood, on the scene in the West Indies, perceived serious weaknesses. "From a strange fatality," he said, "that seems to have attended the operation of His Majesty's fleet in these seas for some time past, not four ships in the whole are in a fit state to go to any distance with a view of meeting the enemy, being totally destitute of spare masts, yards, sails, and every other species of stores." Among the ships which Rodney regarded as sick, but well enough to stand the voyage to England was the *Gibraltar*, 80 guns, which had been the flagship of Rear Admiral Francis Drake until it was appropriated by Rodney to replace his *Sandwich*. The *Gibraltar* was no ordinary warship; Rodney hailed her as "the noblest ship of his rate in the world."[13] Originally the *Fénix*, flagship of Admiral de Langara at Cape St. Vincent, where he had captured her the year before, she had been built in Havana of cedar and mahogany. Why then remove her from the battlefront?

Rodney was severely criticized for coming home in the *Gibraltar*, some of his critics maintaining that he had placed a sick man's comfort ahead of Hood's necessities. To Sandwich he explained that the *Gibraltar*'s "pintails and braces, and the rudder being of iron," they could not survive six more months in the tropics. Apparently the ship's copper sheathing had corroded the iron fastenings of the rudder; and it was also said that *Gibraltar*'s great draft of twenty-seven feet would have prevented her from crossing the bar at New York. Along with the *Gibraltar*, Rodney took the *Triumph*, 74 guns, long in need of repairs, and the *Panther*, 60 guns, all three described by Rodney as "invalids like myself."

Rodney's homeward-bound squadron and convoy sailed on August 1, 1781, accompanied by the frigate *Pegasus*, which he planned to send to Graves in New York in case he decided not to go there himself. He seems to have hoped that the invigorating effect of the sea air would make that possible, but when he reached the "point of no return" near Bermuda on August 13, and found himself physically no better, he sent the *Pegasus* off with dispatches for New York. He relayed the intelligence which had come to him from St. Thomas on July 31, the day before he had sailed, to the effect that De Grasse's fleet "when he left the Grenades to collect his convoy, consisted of twenty-six sail of the line and two large ships armed *en-flûte*; and I imagine that at least twelve of these ships, and in all probability a part of M. De Monteil's squadron will be in America; and it is not impossible they may be joined by some Spanish ships." He added that he had sent Hood "to the Capes of Virginia, where I am persuaded the French intend making their grand effort."[14]

Unfortunately the *Pegasus* was not a fast sailer, and took twenty-six days to reach New York, arriving there three days *after* the September 5th battle. But the truly astonishing thing about Rodney's August 13 letter is the fact that he had all the information contained in it eleven days before Hood left Antigua, only seventy miles from where he was at St. Eustatius, and yet not a scintilla of it was communicated to Hood, the man who was most concerned.

By the losses already enumerated, Hood's force had been cut by exactly one-third, from twenty-one ships to fourteen,

which was the number he commanded when he sailed north from
Antigua on August 10. He did not then know it, but he was
engaged in a race with Admiral de Grasse, who had left Cap
Français on August 5. With his faster coppered ships and the
usual sea lane in his favor Hood won that contest hands down,
for he arrived off the Capes of Virginia on August 25, nearly
a week ahead of the French admiral. Looking into the Chesapeake, he saw no signs of the enemy there, and the same was
true of the Delaware. What has never been explained was his
failure to encounter any of the cruisers which Graves had stationed at those two points to meet him.

Pausing at the Chesapeake on August 25 long enough to send
off letters to Graves and Clinton by the *Nymphe,* he resumed
his voyage to New York. He could tell Graves nothing about
any movements of De Grasse. When his fellow admiral replied
to the letter on August 28, he showed very clearly that he shared
Hood's ignorance regarding that all-important subject, for he
wrote to Hood: "We have as yet no certain intelligence of De
Grasse, the accounts say that he was gone to Havana to join the
Spaniards and [they are] expected together upon this coast. A
little time will show us." Hood assured Clinton that "the force
he had with him was equal fully to defeat any designs of the
enemy, let De Grasse bring or send what number of ships he
might to aid those under Barras."[15] This over-confidence was, of
course, to have a most unfortunate effect upon Clinton's subsequent strategy.

On the evening of August 26, while Hood was at sea, one of
his advanced ships spoke with a brig from Jamaica, and learned,
according to a letter from Hood's secretary Joseph Hunt to
Charles Middleton, dated August 29, 1781, "that on the 28th
of July the Count de Grasse, with his whole fleet, consisting of
thirty sail of the line, was at the Cape, and that the Jamaica
convoy only waited his departure to pursue their voyage to
England." From this circumstance, said Hunt, "we know that,
at the above period, no detachment could have been possibly
made to this country, which we are taught to expect as a certain
event; and therefore, our previous arrival on the coast will
operate greatly in our favor, as it will not only effectually enable
the commanders-in-chief to counteract the motions of the

enemy, but will also allow of their adopting such measures as will be most efficacious toward preventing a junction of their squadrons, which cannot fail to lessen the French interest in the Colonies; and will, in its consequences, prove a decisive blow to the American cause, which, from all accounts, is in a tottering state and verging toward its decline." Hunt goes on to predict that "from the state of the French fleet in the West Indies, I imagine they will not venture to detach more than twelve sail (about the number they had coppered), it is very probable we may find ourselves in superior force."[16]

This was the first specific news of De Grasse, and much too reassuring in its false premises. It was alarming enough, nevertheless, to send Sir Samuel Hood in all haste to Sandy Hook on the morning of August 28 with an urgent message for Rear Admiral Graves. What he found there was Graves's reply to his letter of August 25 informing him that he had "sent up for pilots to bring your squadron over the bar." But that was the last thing Hood wanted to do, "foreseeing the great delay and inconvenience which might arise from going within the bar." Instead, he resolved to keep his fourteen ships outside and ready to go after the French. He learned that Rear Admiral Graves had gone to Denis's on Long Island to confer with Sir Henry Clinton. Sir Samuel was not a man to temporize on such an occasion. "I got into my boat," he said, "and met Mr. Graves and Sir Henry Clinton on Long Island, who were deliberating upon a plan of destroying the ships at Rhode Island. This was an additional argument in support of my opinion against my going within the Hook, as the equinox was so near at hand, and I humbly submitted the necessity which struck me very forcibly, of such of Rear Admiral Graves's squadron as were ready coming within the bar immediately, whether to attend Sir Henry Clinton to Rhode Island, or to look for the enemy at sea . . . You have no time to lose; every moment is precious. My arguments prevailed, and he promised to be over the bar next day." The long row which Hood had taken to his Long Island rendezvous with Graves and Clinton had not been in vain. "They expressed great surprise," added Hood, "at seeing me."

Once more Hood was moved to comment on "the strange fatality which seems to hang over us, for had Mr. Graves kept his ships collected together and ready to join the West India squadron upon my appearing off the bar, he might have had ten ships rather than five . . ." In these figures, however, Hood was including three heavy frigates, the *Chatham*, 50 guns, *Warwick*, 50 guns, and *Assurance*, 44 guns, which were either cruising or conducting convoys. The other two of the missing, however, were line ships: the *Robust*, 74 guns, and *Prudent*, 64 guns. Both had long-standing defects which had been worsened during the futile excursion to Massachusetts Bay. The *Robust* had not had any repairs for two years; and on July 4, 1781, Graves reported to Sandwich that she was "in a state to require going home for repair, having several complaints in her bottom," which was uncoppered.[17] By August 21 Graves said that "the *Robust* is so bad that I am forced to send her to the wharf, and my highest expectations are that she may be made fit for sea without heaving down, a work of greater magnitude than has ever been undertaken at New York." Like all other commanding officers, Graves had pointed out the uselessness of wooden-bottomed ships in the American theater of war. "The wooden bottoms in the Chesapeake and at Carolina are eat up presently," he wrote to Stephens on August 20, 1781, "the small men-of-war upon the out posts here, are so perforated by the worm, we find a necessity of hauling them frequently on shore to prevent their sinking, this will oblige me to keep every thing upon copper in this country, and to send home as convoys all the wooden bottoms . . ."[18]

The *Prudent*, 64 guns, was an old-fashioned ship with mast trouble, and, according to Clinton, Graves thought that while the *Robust* had to be in the yard, "he should take the opportunity of shifting a mast or two in the *Prudent*." When Hood arrived on August 28 neither the *Robust* nor the *Prudent* was ready to leave. But the news that seems really to have shocked Clinton came that evening, to the effect that the Count de Barras and his squadron had sailed from Newport on August 25. "Thus, to the admiral's great mortification and my own, was lost an opportunity of making the most important attempt that had offered the whole war."

Rear Admiral Graves was not disposed to take the news of De Grasse's coming as seriously as Hood did. The frigate *Richmond* came in from the Chesapeake on August 29 and reported

"Everything is quiet . . . whether the French intend a junction or whether they have left the coast is only to be guessed at." Graves guessed that the whole thing might be a false alarm. On August 30 he wrote to Hood at Sandy Hook, "No intelligence yet of De Grasse . . . For my part I believe the mountain in labor." What was to come forth was not a mouse!

18

THE BATTLE OF
THE CHESAPEAKE:
FIRST PHASE

"It was a dramatic moment at this crisis in the world's history. Both sides were equally surprised . . ."
—Captain Dudley W. Knox, U.S.N.

Despite the need for haste so urgently set forth by Sir Samuel Hood, three days (August 29-31) were spent by Rear Admiral Graves in delivering a line of battle and awaiting a favorable wind. "The moment the wind served to carry the ships over the bar, which was buoyed for the purpose," he said, "the squadron came out" on September 1. Graves had only five serviceable ships of the line: his flagship the *London*, 90 guns, *Royal Oak*, 74 guns, *Bedford*, 74 guns, *America*, 74 guns, and *Europe*, 64 guns, together with the *Adamant*, 50 guns, and some frigates.

On joining the impatient Hood off Sandy Hook, salutes of fifteen guns were exchanged between the two admirals, and without coming to anchor the combined fleet of nineteen warships put out to sea at 7:00 P.M. under Graves's command. He had no accurate information about either De Barras or De Grasse, except that both of them were at large. He set his course southward "on the chance of falling in with one of the French squadrons before joined with the other." It was his intention to go to the Chesapeake, "as the enemy's views would most probably be on that part," for "that place seemed to be the object of contention."[1]

The British fleet proceeded under a press of sail, "the winds being rather favorable, without any interruption," said Graves, "but from the complaints of the West Indian squadron." On the third day of sailing, the *Terrible*, 74 guns, made the distress signal. The whole fleet had to be brought to, and it was found that the *Terrible* had come from the Leeward Islands with five pumps at work. But that was not all. It was further discovered that Hood's *Ajax*, 74 guns, was, in Graves's words, "but little better; the *Montagu*, 74 guns, a leaky thing; some of the rest had masts sprung, and several were very short of water and bread." These members of Hood's squadron, in his superior's eyes, "were the shadow of ships more than the substance."[2]

Admiral Graves was understandably annoyed by such revelations, because Hood had just assured him, on arriving at New York only a week before, that his squadron was "fit for sea for a month." It took some time to remedy the deficiencies "as well as the situation would permit," so that the fleet could proceed "with the utmost expedition." Of his own ships, Graves was none too sure of the *Europe*, 64 guns. Her condition was so poor that he had already given orders to her captain, Smith Child: "if unable to keep her position in the line of battle, to fall to the rear and be replaced by the *Adamant*."[3]

As the fleet passed the entrance to the Delaware Graves found that the two cruisers which he had stationed before it, and which Hood had so mysteriously missed on his passage north, could give him "no certain information" concerning the whereabouts of either of the French squadrons, and the same dearth of information continued as they neared the Chesapeake.

It was not until the morning of September 5, 1781, the day on which General Washington at Chester first learned with joy of De Grasse's arrival in the Chesapeake, that Graves and Hood reached the broad entrance of the bay between Capes Charles and Henry. It had taken them three and a half days to cover the two hundred and forty nautical miles, at the rate of something less than three nautical miles an hour. "As the mouth of the bay began to open" before them, the scouting frigate *Solebay*, which had been sent on ahead to look into the Chesapeake for signs of the enemy, signalled at about 9:30 A.M. that she had descried some hostile ships in Lynnhaven Bay under Cape Henry, then about ten or twelve miles distant. "About an hour-and-a-half after the frigate had left Admiral Graves," says an account in the *Political and Military Journal* for 1782, "the man at the masthead gave notice of a fleet at anchor in Lynnhaven Bay. The commanding officer, thinking the man might have mistaken the tall stumps of trees for masts, since it is customary there to burn the trees as they stand for tar, and many of the bare stumps remain standing twenty-feet high, went himself to the masthead, and saw the French fleet at anchor, and not even in any posture of defense."[4] At first they were taken to be the eight warships of De Barras's squadron from Rhode Island, plainly no match for the British nineteen.

In the meantime Admiral de Grasse, with twenty-four of his twenty-seven ships of the line at anchor in three irregular lines, was hopefully awaiting the arrival of De Barras from the north. Three of his line ships and two fifties had been detached to block the mouths of the York and James rivers, and three more were on the point of proceeding up the bay, when his advance frigate *Aigrette*, cruising off the entrance of the Chesapeake, discovered the approaching British fleet. It too underestimated the strength of the enemy at ten ships rather than nineteen. This gave rise to a brief period of rejoicing among the French crews in the belief that the incoming vessels were indeed those of De Barras. Curiously enough, both admirals had mistaken each other for a third who was not present.

Both of them were disillusioned as their forces slowly converged. At 10:00 A.M., when the British were still a long way from Cape Henry, the French were seen from the *Bedford* to number at least fifteen or sixteen sail; and by 2:00 P.M., to the extreme astonishment of Graves, the count of "very large ships" had risen to the dismaying total of twenty-four. "Whereupon," says Graves, "it was universally taken for granted" that the dreaded junction of the two French squadrons must already have taken place, although this was not, in fact, the case. It was still inconceivable to the British commanders that De Grasse could have been rash enough to denude the West Indies by bringing so many capital ships to the Chesapeake. They assumed that he had come with sixteen of his fleet to join De Barras's eight.

During these same morning hours of September 5, the French estimates of the size of what was now seen to be an enemy fleet jumped from ten to twenty-five. This was an exaggeration in

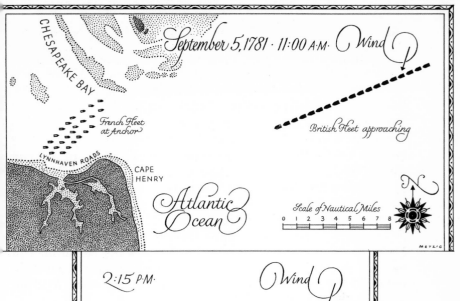

CHESAPEAKE BAY

September 5, 1781 · 11:00 A.M. · Wind

British Fleet approaching

French Fleet at Anchor

LYNNHAVEN ROADS

CAPE HENRY

Atlantic Ocean

Scale of Nautical Miles
0 1 2 3 4 5 6 7 8

N

METZIG

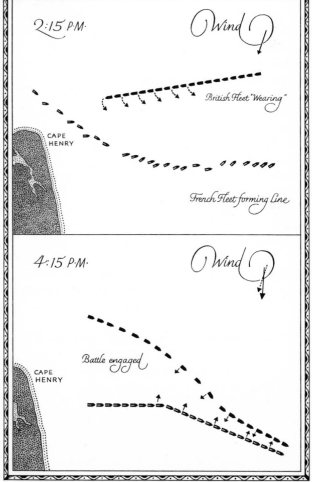

2:15 P.M.

Wind

British Fleet "Wearing"

CAPE HENRY

French Fleet forming Line

4:15 P.M.

Wind

Battle engaged

CAPE HENRY

terms of ships of the line, since of the twenty-seven sail of all kinds with Graves and Hood, only nineteen carried more than the required sixty guns. The British were inferior in numbers by five, and in aggregate fire power by roughly five hundred cannon, having about fifteen hundred guns against nearly two thousand. Besides, five or six of their lineships were in doubtful condition to do battle. Their greatest advantage lay in the fact that all of their ships were coppered as against about half of the French vessels. This probably more than offset the qualities of speed and maneuverability provided by the superior ship designs of the French naval architects.

The British warships were, moreover, fully manned, whereas De Grasse had been called upon to dispatch the best-drilled of his boat crews, amounting to ninety officers and fifteen hundred sailors, up Chesapeake Bay to assist in the landing of the Marquis de Saint-Simon's corps and in watering the fleet. Signals were hoisted ordering their immediate return, but mostly in vain, since only a few of the boats were near enough to see them. One of the French seventy-fours, the *Citoyen*, was short five officers and two hundred seamen, to the point where, even after drafting every last man of the ship's marines, the upper-deck tier of guns could not be manned. "Much the same may be said of the others of the fleet." It was reported that "every vessel had a hundred men in the boats," which meant also that the French warships were virtually boatless in going to sea. In an action, however, that was not wholly a drawback, since "boats lumber the decks," and splinters from them, when smashed by enemy cannonballs, were notorious sources of battle wounds. Graves's critics were not slow to point out that, with three of De Grasse's line ships, two fifties, and perhaps a sixth of his crews absent, the naval engagement "could not have been at a more opportune time for the British, and, had it been successful, it must have relieved Lord Cornwallis effectually."[5]

Yet Rear Admiral Graves was outnumbered; and of his personal courage in ordering an immediate attack against odds there can be no question. It was concerning the manner of his approach, and his tactics during the engagement, that there was bitter controversy. Over a century earlier, George Monk (1608-69) had said that the nation which would rule upon the sea must always attack; and that dictum, according to Mahan, "had set the keynote to England's naval policy." Yet the notion also has about it the flavor of the blindly charging bull, and in Graves's case, "once the attack failed, he was a commander without a plan."

True to the Royal Navy's tradition of attack from the windward without undue regard for the numerical odds against him, Graves made the preparative signal to clear for action at 10:05 A.M., and called in his cruising frigates a half-hour later. The admiral's orders were immediately repeated by the boatswain and his mates at all hatchways. At the cry of "Up all hammocks!" the crews went about the task of stowing them away, or lashing them to the rails to absorb splinters. Next came the securing of all yards, the fastening of nets over the upper gun deck to catch broken spars or men falling from the tops, and the assembling of cordage to be used in repairing damaged rigging. The ships' carpenters began the preparation of wooden and lead plugs for holes inflicted by enemy fire. The gun crews commenced the clearing of their positions, and the securing of a supply of powder and ball. Last of all the decks were sprinkled with sand to prevent slipping in the gore which might be expected to cover them before long.

After a previous night of high winds and heavy seas billowing from the northeast, the morning breeze was fresh and from the north-northeast. Thus Graves was coming in under foresails and topgallant sails on a leading wind and tide, the most favorable conditions that could be imagined for his attack. Said the Chevalier de Vaugirard of their approach: "They came down upon us with a following wind and with an assurance which made us think they did not know our strength."[6] Admiral de Grasse, on the contrary, was placed in a most embarrassing initial situation, with his fleet anchored "promiscuously" in three lines. He was faced with the task of coming out against an inflowing tide from a lee shore and around Cape Henry on a tack opposite to that of the British fleet. As Lieutenant Tornquist noted, the latter was advancing with its heavy ships, the two three-deckers *Barfleur* and *London*, each with 90 guns, well to the fore. The only French warship of their rating or better was

De Grasse's flagship *Ville de Paris*, mounting over one hundred guns and regarded as the most powerful battleship then afloat.

De Grasse showed no more hesitation than Graves in giving the order to his captains to clear their ships for action and to slip their cables, attaching their anchors to buoys, in order to gain sea room at the earliest possible moment. Only by getting out to the open sea could he take advantage of his numerical superiority, and also insure the safe arrival of De Barras. Rear Admiral French E. Chadwick, U.S.N., editor of *The Graves Papers*, has argued that De Grasse was "in a position he never should have left," on the ground that he could have assured the surrender of Cornwallis without ever leaving his Lynnhaven moorings. With only nineteen ships of the line, Chadwick believes that Graves would have had trouble in forcing an entrance against the French twenty-four, no matter how great the confusion among the latter.[7]

It must be granted that if Graves had succeeded in making a dash directly into Chesapeake Bay, he might indeed have upset the plans of Washington and Rochambeau for the siege of Yorktown, of which, incidentally, he had no inkling. But by sea he would have found himself completely bottled up by the combined naval might of De Grasse and De Barras, and would probably have been obliged to surrender his fleet along with Cornwallis's army. He would, moreover, have left New York entirely undefended and at the mercy of the French admirals if they had decided to force the surrender of Clinton instead of that of Cornwallis. For De Grasse to have remained passively at anchor merely for the purpose of keeping Graves out of the Chesapeake would probably have meant the sure annihilation of De Barras's squadron and its convoy. That would have deprived the land generals of the valuable train of siege artillery and the supplies of food which De Barras was bringing them from Newport.

Soon it became evident to the British that De Grasse was coming out to fight. During the forenoon, however, the rising tide was still flooding into Lynnhaven Bay against Cape Henry so violently that De Grasse was forced to wait until almost noon before it made, and his ships could get under way. The *Ville de Paris* quickly came alive with signal flags, ordering all hands to set sail and to form a line of battle according to speed without regard to particular stations, and in reverse order. This placed Commodore de Bougainville's blue squadron, normally that of the rear, in the van as the fleet slowly emerged.

"The axes of the carpenters," writes Lieutenant de Loture, "soon bit into the anchor cables." Such was the ardor of the ship captains that, despite the absence of so many of their personnel, "within minutes, all the ships were under sail, and, in three-quarters of an hour, nothing was left at the Lynnhaven anchorage except the buoys dancing at the ends of their cables."[8] But it was one thing to leave the anchorage and another to escape from the shoals and shores of Lynnhaven Bay through the ship channel and around Cape Henry to the open sea.

Second to none in his eagerness for action and also in his navigational skill was Commodore Louis Antoine de Bougainville. "I was anchored [in his flagship *Auguste*, 80 guns]," he recorded in his *Journal*, "to the windward of almost the whole fleet, and particularly to the windward and behind the *Ville de Paris*. In addition, I was covered by the head of a shoal which obliged me to turn about, and which forced the *Hercule*, 74 guns, which was moored next to me, to make a tack in order to clear it. By the aid of a previously-rigged stern-cable (*croupiat*), I got under way with the wind in all my sails. Thanks to this maneuver, I doubled the shoal, and gained the head of our line."[9]

Others of De Grasse's ships had much greater difficulties in extricating themselves. "One of them, the *Souverain*, 74 guns, was so entangled with the shore that she was for some time in only four fathoms of water." The admiral's orders were "to follow the movements of the van, successively lining up behind them in order of speed." This invited a pell-mell race for positions of honor in combatting "the hereditary enemy." Chevalier d'Ethy, captain of the *Citoyen*, said that he managed to get moving "under topsails and staysails, at 12:45 P.M. I was trying to raise and secure my anchor when the frigate *Aigrette*, which entered the bay at that moment, hailed us, and, speaking to Monsieur de Koefold, who was acting as lieutenant in the forecastle during the absence of Monsieur de Saint-Marc, told him that unless I tacked at once I would run aground on Cape Henry. I found it hard to believe this. . . . So I myself asked the *Aigrette* what it was that they had shouted to us. They answered that their pilot had assured them that if I continued on my present course I would run into a sandbank. I made the tack and ran along the north-northwest shore, being obliged to pass under the stern of the Admiral, who was getting under sail and whom I did not wish to disturb in his maneuver. Finally at 1:15 P.M., finding myself clear of all the ships that were under sail and running out of the bay, I tacked back to larboard and made my way out also. It was about 1:45 P.M. when I was able to double Cape Henry."[10]

Even then the *Citoyen's* commander found himself faced with sharp competition from other captains who were trying to get ahead of him in the ragged battle line that was slowly evolving from the previous checkerboard formation created by "the contrariness and feebleness of the wind." Four of the French seventy-fours, the *Northumberland, Palmier, Solitaire,* and *Scipion* came out at about the same time as the *Citoyen.* There had to be a great deal of anxious backing and filling, pressing forward and giving way, before they managed to form some sort of column behind the *Ville de Paris,* which had been the twelfth vessel to emerge. So great was the zeal of Commodore de Monteil, accustomed to leading the van in the *Languedoc,* 80 guns, but whose proper post in reverse order was in the rear, that he found himself in advance of the *Ville de Paris.* Admiral de Grasse, perceiving that there was no officer of flag rank in his rear, gave De Monteil a verbal order to leave at once and take command there. The latter was barely able to do this by tacking boldly between the two fleets at about 3:30 P.M., just before the British opened fire.

But the greatest peril to the French was created by the very dash and speed with which De Bougainville's van had extended itself toward the open sea ahead of the center and rear, thus depriving itself of their support. At 2:00 P.M. and again at 3:15, De Bougainville had made the signal to his squadron to press on sail. At 3:45 P.M. they were so far to the windward that De Grasse ordered them to bear two points large so as to re-establish and tighten his line of battle. In the words of an anonymous French officer: "The fleet formed in very bad order, for, to tell the truth, there were only four vessels in line, the *Pluton,* 74 guns, *Bourgogne,* 80 guns, *Marseillais,* 74 guns, and *Diadème,*

74 guns. The *Réfléchi*, 64 guns, and *Caton*, 64 guns, came next, half a league to the lee of the first, the rest of the fleet were more to the lee of the latter, the *Ville de Paris* in the center. The British were in the best possible order, bowsprit to stern, bearing down on us."[11]

Some of the confusion that prevailed in the forming of the French line of battle seems to have communicated itself to the various reporters of the event, for no two of them agree exactly concerning the ships which formed the van, or the order in which they fought. All versions, however, state that the *Pluton* was the leading ship, with *Marseillais* either second or third. Even their commander De Bougainville himself gives varying lists. In his *Journal* he first wrote: "The only ones to fight were the *Pluton, Auguste, Scipion, Marseillais, Diadème* and *Hercule*." Later on he crossed out that sentence and wrote in the margin: "*Pluton, Marseillais, Réfléchi* (under press of sail), *Auguste, Saint-Esprit, Diadème* (under press of sail). I did not see," he added, "the rest of the line of battle."[12] In spite of these discrepancies in the listings, it seems clear that there were four or five of De Bougainville's van which were "in line" considerably to the windward and in advance of three or four others, and that all of his ships, which did the bulk of the fighting, were well to the windward and out to sea ahead of the rest of De Grasse's fleet.

Right here, it was argued by Graves's critics, was his first golden opportunity to bring his whole force down upon the French van at odds of at least two-to-one, cutting it off and destroying it before the center and rear could come up sufficiently to give it support. He had only to abandon his orthodox "line-ahead" and order instead a "general chase," but whether he could reasonably have been expected to make such a move, or even had the signals for it in those circumstances, remains a matter of controversy.

Of one thing we can be certain, and that is, that no such idea entered Graves's mind at the critical moment. His own explanation of his tactics, written to Lord Sandwich nine days later, reads like a condensed version of the *Fighting Instructions* as the admiral understood them: "My aim was to get close, to form parallel, and attack all together . . . I therefore came to the same tack as the enemy, and lay with the main topsail to the mast dressing the line and pressing toward the enemy, until I thought the enemy's van were so much advanced as to offer the moment for successful action; and I then gave the signal for close action."[13]

The British admiral had been coming down before the wind with his ships at two cables' length asunder (1,440 feet), which extended his nineteen vessels over a distance of about five miles, heading southwest for the mouth of the Chesapeake. His main preoccupation at the moment was to get and keep his ships in their assigned positions in line, and to close the interval between them. As a French officer noted: "Admirals Graves, Hood and Drake made an immense number of signals to each other before engaging us."

At 12:45 P.M., about the time that the *Ville de Paris* was clearing Cape Henry, Graves made the conventional signal for "Line ahead at one cable's length," followed at 1:00 P.M. by that for an "East-and-West line" at the same interval. Since it was "inclinable to be squally" he called for a reef in the topsails. But Drake's rear division began to lag somewhat, and had to be ordered at 1:25 P.M. to make more sail. Already there were difficulties in forming and preserving an orderly east and west line. At 1:30 the *Centaur* was told "to keep in her station," and at 1:39 P.M. the same signal was made to *Resolution, America,* and *Bedford,* all of them in Graves's own center division of the fleet.

Although the mouth of Chesapeake Bay is about ten miles wide, the ship channel at that period was only about three miles in width and located to the south of a large shoal called the Middle Ground. At 2:05 P.M., Graves perceived that his leading ship, the *Alfred* of Hood's division, was coming dangerously close to this shoal, and gave the signal for all the ships of his fleet to "wear," that is, for each ship to pivot in its place in line, reversing its course by 180 degrees in a west to east line. Thus Drake's squadron, which had formed the rear, now became that of the van, while Hood's became the rear.

The British vessels were now headed for the open sea, close-hauled on the same larboard tack as the French, but not quite parallel with them at a distance of four or five miles. It is

apparent that Admiral Graves was deeply concerned lest De
Grasse might use his numerical superiority to overlap the British
line, for he noted that his own fleet was "by no means extended
with their rear." There was always the possibility that the French
admiral might contrive to "double" the British line with his five
"extra" ships, that is, to attack the enemy rear from both leeward
and windward at the same time. The sure way to prevent this
was to extend the nineteen British ships to cover the French
twenty-four. But then each of the English ships would not have
a single identifiable opposite number in the French line.

At 2:40 P.M. the British fireship *Salamander* was given the
order to prime, but there is no testimony that it figured in the
battle. Reversing the line of the attackers meant that the two
three-deckers that were the flagships of Admirals Hood and
Graves were now to be found in the center and rear instead of
the van and center as previously. Drake's division, which was to
bear the brunt of the fighting, included two of the ships, the
Terrible and the *Ajax* which had come from the West Indies
in poor condition for combat. A French account even states that
"the *Terrible*, which was pumping four pumps, not feeling
in a condition to take part in the action, kept to the windward
of the enemy's line, athwart Drake, who signalled her to take
her position, which she lost some time in doing. But the Rear
Admiral soon persuaded her to take her place by sending her
three cannonballs. Then it was that they tacked to the larboard
as we did, and hoisted a great white flag astern; but they soon
struck it and hoisted their own."[14]

Plainly Graves, in launching his attack in reverse order, was
leading from weakness rather than from strength. De Grasse
was also pitting what was normally his rear division against the
British rear, but at no disadvantage to the French, since De
Bougainville's ships were fully as powerful as those of De Monteil. Once Graves had decided to fight De Grasse in the prescribed formation, with the two fleets facing one another, ship
to ship, in parallel lines at close range, he had two immediate
tactical problems to solve. The first was to induce, or at least
to permit, the French admiral to arrange his somewhat scattered
ships in a presentable opposing line of battle. The second was to
close the range between the two lines.

As Graves himself said, the first four or five ships of the French van were "very particularly extended" in what a French officer called "a disagreeable position." Having missed his chance to exploit this predicament Graves must now, in order to make his line conterminous with that of the enemy, wait for the latter's center and rear to come up with him. Soon after the wearing about, the log of the *London* contains this astonishing entry: "Brought to in order to let ye Center of the Enemys Ships come a Brest of us." Far from seizing the opportunity to profit by De Grasse's slowness of movement Graves, by bringing his fleet to and pressing down, made the French a gift of invaluable minutes (Hood's estimate was "a full hour-and-a-half") in which to close the gaping interval between their extended van and lagging center. As one British account says: "To the astonishment of the whole fleet, the French center were permitted without molestation to bear down to support their van."[15]

Graves's second problem, that of closing the range to musket-shot distance, thereby enabling all arms to fire effectively, could be solved in any one of three different ways. With the wind in his favor the British admiral could order his ships to turn at right angles to their stations in line, bear down directly toward their opposite numbers in the French column, then luff up into a new line to discharge their broadsides. A second alternative would be to maintain the line-ahead with the leading ship bearing obliquely toward the French, resuming a parallel position as, one by one, the proper distance was reached. A third and more radical approach, which contributed to the fearful downfall of Admiral John Byng at Minorca, was called "lasking." By this last method, each vessel turned obliquely in its position in line and came down with the wind on its quarter toward its opponent until within range, then resuming the parallel line.

The potential dangers to the attacker in all three methods were the same, in varying degrees and at different stages. They were: first, the peril of depriving his ships of fire-power (except for their bow guns) during the time when their broadsides could not be brought to bear upon the enemy; and secondly, of giving their opponents a chance to rake or enfilade his ships by sending cannonballs directly or diagonally through their entire lengths.

Each method, of course, had its own signal; and it was

Graves's eventual use of two of them at the same time that was to compound disaster, and to provoke still another controversy. He began by choosing the second of the three alternatives: to edge down toward the French, and to maintain a straight bowsprit-to-stern line while doing so. Orders were given at 2:52 and again at 3:09 P.M. to "lead more to starboard, or toward the enemy," accompanied by sharp injunctions to *Royal Oak, Terrible, Montagu, Princessa*, and *Alcide* "to gett to their stations" in line.

This method of attack condemned the British ships to arrive piecemeal, and at an angle which gave all the advantages to the French. It contravened the first axiom of naval tactics regarding a successful attack by an inferior force, namely—that all must strike at once. At 3:45 P.M. Graves signalled for a line-ahead at one cable's length, but this, according to Hood, was soon reduced to half a cable. The two opposing vans and centers were now roughly parallel, the vans being much closer to one another than the centers, and the rear divisions still many miles apart.

Shortly after 4:00 P.M. Graves noted that his line seemed at last "to be pretty well formed" and his van "able to operate," while that of the enemy was "very particularly extended . . . as many of their rear were not clear of Cape Henry . . . advancing very slow." A British eyewitness relates that "At this period the enemy were, unfortunately, near the shore to leeward of us and not so much out of the bay as we could have wished. However, their ships were coming on very slowly, and their van was already so far advanced as to enable us to act against them about three-to-two in our favor."[16] Perceiving also that not many hours of daylight remained, the British admiral judged that the time had come to open his attack at close quarters. It was now 4:03 P.M., some six and one-half hours after the two fleets had sighted one another, and neither had yet fired a shot at the other. The long preliminaries involved in the formal staging of an eighteenth-century fleet encounter had at last been completed. The battle of the Chesapeake was ready to begin in earnest.

19

THE BATTLE OF
THE CHESAPEAKE:
SECOND PHASE

"In the later stages one signal ruined everything."
        —Captain W. M. James, R.N.,
        The British Navy in Adversity

*"Thus moved by comparatively simple things are even the
greatest affairs of men . . . a missed signal loses an empire."*
        —Rear Admiral French E. Chadwick, U.S.N.,
        The Graves Papers

Having finally made up his mind to press home the attack,
Rear Admiral Thomas Graves hoisted a blue and white
checkered flag with a white pendant over it, which was his
order to "ye Ships to bear down and engage close." He filled his
own main topsail and bore down on the enemy in the *London*,
which was the tenth ship exactly in the center of the British
line. But he did not, at that critical moment, lower his previous
signal for "line-ahead." Not until eight minutes later, at 4:11
P.M., did he, according to the *London*'s log, haul down "ye
signal for ye line-ahead that it might not interfear with ye signal
to engage close."[1] What he had done was to switch to the first
alternative mode of approach, the assault at right angles to the
enemy line, without cancelling the second; and the two signals
were literally contradictory.

    The flagship's sudden onslaught commenced from what Hood
called "a most improper distance"; and the disarray which
promptly developed in the hitherto orderly British formation is

well depicted by Beatson. "In bearing down, when the signal was made for that purpose, the *London* by taking the lead had advanced farther toward the enemy than some of the ships which were stationed immediately ahead of her in the line of battle; and when luffing up, to bring her broadside to bear, they having done the same thing, her second ahead (the *Montagu*) was nearly brought on the weather beam. The other ships ahead of her were likewise crowded together."[2] Graves's sudden change from the oblique column-ahead approach to the bear-down-and-luff method of closing the range, with signals for both flying simultaneously, had not only confused his captains regarding his real intentions, but had also resulted in masking the fire of some of his ships. Meanwhile the *London*'s cannon-balls continued to fall short of their targets, and her commander's valiant efforts to signal his way out of the confusion only served to increase it.

At about 4:15 P.M., the leading ships of both vans were within musket range of one another, and the action began with great spirit on both sides. In an eighteenth-century naval battle, it was always the first broadside which was the most destructive, since that was the only time during an engagement when all of the thirty or forty guns of a broadside were sure to be fired simultaneously. It was said that the *Ville de Paris* shook with the firing of her own guns on such occasions. After the first salvo, the cannon were served as rapidly as their crews could sponge, reload and fire, but seldom in concert. At musket range (150 yards or less), the carnage a first broadside could inflict through wooden walls upon the crowded decks of the enemy was fearful. There was no escaping it, since on coming into close action, the hatchways were closed, and marines were stationed to prevent any gunners from leaving their posts.

At the head of the British line, the *Shrewsbury*, 74 guns, attacked "in a very gallant and spirited manner," meeting a deadly hail of return fire from the *Pluton*, 74 guns, which tore off the left leg of *Shrewsbury*'s grizzled old captain, Mark Robinson, killed the first lieutenant and thirteen of the crew. Later in the action, twelve more of her men were killed and forty-six wounded. The most eloquent testimony to the accuracy of the French gunners is contained in the official reports of damages to the British ships. The French were known as "spar-wreckers," for they aimed almost invariably at the masts and rigging of the enemy vessels in order to cripple them beyond any possibility of pursuit; while the British practice was to fire at the hull in the hope of sinking their opponents. The French gunnery tactics were sounder than the British, for a ship immobilized could be approached by the enemy from a chosen angle that would leave her guns helpless against the maximum firepower of the attacker. In the Chesapeake engagement this tendency of the French to aim high was accentuated, says Beatson, by "their firing from the weather side, while the British ships, on the contrary, fired from the low or lee side."[3]

The reports of damages not only tell the story of the battle, they also hold the key to its eventual outcome, for it was their extent which determined Graves's decision that evening. According to the account submitted to the Admiralty, the *Shrewsbury*'s "topmast was shot through in three different places; there were three shot through the head of the mainmast. Her mizzenmast was almost cut off in two places; all the boats were much wounded; there were five shot in the hull under water, so that on the larboard tack the ship made eighteen inches of water in four hours." In sum, "all her masts, yards and sails were so cut to pieces, that by evening she was unable to keep in line, and at 8:05 P.M. made the signal of distress." Captain Colpoys of the frigate *Orpheus* was "ordered to take command of her, shorten both topmasts, shift her topsail yards, and put her into shape for action."[4]

The second British ship in line, the *Intrepid*, whose captain, Anthony James Pye Molloy, attempted "with the utmost gallantry," said Graves, "to cover the crippled *Shrewsbury*," was even more roughly handled by the *Marseillais*, and emerged "much disabled in every respect." There were "sixty-five shot-holes in the starboard side, nineteen between wind and water; the rudder much damaged; two shot through the middle of the bowsprit; three shot in the foremast; two in the mainmast; main topmast almost cut in two and in great danger of falling; sails and rigging very much cut; all the boats damaged."[5] Like the *Shrewsbury*, at the close of the battle *Intrepid* could not keep her place in the line. She had lost twenty-one men killed and thirty-five wounded.

In fact the total casualties of these two ships at the head of Rear Admiral Drake's division constituted exactly one-half of all the British killed in the action, and about one-third of the wounded. According to Captain Ward's *Naval Tactics*, this was because "all the vessels of the British van on their oblique approach, when only their bow-guns bore, were exposed to a severe diagonal fire from the broadsides of the French van ships, and this diagonal fire was nearly as disastrous as raking fire."[6]

The fate of the rest of Drake's ships was similar, although not quite as harsh as that of the two leaders. The *Alcide* had "three shot through the mainmast; the mizzen topmast, topsail and gaff shot away; boats much hurt; many shot under water which makes the ship leaky." As for the *Ajax*, she had her "mizzen topmast shot through; one shot through the head of the mainmast; boats wounded by shot; running rigging and sails very much cut; two guns wounded and one dismounted." Drake's own flagship *Princessa* had so much damage to her masts and rigging that after the engagement, while getting up another main topmast, he shifted his flag to the *Alcide*, and the two ships exchanged places in line. *Princessa*'s mainmast was also "shot through in three places; one shot went through the middle of the foremast; many yards were shot away; a great part of the running rigging and sails were very much cut; several shot in the side and under water."

But it must not be supposed that all the damage was confined to the British ships. The *Princessa*, for example, retaliated furiously in kind. She poured her first broadside into the *Réfléchi*, killing her captain, M. de Boades, and wounding another officer who died later. According to a French eyewitness: "That vessel soon bore away, as well as the *Caton*, on which the English kept up a brisk fire. The four ships of the French van found themselves, consequently, entirely cut off from the rest of the fleet, and constantly engaged with seven or eight vessels at close quarters. The *Diadème* was near Rear Admiral Drake, who set on fire to her at every shot, the wadding entering her side. This vessel was constantly engaged with two and sometimes three ships. The English could not cut off our van, which they might perhaps have taken, and which they would, at all events, have rendered past repair. They contented themselves simply with cutting up that part of our fleet which kept up a distant fight.[7]

"The *Diadème*," this officer continues, "was utterly unable to keep up the battle, having only four thirty-six-pounders and nine eighteen-pounders fit for use, and all on board killed, wounded, or burnt. At this juncture M. de Chabert, commanding the *Saint-Esprit*, which had for a long time been engaged with the British admiral, and who was himself wounded, seeing the imminent danger of the *Diadème*, hoisted sail and was soon in her wake; then he opened a terrible fire, that the gentlemen of Albion could not stand, and had to haul their wind."

In the meantime, Commodore de Bougainville in the *Auguste* had come so close to the *Princessa* that he was on the point of boarding her, but Drake managed to avoid him, whereupon Bougainville turned all his fire upon the *Terrible*. That was the weakest ship in the British line. Two French cannonballs crashed through her already sprung foremast, in which two more buried themselves. After the battle, said her Captain Clement Finch, "We weighed one of the shots; it weighed thirty-nine pounds." The *Terrible* had been very leaky before the action, in which she received "several shot between wind and water." Her pumps "being blown, and only kept together by tarr'd canvas, lead, and mouldings, the chains worn out, and but few links to repair them, pump leather all expended; she was making two feet, two inches of water every twenty-five minutes"; and there were already doubts that she could keep afloat much longer.[8]

Being of a methodical cast of mind, Commodore de Bougainville noted in his *Journal* that his flagship *Auguste* "had fired six hundred and eighty-four cannon shot during the battle, and had suffered fifty-four hits in the hull and seventy in the sails,"[9] with losses of ten killed and fifty-eight wounded. The leading ship *Pluton*, commanded by Captain D'Albert de Rions, called by Admiral Suffren "the best captain in the French navy," had attacked with "an irresistible impetuousness," and reported that its masts and rigging had suffered "prodigiously." Later in the day *Pluton* was obliged to give up its place at the head of the line to *Souverain*. As for the shattered *Diadème*, according to a French officer in another ship, "We had to go to her assistance immedi-

ately after the battle, as she had lost one hundred and twenty
men and had no sails or rigging, having received one hundred
and twenty-five balls in her hull and twelve under the water-
line." These figures were somewhat exaggerated; but, on the
morning after the engagement, *Diadème* did signal that she was
absolutely "*hors d'état de combattre.*" Recovery must have been
rapid, however, for De Bougainville commented that "we could
see no apparent damage" to *Diadème* on that day. The *Caton*
also made the signal of distress after the battle; but the two or
three partially crippled French vessels were able to make repairs
at sea so effectively that it appeared to the British that "they had
received very little damage in the action."[10]

The Swedish naval lieutenant Tornquist was impressed by the
devotion to honor which was manifested by all ranks in the
French fleet. He cites one incident "among others," he says,
which occurred during the battle as an example of it. "When
Commodore de Bougainville twice had his foretop bowline shot
off and the sailors who, of their own accord, both times tried to
repair it were shot, he observed that no one would make a third
attempt, wherefore he, with his usual kindness, offered his purse
to the person who would put the bowline in shape. A common
sailor immediately went out on the yard and called back: 'My
General, we do not go there for money,' whereupon he tackled
the work and fortunately carried it through."[11]

There can be no doubt about where the fiercest fighting of the
day occurred. It was between the vanguards of the two fleets,
with Drake's squadron having decidedly the worst of it. In Julian
Corbett's words: "The British van was cut to pieces before
Graves got into action at all," even though they temporarily
outnumbered the French. Rear Admiral Charles Ekins, R.N.,
says that "many of the British fleet suffered very severely upon
this occasion, justifying all that has been said about such a mode
of attack from the windward position."[12]

On the other side, the dash displayed by De Bougainville
wrung from the lips of Admiral de Grasse, at their first interview
after the battle, the tribute: "Now that is what I call 'combat'!
For a while I thought you were going to board!" Later the
French commander-in-chief made the public declaration to
Generals Washington and Rochambeau that "the laurels of the

day belong to De Bougainville . . . for having led the van and having personally fought the *Terrible*."[13]

As both center divisions came up at a much greater distance from one another, the pattern of the rest of the battle began to take shape. As already noted, Graves explained to Sandwich after the battle that "My aim was to get close, to form parallel, extend with them, and attack all together." But this excellent intention simply could not be realized by obeying the signals he hoisted, which were understood to call for the continuation of a strict line-ahead veering obliquely toward the enemy. Each time he gave the order to his leading ship to bear more to starboard, the angle of approach of his whole column became steeper, and the ships in the rear had less and less chance of making contact with the French. Meanwhile the latter, described by him as "bearing up as they advanced," delivered their broadsides and wheeled away, uniformly inflicting more damage than they received.

Along toward 5:00 P.M., before all of the British center and any of the rear had come within range, the wind began to shift about four points toward the east-northeast. This deprived the British of some of their previous wind advantage over the French, whom it also affected adversely by placing their van still farther toward the windward of their center. When Admiral de Grasse saw this, says Tornquist, since "with much eagerness he desired a general engagement, he signalled to the van to go more freely in order to invite Admiral Graves to follow, but as the English fleet was already severely punished, the latter determined to keep the advantage of the wind and fight at a greater distance in order to avoid the fire of the last French ships which were approaching all sails set."[14]

While the vans were still mauling each other, De Grasse's order to De Bougainville to bear away could not be obeyed, because "they were fighting within gunshot distance, and would have got a very severe handling had the French presented the stern." When De Bougainville's ships finally began to go away, it seemed to the British that the French, as usual taking the defensive in order to preserve their ships, were in full retreat. Graves in his account of the battle said that "their van bore away to enable their center to support them," and that, at the moment, "the center seemed to have little more in view than to shelter their own van as it went away before the wind." The flagship *Ville de Paris* was portrayed as having "avoided closing with the *London* as much as possible." These reports led to some empty English assertions that Drake had given the French van a trouncing, including such claims as that "Their van was beaten and made off . . . with all the appearance of a flight"; and "the French van suffered most, because it was obliged to bear away."[15]

The behavior of the two fleets looked otherwise from the French point of view. In going away the van ships were simply enabling De Grasse to form a continuous line with his center and rear, so that, if necessary, the whole formation could wear about and receive a second British attack. The French officers were impressed with the apparent reluctance of the British center and rear to come close enough to put up a fight. According to the captain of the *Citoyen*, which was the seventeenth ship in the French column, and hence on the outer fringe of the combat: "The vans were fighting at very close range . . . but the enemy, instead of fully engaging themselves, hauled their wind at the moment that they fired their broadsides. Their admiral [Graves] himself, for fear of approaching too close, laid everything against his mast at 4:30 P.M. The action commenced at the center of the fleet from the van and to the rear of Admiral de Grasse. The enemy, although master of the wind, only engaged from far off and simply in order to be able to say that they had fought. In that part of the line it was not at all the way it was in the vans of the two fleets, where one could see only fire and smoke billowing on both sides."[16]

As applied to the leading ships of Graves's center squadron, the gibe that they engaged "simply in order to be able to say that they had fought" is unjustly harsh. Vaugirard was probably nearer the truth when he guessed that the ships of the second half of the British line had been "obliged to haul their wind to stay in the wakes of their van . . . so closely engaged."[17] The true story of their participation is best told in their battle damages and casualties officially reported. The first two vessels of the British center, the *Europe* and the *Montagu*, both sixty-fours, absorbed almost as much punishment as some of Drake's ships. Captain Child of the *Europe* counted: "Four shot in the mainmast, two of them gone through; twelve shot between wind and water and a great many in the upper works; rigging, sails and running gear much cut; three gun-carriages damaged; the ship strains and takes in water." She had lost nine killed in the battle, and eighteen wounded. *Montagu's* damages were serious enough to make her, by 9 that evening, unfit to keep her place in line. She was reported "in great danger of losing her masts, which might fall at any moment; five shot in the mainmast; mizzenmast cut in half, main yard shot half off; running rigging and sails very much cut; hull much shattered by shot; and four guns dismounted." Her casualties numbered eight killed and twenty-two wounded.[18]

The disfigurements suffered by the next three ships in Graves's column decreased in proportion to their distance from the van. The *Royal Oak* had "five shot in the wales and twelve in the topsides; upper decks shot through in several places; and the mizzenmast wounded." The flagship *London* received "one large shot through the mainmast and two in the foremast; a number of shot in the side, several under water; three guns dismounted, one thrown overboard as useless; sails and rigging much cut; four men killed and eighteen wounded." *Bedford's* mizzen topmast was "rendered unfit for service; there was a shot in the mainmast and two in the foremast; fourteen shot in the side and several under water."

The next three ships came out of the battle virtually unscathed: *Resolution* had her "headrails shot away, mainmast and bowsprit wounded; three men killed and sixteen wounded"; *Centaur* and *Monarch* suffered only minor scratches and had no men killed or wounded. Thus it becomes abundantly clear that only twelve of Graves's nineteen ships took any significant part in the combat. As the admiral himself said: "The action became general as far as the second ship from the center towards the rear," that is, the *Resolution*.[19] Where, a great many have asked ever since, was Sir Samuel Hood?

It is not literally true that, as Sir John Knox Laughton claimed, the last seven British vessels "did not fire a shot." According to Rear Admiral Hood himself, "Only three fired a few shots." What is true of all seven ships, six of them in Hood's command, is that they did not get close enough to the enemy to

suffer or to inflict any casualties or significant damage. Graves
had fought a numerically superior fleet with only about two-
thirds of his ships. Why was this?

We know that when, shortly after 2:00 p.m., Graves wore his
fleet about on a west to east line, "his rear was infinitely to the
windward of his van." Evidently this lagging to the windward
continued, since he made signals at 3:30 p.m. for the ships astern
of him to fill and make more sail. From 4:03 to 4:11 p.m., as
already observed, contradictory signals were flying from the
London. Graves himself told Sandwich that he "only resumed
the signal for the line for about five or seven minutes to push the
ships ahead of me forward, and who were some of them upon my
off beam."[20] The signal for line-ahead came down at 4:11 p.m.,
but at 4:27 the admiral, finding that "all the ships were not sufficiently extended," ordered its rehoisting.

This last move had the immediate effect of relieving the
"bunching up" of the ships ahead of the flagship, but by restoring the contradictory signals it placed Hood and all the captains
astern of the flagship in a dilemma. Once more they were caused
to believe that they were being ordered to do two contradictory
things: to seek out and attack their opposite numbers in the
French line (at a great distance), and at the same time to keep
their ships on a straight line running from the leading ship of the
van through the flagship of Admiral Graves. There were excellent reasons why the second signal was, in the words of Captain
James, "one that none of the commanding officers were prepared
to disobey."

Graves's claim was, according to the log of the *London*, that
"within five minutes" after 4:22 p.m., the line-ahead signal had
been lowered once more, and never hoisted again during the battle. He maintained that it was replaced, at about 4:27 by the
signal for close action, which was repeated at 5:15, when Hood
saw it and came up. Hood and at least one of his captains swore
vehemently that the line signal was flying continuously until
about 5:30 p.m. In a "Transcript of proceeding aboard the *London*," as minuted at the time by the admiral's secretary, there is
the entry: "40 minutes past 4 the *Royal Oak*'s signal to keep her
station; 11 past 4 the *Montagu*'s signal to get into her station."
These entries would indicate that Graves was still concerned

with preserving his line, although possibly he meant something other than a bowsprit-to-stern formation.

The log of Hood's flagship *Barfleur* and its record of his "Signals Made" during the battle say only that "At ½ past 4 the van ships began to engage at the same time the signal was made for engaging . . . At 20 minutes past 4 hauled down the white pendant and kept the Blue & Yellow chequered flag flying under the red flag . . . 55 minutes past 5 the admiral made the signal for the *Alcide* to keep her station in the line more regularly . . . 25 minutes past 5 hauled down the signal for the line, at the same time the signal for closer action was flying . . . ¾ past 5 the enemies' shot went over us. About 50 minutes past 5 the *Barfleur* and *Monarch* opened their fire on the enemy . . . At half past 6 the admiral hauled down the signal for engaging, as did the *Barfleur*."[21]

These records give strong indications that Graves showed the same concern for his line-ahead after 4:27 P.M. as he had manifested earlier. What is certain is that he was correct in reporting to Sandwich that "Unfortunately, the signal for the line was thought to be kept up until half after five, when the rear division bore down; but the fair occasion was gone." Hood and his captains acted as if the line-ahead signal was the controlling order of the day; and after the change in the wind, the angle at which they were approaching the French became steeper and steeper, keeping them farther and farther from the enemy.

A furious controversy soon raged between the defenders of Graves, who denounced Hood for his apparent "shyness" and "great dilatoriness" in coming to grips with the French, even suggesting that he was deliberately sabotaging his superior officer; and Hood's partisans, who blamed Graves for his contradictory orders, and the Admiralty for furnishing him an antiquated signal-book. So flatly do the claims of the two admirals contradict one another that Sir John Knox Laughton has suggested the possibility that Graves saw the line-ahead signal lowered, but that "a too active-minded signalman" restored it without his knowledge.

To the French at 5:00 P.M. it looked as if De Grasse were trying, in Chevalier de Vaugirard's words, "to afford the enemy the means of making the action general, and fearing also that perhaps the ships of his van might be cut off, gave them the signal to come up two points, but, far from profitting by this, the enemy fleet held to the wind in such a way as to render futile all efforts by our van and center to approach them."[22] As Tornquist also saw it, "the English rear had no desire to keep within our range." The captain of the *Citoyen* gave this view of Hood's performance: "By 5:15 P.M. the wind was very light and variable from east to east-northeast. Our rear squadron found itself close-hauled by the dropping-away of the light breeze. At 5:45 P.M. the three-decked ship [the *Barfleur*] commanding the enemy rear came up, as well as the two ships ahead of her, opposite the *Palmier* and *Solitaire*. Some moments after their arrival, they hove to and experimented to see whether their cannonballs would reach our ships. The enemy admiral [Hood] began by firing several shots and the other ships, which had also hauled their wind, followed suit. The ships of the enemy rearguard always held the windward position; their fire became general up as far as my ship, but it did not last long, the enemy remaining hove-to . . . I had much the better of the exchange with the three-decker, for it appeared to me that nearly all her cannonballs fell into the sea before they reached us, while the few that we fired were not wasted, or if so, it was because they overshot the enemy."[23]

Another French account by an officer who is critical of De Grasse says: "The two vans having come so close as to be almost within pistol-shot, the fire was long well sustained, and the affair seemed to be decisive, when Admiral Hood made a signal to the English rear division, which he commanded, to bear down upon the French rear. Admiral de Grasse witnessed this movement with pleasure and prepared to tack his whole fleet together, bearing north-northwest, which would inevitably have thrown the English fleet into confusion; but Admiral Graves anticipated him and signalled his whole fleet to keep the wind. The heads of the two fleets gradually fell off in consequence of this new order of the English admiral, and the fire ceased at 6:30 P.M."[24]

By that hour the French in the ships of the van "were so tired that though within gunshot, the vans no longer fired. The contest was kept up in the center for a half an hour longer. At sunset, the battle closed." Both admirals insisted that they were determined to renew the engagement next morning. De Grasse reformed his battle line and headed for the open sea. Graves maintained that "After night I sent the frigates to the van and rear, to push forward the line and keep it extended with the enemy, with the full intention to renew the engagement in the morning."

20

THE BATTLE OF
THE CHESAPEAKE:
THIRD PHASE

*"All depended on a fleet. Sir Henry Clinton was promised
one. Washington had one."* —Sir Henry Clinton

At sunset or soon after on September 5, when the cannonading
at a distance had died down, the two fleets remained on the same
larboard tack that had already carried them about ten miles
southeast of Cape Henry. At 6:15 P.M., just before the end of
the firing, Admiral Graves had dispatched two of his frigates, the
Fortunée to the van, and the *Solebay* to the rear, with his orders
for the night. The British ships were told to keep a parallel line
at two cables' length and well abreast of the enemy who, although without the advantage of the wind, were in possession of
the initiative. The *Fortunée* did not return from her mission until
10:00 P.M., bringing bad news of the damages sustained by
Shrewsbury, Intrepid, and *Princessa.* An hour earlier *Montagu*
had hailed the flagship and informed Graves that she was in imminent danger of losing her masts and could no longer keep
her place in line.

Graves also knew that the *Terrible* and *Ajax* had very leaky
hulls, and that his own ship *London* needed repairs. He noted
that "the French had not the appearance of near so much damage
as we had sustained." He had seen no evidence that more than
two or three of them, at most, had suffered any serious injuries
during the battle. It began to seem doubtful that any renewal of
an attack upon the French in the morning would be feasible. His

initial shortage of five ships had now been doubled by the partial crippling, especially aloft, of at least five more.

Nevertheless the English admiral clung tenaciously to a windward position that would enable him to decide whether or not an attack was to be made next morning. De Grasse's orders for the night were to form on himself and keep the line in readiness for combat. According to a French account: "The fleet passed the night in the presence of the enemy in line of battle, the fires in all the vessels lighted. These signs of victory were not belied in the morning, for we perceived by the sailing of the English that they had suffered greatly."[1]

At dawn on September 6 the weather was "moderate and clear" with only a feeble north wind until 4:00 P.M. This relative calm favored the tasks of refitting at sea by both fleets: everywhere the sailmakers and riggers were busy repairing the damaged upper works. At 5:45 A.M. the British fleet was ordered to form a battle line at half-a-cable's length; but at 6:00 there was much activity by the messenger frigates, the *Nymphe* reporting that *Shrewsbury* and *Intrepid* wanted to speak to the admiral. At 11:00 A.M. Rear Admiral Drake shifted his flag from *Princessa* to *Alcide*. As seen from the French warship *Citoyen* about seven miles away toward the south, five of the British ships "were occupied in changing their topmasts, and one seemed to have a damaged mainmast."

During the afternoon of September 6 it became ever more apparent to Rear Admiral Graves that his fleet was in no condition to resume the attack, even though Hood's squadron was undamaged and full of fight. The British had sustained no great losses in either men or guns. They had had ninety men killed and two hundred and forty-six wounded, as against total French casualties of two hundred and nine. Sixteen of the English guns had been put out of action, or a little more than 1 percent of their armament. Their real losses were in speed of sailing and maneuverability, thanks to the French gunners' customary skill in disabling masts and rigging. With a "mutilated" fleet unable to attack, Graves had no other strategic plan on which to fall back. What Rear Admiral Chadwick calls his "wooliness of mind about his mission" prevailed during the aftermath of the engagement.

He did not want to offend the bellicose Hood still further by appearing not to consider a renewal of the action. So he asked for Hood's advice. "This forenoon," Hood recorded, "Captain Everett came on board the *Barfleur* with a message from Rear-Admiral Graves to Rear-Admiral Sir S. Hood desiring his opinion whether the action should be renewed. Sir Samuel's answer was: 'I dare say Mr. Graves will do what is right. I can *send* no opinion, but whenever he, Mr. Graves, wishes to see me, I will wait upon him with great pleasure.' " (Italics his.)[2]

This icy reply could hardly have helped the commander-in-chief to decide upon the fleet's next move. That evening he summoned Admirals Hood and Drake to a conference on the *London*. During the day Hood, in his cabin, fuming with indignation at Graves as the one responsible for his own failure to get into action on the day before, had been writing down his "Sentiments upon the Truly Unfortunate Day," which were to set forth his side of the coming controversies with his superior officer. He wrote to George Jackson, Assistant Secretary to the Admiralty, on September 16 that he "mentioned these sentiments to Mr. Graves when I attended his first summons on board the *London*." Sparks must have flown at that conference.

According to an account published in the London *Political and Military Journal* for 1782, the following conversation ensued: "Admiral Graves asked Admiral Hood why he did not bear down and engage? The answer was: 'You had up the signal for the line.' Admiral Graves then turned to Admiral Drake, and asked him how he came to bear down? He replied: 'On account of the signal for action.' Admiral Graves then said: 'What say you to this, Admiral Hood?' Sir Samuel answered: 'The signal for the line was enough for me.' "[3]

In his letter to Jackson on September 16, Hood became confused about his encounters with Graves when he wrote: "On the 6th it was calm the whole day, and in the evening Mr. Drake and I were sent for, when Mr. Graves communicated to us the intelligence he had received from the captains of the *Medea* and *Iris*, who had reconnoitred the Chesapeake." Hood evidently telescoped in his memory the meetings with Graves on September 6 and September 8, because Captain Duncan of the *Medea* was not ordered by the admiral to look into the Chesapeake until

September 6, and it was not until the next day that the *Medea* and *Iris* actually entered the bay, observed the French ships there, and cut away the buoys left behind by De Grasse's fleet. Thus the earliest day on which Graves could have had their intelligence was on September 8, when they returned and reported "three large ships, which they thought were ships of the line" with a 40-gun ship and a frigate in the Chesapeake.[4]

Hood's account of the September 6th conference in his letter to Jackson continues: "Mr. Graves also made known to us a letter from Sir H. Clinton to General Cornwallis which he was desired to convey to his Lordship if possible. The *Richmond* and *Iris* were detached upon that service, I fear to be cut off." This also refers to a date later than September 6, since those two frigates did not leave Graves's fleet until September 8; and Hood was quite correct in prophesying their ultimate fate. Then comes Hood's highly significant comment: "The whole squadron should have gone [to the Chesapeake]; they might then not only most effectually have succored Lord Cornwallis, but have destroyed the enemy's ships there."[5] Here began still another controversy between Graves and Hood, for what the latter had in mind, if not on September 6 then surely on September 8, was something far more drastic than anything Graves was contemplating. Hood was proposing to turn the fleet about and hasten to beat De Grasse in a race for the Chesapeake Bay anchorage, a maneuver that Hood was to execute successfully against this same French admiral only four months later at Basseterre Bay, St. Kitts.

But whenever Hood's bold scheme was conceived or suggested to Graves, it found no acceptance on the part of the latter. Graves continued to be lured farther and farther in the opposite direction, away from what should have been his prime objective, the relief of Cornwallis. Yet Admiral Sir Vesey Hamilton points out that "Graves had no information showing him the extreme and immediate importance of relieving Cornwallis, and as a dull though honest and brave man, he did not appreciate it aright. Hood seems to have done so, but intuitively, certainly not of positive knowledge, but he was unfortunately only second in command."[6] Graves had furnished Hood with one more grievance against his superior.

While the British fleet continued to hold the windward position, De Grasse was content to wait and see whether they would
make use of it to renew the attack. "It seemed unlikely that they
would fight this day," wrote De Bougainville in his *Journal* on
September 6. Next day at 7:00 A.M. the sea was still calm, but
then a breeze sprang up from the south-southwest, and it became
possible for the French to begin jockeying for the windward
position. The two fleets were still in sight of one another at a
distance of seven or eight miles, bearing southeast away from the
Chesapeake, and occasionally within sight of land. Both admirals
seemed temporarily to have forgotten their true strategic bone
of contention, the control of the Chesapeake.

It was on September 7 that Admiral de Grasse made two extraordinary gestures toward his subordinate, Commodore de
Bougainville. Lieutenant Tornquist had already noted a change
for the better in their personal relationship, just after the battle
of September 5. "De Bougainville," he says, "became the most
intimate friend of the Count de Grasse. These two gentlemen
had since the 29th of April been at loggerheads, but now and
thereafter became attached to one another."[7] It is sad to reflect
that this amicable *entente* did not survive the battle of the
Saintes seven months later, when the breach between the two
officers became irreparable. But at 11:30 A.M. on September 7,
1781, De Bougainville was surprised and pleased to receive an
unusually cordial letter from his *grand chef*.

After the routine admonitions to keep his squadron well-
formed "upon the center, which is myself," and in a tight line,
De Grasse wrote: "Thus, Monsieur, on this present occasion and
in all other circumstances, I beg you to regard the squadron
which you command as if it were a fleet attached to my own, of
which you have all the discipline (*police*)." This letter was followed by another on the same day assuring "My dear Bougainville" that he was being sent De Grasse's own chief surgeon to
serve on the *Auguste* until that vessel's own chief doctor, who
was absent, returned to duty. This letter went on to say: "If the
wind continues and the English do not escape us tonight, we
shall meet them at closer range tomorrow morning, and I hope
the day will be a happier one, which will permit us to go back
and take those Johnnies in the Chesapeake. What a joy it will be

to have the ships of De Barras united with ours! What a body blow that will be, and decisive, too, instead of this uncertain state of affairs where the forces are only equal and poorly manned. I have great hopes based upon the damages to the enemy which I can see. I judge by them that they are not as well-outfitted as we are, and by the slowness of their movements that they are not as ready for battle. If we can have a sample we shall become better informed about this."[8]

The contrast between the personal relationships existing in the highest echelons of the French and the British commands hardly needs pointing out. Admiral de Grasse's entrusting of the discipline of the van squadron to De Bougainville was, as De Loture says, "an exceptional mark of confidence" in that officer's ability, demonstrated at the Chesapeake, to act independently and to control the captains under him. De Grasse's letter also indicates his apparent belief that the two fleets were more nearly equal in strength than was actually the case, and may account in part for his disinclination to attack the British when changes in the wind temporarily afforded him that privilege.

"On the 8th of September," says Graves in his report of events, "it came on to blow pretty fresh" with thunder and lightning. At 7:00 A.M. Rear Admiral Hood went on board the *London* for half an hour, to learn what has already been related above. At 11:00 A.M., when, standing against a head sea, the *Terrible* made the signal of distress, and the *Orpheus* and *Fortunée* had to be sent to her assistance. At times on the preceding day and night the French, even though many of their ships were poor sailers, had gained the windward position. "But on the 9th," writes Tornquist, "the wind again became favorable for the English admiral, who took the luff from the French fleet . . . Count De Grasse turned immediately on the spot, so that his fleet lay to port in good order, steering down on the enemy which came on the opposite tack, in poor formation, nevertheless with the determination to dispute the advantage of the wind with the French. De Grasse signalled his foremost ship to pass within the distance of a pistol-shot of the enemy, who now began to turn by the wind in each other's wake, in order to come on an equal bow with our ships. Graves finally saw the danger of such a movement which, if it had been followed out would have given occasion for our fleet to have attacked the enemy in an evolution only half-performed; therefore he gave the signal, when three of his ships had already turned, to his whole fleet to hold before the wind . . . Through this movement Count de Grasse became completely master of the wind, while the enemy sought their escape with all sails set. During the night a change of wind again made them master, but the following day towards evening Count de Grasse once more won the luff back again, because he had a smaller number of damaged ships."[9]

That Graves was becoming more and more aware of the cripples in his fleet is apparent from his report of later developments on September 8: "At night about an hour after the fleet had been wore together, the *Intrepid* made the signal to speak with the admiral, upon which the fleet was brought to, and I was soon informed that her main topmast was gone over the side and they expected the fore-yard would go at every minute. These repeated misfortunes in sight of a superior enemy who kept us all extended and in motion, filled the mind with anxiety and put us in a condition not to be envied."[10]

As Graves's distresses multiplied, and he seemed to have no plan but to stick to De Grasse, the two fleets lost sight of one another on September 9. When this happened, said the *Political Journal*, Graves seemed to have concluded that his "maimed plight prevented his keeping pace with the French and put it out of his power to hinder them from getting back into the Chesapeake."[11] That he saw no hope in Hood's proposal to go there is evidenced by a letter written by Sir Henry Clinton on September 26, 1781, saying that in a letter from Rear Admiral Graves dated September 9 he had been informed that "the enemy being absolute masters of the navigation of the Chesapeake, there was little probability of getting anything into York River but by night, and at infinite risk to any supplies sent by water; at the same time acquainting him that he had had on the 5th a partial action with the French fleet of twenty-four sail of the line, and that the two fleets had been in sight of each other ever since; which making it inexpedient to send the reinforcements immediately, under such dangerous circumstances . . . a council of war decided to wait for a more favorable account from Rear Admiral Graves."[12]

But if the two commanders-in-chief had become so absorbed in out-maneuvering one another as to forget the prize for which they were contending, the same was not true of their immediate subordinates. On September 9 De Bougainville confided to his *Journal:* "I was very much afraid that the British might try to get to the Chesapeake under a press of sail ahead of us. It is what we ought to have been doing since the battle: that is, our very best to get back into that bay, recover our ships, barges and boats, or at least the men who man our rowboats. Perhaps we would also find the squadron of M. de Barras."[13]

The British were not alone in feeling some of the after-effects of the "partial engagement" of September 5. At 3:00 P.M. on September 9 the French warship *Caton* signalled that it was taking a lot of water, "doubtless because of a cannon-shot at the waterline," said Bougainville. "We saw a number of men working above the rigging-platform of her mizzenmast, and at 4:00 P.M. she rejoined the line." By that evening, Admiral de Grasse had made up his mind to go back to the Chesapeake. The wind being favorable, a press of sail was ordered, and the French headed back toward the northwest. As Dudley W. Knox remarks: "Count de Grasse has sometimes been criticized for thus abandoning the field to an inferior fleet, but this is scarcely warranted when we consider that his main mission was to co-operate with armies in the capture of Cornwallis. While the destruction of the British fleet would have made this end more certain, an indecisive or unsuccessful action, on the other hand, might well have rendered his principal object more difficult and perhaps impossible."[14]

The commander who was most upset by the disappearance of the French was not Graves but Hood, who next day addressed this letter to his chief, dated *Barfleur* at sea, September 10, 1781: "I flatter myself you will forgive the liberty I take in asking whether you have any knowledge where the French fleet is, as we see nothing of it from the *Barfleur*. By the press of sail De Grasse carried yesterday (and he must have done the same the preceding night by being where he was at daylight), I am inclined to think his aim is the Chesapeake. In order to be strengthened by the ships there, either by adding them to his present force, or by exchanging his disabled ships for them. Admitting that to be his plan, will he not cut off the frigates you have sent to reconnoitre, as well as the ships you expect from New York? And if he should enter the bay, which is by no means improbable, will he not succeed in giving most effectual succor to the rebels? I trust you will pardon the offer of my humble sentiments, as they are occasioned by what passed between us, when I had the honor of attending your summons on board the *London* on the 8th in the morning."[15]

Once again Hood's vision of the British predicament was accurate, and once more it had no effect upon the mind of Graves, which seems to have been on troubles closer to his ship. On September 9, Captain William Clement Finch of the *Terrible* had reported that his ship was taking in water at the rate of six feet per hour, and that, with all workable pumps going, he was "apprehensive that the ship cannot be saved." On the 10th the rate had gone up to eight feet an hour; five of the lower-deck guns had been thrown overboard "while it was still in our power to do so," and others were marked to follow them. "Although we do not make quite so much water on this tack," her captain declared, "we make too much to give us any great hopes of being able to carry her into port."[16]

An eight-man survey party headed by First Lieutenant Richard Nash examined the *Terrible*, and concluded unanimously that it was "absolutely impracticable to carry her into port," even with help from other vessels of the fleet. On September 11, Graves summoned Hood and Drake to another council of war. Their laconic verdict was: "We are of opinion to take out People and sink her." Accordingly the *Terrible* was stripped, with her men, powder, and supplies being distributed to other ships of the fleet; and on the evening of "the first calm day," which was September 11, she was set on fire and burned. Graves now found himself with only eighteen bona fide ships of the line, the 50-gun *Adamant* having been substituted for the *Terrible*.

In England, voices were raised in protest over the deliberate destruction of the *Terrible* "because she made six feet of water an hour. It was," said a writer in the *Political and Military Journal*, "a very wrong step. Sir Samuel Hood in coming from the West Indies never thought of destroying her, though she made the same quantity of water during that passage. Besides, there are other facts to go upon. After the action she made no more water than she did before it. But when it was deemed necessary to sink her, and the men were taken out, in order to hasten her sinking, they opened a large cock of nearly two inches in diameter, to let the water into her hold, and left her a whole night, *yet with this assistance she would not go down;* therefore the next day, that she might not continue to swim, and perhaps fall into the hands of the enemy, she was set on fire. If an able officer had been at the head of the fleet, the *Terrible* would not have been destroyed." (Italics his.)[17]

At about 9:00 P.M. on the same evening of the 10th, Graves ordered the fleet to turn back toward the Chesapeake, and sent the *Medea* ahead to reconnoitre that bay. His explanation was that "the fleets had continued in sight of each other for five days successively, and at times were very near. We had not speed enough in so mutilated a state to attack them had it been prudent, and they showed no inclination to renew the action, for they generally maintained the wind of us and had it often in their power."[18] What the admiral never did succeed in explaining was why he kept on, day after day, sparring with an enemy which he dared not attack, and a commander who might turn upon him with an excellent chance of destroying the only shield of the British armies in both New York and Yorktown. If he did not want to adopt Hood's rash scheme for capturing the Chesapeake anchorage the sensible alternative was to hie himself speedily to New York to refit. He knew that Rear Admiral Digby was expected from England with naval reinforcements, although he did not know how many, or exactly when he would arrive. But his letter to Clinton on September 9 shows clearly that he had conceded absolute control of the Chesapeake to the French. The British problem now was to get into condition to dispute it.

A contemporary British account says with sarcasm that "De Grasse, afraid that the idea of returning to the Chesapeake would at last come into Graves's head, thought proper to prevent him by going back there again himself."[19] From the French point of view, said Chevalier de Vaugirard: "Everything called Count de Grasse back to Chesapeake Bay: the operations of the land army were entirely suspended in his absence; no one knew the fate of

De Barras and one hoped to find him there. Finally, our armed boats with about ninety officers and eighteen hundred of our best sailors were for all our ships an object of very lively uneasiness."[20]

By pressing on all possible canvas the French fleet got back in sight of Cape Henry at 11:00 A.M. on September 10. "Behind the point of land," says De Loture, "there appeared the high masts of ships. They were at anchor, close to the entrance of the bay, twenty vessels of good size, approximately the number in Graves's fleet. Immediately orders were given to clear for action, and the Commodores of De Grasse's squadrons waited for the word to form a line of battle. But if it were only De Barras!

"Already a frigate had been sent on ahead, with the recognition signal flying from its mainmast. Bravo! There, on one of the ships in the distance, the signal agreed-upon is unfurled. It is indeed De Barras, who, finding the way open, had entered in the nick of time with his eight warships and the ten vessels of his convoy carrying the siege train."[21] De Barras had eluded the British by going far out to sea and as far south as Albemarle Sound before circling back toward the Chesapeake. He had been aware of the battle on September 5, but had been unable to distinguish the nationalities of the ships engaged. When first sighted, he had taken De Grasse's approach for that of an enemy fleet, and "maneuvered to protect and preserve his convoy and gain the anchorage before nightfall."

"Now the fleet sails back to its former anchorage," writes De Loture, "but then they notice that first one, then two, and then a whole garland of buoys which the current of the ebb tide is carrying gently toward the entrance of the bay. And yonder is the cause of this new kind of launching, two smart English frigates, the *Iris* (before her capture the *Hancock*) and *Richmond* which, not expecting the French to return so soon, were engaged in the little game of cutting the cables attaching the anchors to the buoys and now found themselves promptly punished for their temerity."

All hope of retreat being cut off, the British ships lowered their flags and prize crews took over. De Grasse's captains set about the "long and delicate operation of recovering their anchors by means of ship's boats rather than buoy-ropes."[22]

When Captain Duncan of the *Medea* returned on the morning of September 13, he reported to Rear Admiral Graves that the French fleet was indeed back at their anchorage in the Chesapeake, but made no mention of their exact numbers. Hence he did not convey the vital information concerning the arrival of De Barras's squadron and its junction with De Grasse's. Consequently Graves persisted in his mistaken belief that on September 5 he had fought the combined French fleets. His arithmetic would have it that the twenty-four vessels he had encountered consisted of eight from Rhode Island and sixteen brought from the West Indies. This gave continuing substance to his hope that, if Digby arrived with reinforcements, the British fleet might soon outnumber that of the French.

But for the present he must act a different role, and in his uncertainty in regard to it, he turned once again to Sir Samuel Hood for advice. "Admiral Graves," he wrote to the latter on the morning of the 13th, "presents his compliments to Sir Samuel Hood, and begs leave to acquaint him that the *Medea* has just made the signal to inform him that the French fleet are at anchor above the Horse Shoe in the Chesapeake, and desires his opinion what to do with the fleet?" Hood replied with his usual bluntness: "Sir Samuel Hood presents his compliments to Rear Admiral Graves, though it is not more than what he expected, as the press of sail the fleet carried on the 9th and in the night of the 8th made it very clear to him what De Grasse's intentions were. Sir Samuel would be very glad to send an opinion, but he really knows not what to say in the truly lamentable state we have brought ourself."[23]

There was nothing to do but call another council of war, and to face the fact that, as Hood phrased it, "We should have barred the entrance [of the Chesapeake] to De Grasse; now he has barred it to us." The resolve adopted by the three admirals on board the *London* is of such transcendent importance for the outcome of the Yorktown campaign that it deserves citation in full. As Stephen Bonsal has truly remarked: "That was indeed a war council that should be gratefully remembered in our annals. Its members contributed powerfully to the founding of the United States of America."[24]

"At a council of war held on board *H.M.S. London* at sea on the 13th of September, 1781, upon a report from Captain Duncan of the *H.M.S. Medea*, that they had seen the evening before, the French fleet at anchor off the Horseshoe Shoal in the Chesapeake, that the large ships appeared more numerous and to be in divisions, but that it was too late to get near enough to form a close judgment. Upon this state of the position of the enemy, the present condition of the British fleet, the season of the year so near the equinox, and the impracticability of giving any effectual succor to General Earl Cornwallis in the Chesapeake, it was resolved, that the British squadron under the command of Thomas Graves, Esq., Rear Admiral of the Red, Sir Samuel Hood, Bart., and Francis Samuel Drake, Esq., Rear Admirals of the Blue, should proceed with all dispatch to New York, and there use every possible means for putting the squadron into the best state for service, provided that Captain Duncan who is gone again to reconnoitre should confirm his report of the position of the enemy and that the fleet should in the meantime facilitate the junction of the *Medea*."[25]

The meeting with the *Medea* off the Chesapeake must have been visible from the French fleet, since De Barras reported that "the English fleet appeared in the distance on September 13-14, and the signal was made to the French fleet to prepare to weigh anchor." Since the British soon made off toward the north, that order was quickly rescinded. When the *Medea* reported on September 14, with no more information than on the day before, Captain Duncan was ordered to proceed to England with Graves's dispatches, with positive commands neither to wait for any private letters, nor to touch at New York. The *Medea* left at dark, and at daylight met with the *Prudent*, finally refitted at New York, and on its way with two frigates and a sloop-of-war to join Graves's fleet. Captain Duncan landed at Weymouth on October 5, and reached London the same evening, bringing the first news of the battle of the Chesapeake, just one month after it had occurred.

21

"TOO LITTLE, TOO LATE"

"Clinton and Graves promise every exertion to relieve Cornwallis . . . and go about it after His Lordship is taken."
—Headline in *Political and Military Journal*, II (1782)

With the lost *Terrible* replaced by the repaired but smaller *Prudent*, and with provisions running short, Graves's fleet limped back to New York. One of the officers on board the frigate *Nymphe*, which was employed in repeating the admiral's signals, stated that "By this time, too, when we had been but ten days at sea, Sir S. Hood's ships complained generally of want of water and bread, five or six of them having scarcely any water at all, and three others having only sufficient provisions for eight days longer."[1] Graves knew only too well how slender were the supplies to be had in New York. "We are," he wrote to Stephens on September 14, "without resources in New York, there having been neither stores nor provisions but what has been purchased for many months past, and a very slender quantity even of that."[2] One of the reasons that the admirals had been moved to return to New York was the fear that the equinoctial gales might wreak damages to their already weakened masts and rigging which could not be repaired at that port.

Even before his mutilated ships reached New York harbor, rumors had begun to circulate that Graves had received "a severe drubbing." On September 17, "when a packet arrived at New York," said Major General William Heath, "three thousand people were said to be waiting on the wharves to learn the news, but not a word transpired, nor did the countenance of the officer who landed appear to beam with the smiles of fortune." Graves and his fleet arrived on September 20, ten of his vessels going to the dockyard for repairs, whereupon "the inhabitants were in great consternation, many were packing their goods."[3]

Most of our information about what happened in New York during the next anxious weeks comes from two impatient and frustrated men: Rear Admiral Sir Samuel Hood, who was almost frantically eager to get back at De Grasse ("Every moment is precious," he wrote to Jackson); and General Sir Henry Clinton, army commander-in-chief, whose thousands of inactive garrison troops were so desperately needed for the relief of Earl Cornwallis. Graves himself was content to maintain that everyone was laboring "with the utmost alertness" to get the rescue expedition to sea as soon as possible.

By September 2, Clinton realized that Washington and Rochambeau had outwitted him in moving their armies to Virginia, although he managed to convince himself that he had not really been "deceived," since in any event he could not have spared men enough to stop them. He was sure that the Franco-American army numbered eleven thousand men instead of about seven thousand; and while Germain in London credited him with a garrison of twelve thousand, "not above nine thousand three hundred of them were fit for duty," and at least six thousand of those must be kept to defend New York. At the same time he had "the strongest reasons" for thinking that the British still had naval superiority in the Chesapeake. He was still "relying on the repeated promises made me by both Ministers and Admirals that Sir George Rodney would be watchful of the Count de Grasse's motions and bring or send me timely succor to prevent his doing me any mischief."[4] It was not until September 17 that Clinton received the first account, written by Graves on September 9, saying that "the enemy have so great a naval force in the Chesapeake that they are absolute masters of navigation."

Even then Clinton had every reason to think that the British loss of control by sea was only temporary. Neither he nor Graves yet knew the true strength of the French, because they did not know that, when Graves had fought De Grasse on September 5, De Barras had not yet arrived. They believed that

the maximum French strength stood at twenty-four ships of the
line, the ones which Graves had failed to defeat. They also
knew that Rear Admiral Digby was on his way from England
with a minimum of three fresh ships, that two more should be
coming from Jamaica, and that the *Robust* could probably be
repaired in time to be of service. Added to the nineteen which
had fought with Graves and Hood, that would make twenty-five
ships of the line to be arrayed against De Grasse's and De Barras's
supposed twenty-four. The same optimistic brand of arithmetic
prevailed in London also, where it was reckoned that "thirteen
ships of Graves added to thirteen of Hood would make twenty-
six, which we hope," said the *Political and Military Journal*, "will
be able to face with some effect the Count de Grasse."[5]

As early as September 4, Cornwallis had notified Clinton of
De Grasse's arrival within the Capes of Virginia, and of the
landing of French troops in the James River. When Clinton
finally became convinced on September 2 "that Mr. Washington
was decidedly marching south," he called several conferences of
his generals to debate the possibility of relieving the Yorktown
army by diversionary operations elsewhere. They concluded
that the only way "to be of the least use to Lord Cornwallis
was the direct one of joining him in Virginia."[6] On September
13 Major General James Robertson proposed to send one ship
of the line with five thousand soldiers on the chance of slipping
reinforcements to Cornwallis through the enemy cordon, but
this plan was vetoed.

It was not until September 17, a whole week after De Grasse's
return to his anchorage, that Cornwallis became aware of the
actual strength of the combined French squadrons blockading
him by sea. He knew then that his chances of escape by that
avenue had disappeared. By land, however, the trap had not
yet completely closed around him, since the four armies of
Washington and Rochambeau, Lafayette and Saint-Simon were
not fully deployed until September 27. Clinton confessed himself "at a loss to account for Cornwallis's not attempting to cut up
Monsieur St. Simon's three thousand enervated troops on their
landing within a few miles of him on the 1st of September, or by
placing himself between them and Lafayette's small corps of
Continentals to prevent their junction [which did not take place

until several days after] and strike at either or both as occasion offered, it being obvious that success even against the one or the other must have retarded the enemy's operations against him, and perhaps induced their relinquishing them altogether."[7]

Clinton was justified in expressing amazement at Cornwallis's failure to attack Saint-Simon's men at their landing (an amazement shared by Saint-Simon himself), but he underestimated the strength of Lafayette's and Saint-Simon's forces, once they were combined, which stood at fifty-five hundred regulars and upwards of three thousand militiamen. By stripping all his posts, Cornwallis might have been able to send six thousand regulars against them, with less than two thousand sailors and loyalist militia in reserve.

As for Cornwallis's own attitude, his changing state of mind can be perceived in an important letter which he wrote to Clinton on September 16-17. On the first of those two days, he said: "If I had no hopes of relief, I would rather risk an action than defend my half-finished works. But, as you say Admiral Digby is hourly expected and promise every exertion to assist me, I do not think myself justifiable in putting the fate of the war on so desperate an attempt. My provisions will last at least six weeks from this day. I am of opinion that you can do me no effectual service but by coming directly to this place." Though he did know that Digby was on the way, Cornwallis did not know how many ships he was bringing with him, and almost certainly guessed that it was many more than three. On the very next day, September 17, his whole tone changed, and he announced what was virtually the end of all his hopes of rescue by sea in this postscript: "Lieutenant Conway of the *Cormorant* is just exchanged. He assures me that, since the Rhode Island squadron has joined, they have thirty-six of the line. This place is in no state of defense. If you cannot relieve me very soon, you must be prepared to hear the worst."[8]

General Sir Henry Clinton received this catastrophic news on September 23; and from that moment on, the problem of rescuing Cornwallis took on a radically changed character. Any possibility of restoring British naval superiority in the Chesapeake had vanished. France simply had about ten more ships of the line in place than Great Britain could summon before the land campaign was over. If Cornwallis was to be extricated, it must be by some strategic device that could be utilized successfully by a fleet and army at least one-third smaller than the Franco-American forces. Since the enemy now held the defensive, the numerical odds were overwhelmingly in their favor. An attack upon a prepared position required a superior, not an inferior force. Yet Clinton in his wilful blindness persisted in displaying, in public at least, a high degree of optimism.

The commanders of both services were called into a joint conference. On September 24, writes Hood: "I attended a consultation of generals and admirals at Sir H. Clinton's when it was agreed to attempt the united efforts of army and navy to relieve Lord Cornwallis in the Chesapeake, and I proposed to have three or four fireships immediately prepared, with which the enemy's fleet may possibly be deranged and thrown into some confusion, and thereby give a favorable opening for pushing through it. This was approved, and upwards of five thousand troops are to be embarked."[9] Graves's account of this same meeting noted that "It seemed to be the opinion of the army that no diversion which they cou'd make by land would afford relief to Lord Cornwallis, that unless the navy cou'd land them in York or James rivers, they saw very little probability before them: the State of the Chesapeake, the Strength and Situation of the enemy's fleet, and the condition of our own was considered, and it was concluded upon, that the ships of war should take on board what provisions they could for the army, and embark the General Sir Henry Clinton and six thousand troops if possible, and so soon as it cou'd be got ready, to make an attempt to force its way, and that three fireships should be added to the one already here which are now preparing with every possible exertion, and it was hoped that the whole might be ready in ten days."[10]

The joint board of officers present (Generals Clinton, Knyphausen, Robertson, Leslie, and Patterson, and Admirals Graves, Hood, Drake and Commodore Affleck) then voted that the following letter be sent to Lord Cornwallis: "At a meeting of the flag and general officers held this day, in consequence of Your Lordship's letter of the 16th and 17th instant, it was unanimously determined that above five thousand men shall be embarked on

board the King's ships, and the joint exertions of the fleet and
army shall be made in a few days to relieve you. There is every
reason to hope that we shall start from hence about the 5th of
October."[11]

Much of this false optimism must be charged to Sir Henry
Clinton. His later defense of it acknowledged that "some persons
regarded this attempt to relieve the army at Yorktown by
forcing a passage to it through the French fleet as a chimerical
project, because they doubted the possibility of twenty-five sail
of the line and two fifties being able to penetrate a compact line
of thirty-six sail in the advantageous position De Grasse had
taken, or of afterwards escaping being all captured, supposing
it possible for them to have effected it."

Yet Clinton claimed that "the flag officers of the fleet, who
were present when this matter was debated in council [Septem-
ber 24], were all clearly of the opinion that thirty-six ships of
the line could not, in the position the French fleet had taken
between the Middle Ground and Horseshoe Flats, prevent even
twenty-three from passing (with a leading wind and tide) into
either York or James rivers." In the absence of any minutes of
the debate in the council it is impossible to tell whether the naval
officers present were genuinely sanguine regarding Clinton's
absurd hopes, or merely gave polite and silent assent.

Sir Henry's logic was that of a landsman very much at sea.
He argued that the enemy's ships, "being unable from the violence of the tide and the great swell of the sea in that channel to
avail themselves of the springs on their cables, would find that
their broadsides could not be brought to bear on ships approaching them end on, and, after a passage had been effected, would
not dare suddenly to weigh anchor for the purpose of following,
lest they should be driven ashore."[12] Clinton apparently dreamed
of landing on the Gloucester side of the York River, there to join
Tarleton and assure the safety of at least a part of Cornwallis's
army. As for the possible capture of the ships of the fleet after
the British reinforcements might have been landed, says Clinton,
"no idea of the sort was stated at the council of war, from
whence it may be inferred that the naval gentlemen present did
not look upon the possibility of such an event as very alarming."
If they did not, Professor Willcox wryly suggests that the chance

of exposing the entire British West Indies to capture by the French was of no great concern to the men supposed to be guarding it.

On the first day of October, Captain Frederick MacKenzie of Clinton's garrison noted in his diary that among "the navy captains downward . . . they talk very freely of the conduct of the Admiral on the 5th of September, and appear more ready to censure the conduct of others than to refit their own ships." One result was that, as late as October 10, the *Invincible* still lacked a foremast and the *Intrepid* a mizzenmast.

That the alleged optimism of the naval high command was hardly undiluted can be seen from Hood's angry comments on a conference of admirals called by Graves on the *London* on October 7. "Soon after we were assembled," Hood wrote to Jackson, "Mr. Graves proposed and wished to reduce to writing the following question, 'Whether it was practicable to relieve Lord Cornwallis in the Chesapeake?' This astonished me exceedingly, as it seemed plainly a design of having difficulties started against attempting what the generals and admirals had most *unanimously* agreed to, and given under their hands on the 24th of last month."[13] (Italics his.) Hood said that he replied at once to Graves that this seemed to him "a very unnecessary and improper question, as it had already been maturely discussed and determined upon to be attempted with all the expedition possible; that my opinion had been very strong and pointed (which I was ready to give in writing with my name to it) that an attempt under every risk should be made to force a junction with the troops the commander-in-chief embarks in His Majesty's fleet with the army under General Earl Cornwallis at York; and admitting that junction to be made without much loss, and the provisions landed, I was also of opinion that the first favorable opportunity should be embraced of attacking the French fleet, though I own to you that I think very meanly of the ability of our present commanding officer. I know he is a *cunning* man, he may be a good theoretical man, but he is certainly a bad practical man, and most clearly proved himself on the 5th of last month to be unequal to the conducting of a great squadron."

All such questions, however, would be academic unless speedy repairs could be made to Graves's damaged ships. Cornwallis could not be expected to hold out indefinitely. What were the prospects of speedy repairs? On his arrival in New York, Graves had written to Clinton on September 21, 1781, telling of his willingness "to undertake any service in conjunction with the army that shall be thought advisable," but adding these words of caution: "At the same time I should be greatly wanting were I not to apprise Your Excellency that the injuries received by the fleet in the action, added to the complaints of several very crazy ships, makes it quite uncertain how soon the fleet can be got to sea. One ship we have been obliged to abandon, and another is in a very doubtful state."[14]

On the evening of September 24, the date of the combined services conference, some good news was received of the arrival off the bar in New York of Rear Admiral Robert Digby in the *Prince George*, 90 guns, with the *Canada*, 74 guns, and the *Lion*, 64 guns. Digby had been sent to take over the command, and was accompanied by young Prince William, later King William IV. Rear Admiral Hood wrote to Jackson that "as the wind was against their entering the port, I went out to the *Prince George* the next morning early and had the happiness to find His Royal Highness and all on board in most perfect health." There was one other bright spot amid the general gloom of those who understood the true plight of the British. The frigate *Carysfort* providentially brought into port a captured ship bound from New England to France with a precious cargo of masts. "This was," said Graves, "a most valuable acquisition at this time of scarcity, there being hardly a spar left in the yard at New York" for the repair of his ships. Even so, the captured masts, says Professor Robert G. Albion, "were insufficient, and several of the ships had their masts patched up for want of proper materials. These masts were so weak that they could carry only a moderate sail to prevent them from tumbling over the side."[15]

Hardly had Lord Cornwallis been assured of a departure "about October 5" when delays began to threaten. On the very next day after the comforting words had been sent, Clinton reached for a little elbowroom, writing to Cornwallis: "It is supposed the necessary repairs of the fleet will retain us here to the 5th of the month, and Your Lordship must be sensible that unforeseen accidents may lengthen it out a day or two longer."

One day later Graves wrote to Stephens in London with hints of further delays: "The whole fleet are as busy as they can be, but I am very apprehensive that so much as is wanted to the fleet, such a poverty of every kind of stores and provisions, and so much to do for the army afterwards, will consume more time than was foreseen. Every exertion of mine and of any other officer in the fleet I may venture to affirm will not be wanting."[16] Two days later Admiral Graves was informed by the officers of the yard that the fleet could not be ready before October 8. Two days after that Graves was giving assurances that his ships might pass the bar on October 12.

As Hood wrote to Jackson on October 14, still from New York, "The repairs of the squadron have gone on unaccountably tedious, which has filled me with the apprehension that we shall be too late to give relief to Lord Cornwallis. I pray God grant my fears may prove abortive!"[17] Some of the delays, however, were wholly accountable, such as the accident on October 13, when "in a squall wind the *Alcide* parted her cable and fell on board the *Shrewsbury* which carried away her foreyard and bowsprit that had just been repaired. This ugly incident," said Graves, "threw us back just at the time the troops were embarked to fall down with the first division of the men-of-war from Staten Island to Sandy Hook. Two ships parted their cables at Staten Island and several drove in the North River."[18]

Among the many charges brought against the hapless Rear Admiral Graves was the claim that he refused to move on several occasions, of which this was cited as one, "until every last ship" of his fleet was in complete readiness for action. In this instance it could be said in his defense that, knowing his great numerical inferiority to De Grasse, he could hardly have afforded to spare a single one of his ships. On the other hand, it could be argued that, in making such a desperate gamble against overwhelming odds, speed was what was of primary importance if Cornwallis was to be saved. As Hood expressed it: "*Desperate* cases require *bold* remedies." (Italics his.)

On October 13 the *Torbay* and *Prince William*, hailed by Hood as "a noble acquisition, that makes my heart bound with joy," finally reached New York from Jamaica. By October 16 the departure of the expedition seemed only a few days off, but dispatches from Lord Cornwallis did not encourage hopes of breaking through into either the York or the James river. "With the French advantage of position and numbers, the enemy having collected all their naval strength between the Horse Shoe (shoal) and York spit, they think there is little to apprehend from an attempt to force either river."

When Graves wrote to Stephens on October 16, the prospects, even for getting under way, seemed very dark indeed. "The excessive want of stores and provisions and the immense repairs for a crazy and shatter'd squadron, with many cross incidents which have interven'd. has thrown back the equipment of the squadron to a great distance. They are not quite ready. They are now very short of bread, and all the ovens will not keep up the daily consumption. Several ships have parted their cables, others broke their anchors, and three been on shore; that I see no end to disappointments."[19] To Captain MacKenzie on the same day it appeared that the Navy men did "not seem to be hearty in the business, or to think that the saving of that Army is of such material consequence. One of the captains has exposed himself so much as to say that the loss of two line-of-battle ships in effecting the relief of that Army is of much more consequence than the loss of it. . . ."

By October 17, most of the ships had assembled for the purpose of taking on Clinton's troops. The commander-in-chief had exceeded his estimate of five thousand men by ordering no less than seven thousand one hundred and forty-nine of his soldiers to take their places on board the ships of the fleet, a process completed on the 18th. When finally assembled, the fleet consisted of twenty-five ships of the line, three of them three-deckers mounting ninety guns with eight additional carronades, fourteen seventy-fours, one seventy, and seven sixty-fours, the whole still under the command of Rear Admiral Graves even though Rear Admiral Digby had brought orders for Graves to proceed to Jamaica, there to be under Vice Admiral Parker, "a painful situation" in Graves's eyes. The date of their sailing was to have an ominous ring, for it was October 19, the very day on which Lord Cornwallis and his entire army laid down their arms.

In ignorance of this devastating development, Clinton and Graves sailed for the Chesapeake. "On October 24," Graves told

Stephens, "we received intelligence from James Robinson, a black man who was pilot of *H.M.S. Charon*, a white man who belonged to the Quartermaster General's department, and Jonas Rider, another black man, who had made their escape together from Yorktown, that Lord Cornwallis had capitulated on the 18th instant, the day before the fleet sailed from Sandy Hook, . . . The 26th one of our boats brought off some people from the shore near Cape Charles, who have the same report of the capitulation. The 25th *H.M.S. Nymphe* joined us from New York and brought dispatches from Lord Cornwallis dated the 15th, . . . which leave little room to question the truth of the other intelligence . . . I therefore determined to detach the *Rattlesnake* for Europe, to give the earliest information to their Lordships, that Government may be prepared to receive the particulars of so sad a catastrophe. My former letter to their Lordships did not abound in hopes of success."[20]

When Graves reached the mouth of the Chesapeake, he found De Grasse's and De Barras's mighty armada of thirty-six ships of the line arranged in a crescent before him, in a position where, as he said, "Our ships must have had the disadvantage of banks, shoals, and tides, to limit and obstruct their operations. However, we stood close into the back of the sands, to offer them battle, for two successive days." Graves would have been happy, he maintained, to have "tried the fortune of another action in free water . . . but the French showed no disposition to come out." There was no more brave talk about Clinton's scheme to penetrate the cordon of the French, and the three new fireships which Graves had purchased and christened *Lucifer*, *Volcano*, and *Conflagration* were never used.

Before the decision was made to return to New York, there was another council of war "to consult on what was to be done." According to the *Political and Military Journal*'s report, "Sir Samuel Hood was of the opinion, that the fleet should remain and block up De Grasse in the Chesapeake. In this bold advice he was supported by Rear Admiral Drake. But Admirals Graves and Digby, the two superior officers, being of a different opinion, the fleet returned to New York."[21] On October 29 it appeared to Graves that "nothing was so proper as to return with the fleet to New York," where the troops were disembarked on November 2. Hood's squadron did not come within the bar, for he deemed it his duty to resume operations in the West Indies.

A young French lieutenant, Comte de Revel, summed matters up in his diary by relating how forty-four sail appeared off the Capes, and then on October 29 "they all disappeared. They were too late. The fowl had been eaten."

22

ROCHAMBEAU
WRITES A LETTER

"We can now see how merciful to the Americans was the non-appearance of Count de Grasse at New York with his fleet...."
—Jacob H. Patton

Action by the French land army in America was to be prefaced by almost a year of inaction. The conditions which surrounded the coming of Count de Rochambeau's troops in the summer of 1780 can hardly be called auspicious. On their way across the Atlantic in the Chevalier de Ternay's squadron, the first news they received, from a captured cutter bound from Halifax to the West Indies, was of the fall of Charleston to the British under Clinton and Arbuthnot. They knew that they were in a race across the ocean with an English squadron under Rear Admiral Thomas Graves, which had left without convoy at about the same time that they had, and which would probably beat them to America. They were apprehensive that a junction might already have been effected between Graves and Arbuthnot, which would give the enemy for their reception committee a fleet about twice the size of De Ternay's. This fear was heightened by the news from another captured prize out of New York, from which they learned that Clinton and Arbuthnot had already returned from Charleston. As Count William de Deux-Ponts said: "The great number of our sick and the hardships we had experienced from lying twenty-seven days in the roads of Brest, and from being sixty-six days at sea, made us wish to avoid the meeting of the forces with which we were threatened."[1]

They headed for Rhode Island, and aside from a cannonade off Bermuda with a small squadron under Commodore Cornwallis, brother of the general, they saw nothing of the British, and arrived safely at Newport on July 11, 1780. There they received a welcome which, according to both De Deux-Ponts and Rochambeau's son the Vicomte, was not as enthusiastic as they expected it to be, "coming from the people who had brought about the most amazing revolution in the annals of the modern world." But with their announcement of their intention to pay hard cash for French purchases, the countenances of the inhabitants brightened perceptibly; and the latter were further cheered by the news that this was "only the first division of a larger reinforcement which they might expect." Another Frenchman, Mathieu Dumas, probably hit upon the true explanation of "the coldness and reserve" which Deux-Ponts thought characteristic of Americans, when he made it clear that the French were welcomed warmly by "the small number of patriots that remained in Rhode Island lately occupied by the British . . ."[2]

Rochambeau was hardly in an enviable position. A "large third" of his army had contracted the scurvy, and a number had died of it during the voyage. A week after the soldiers had been landed, on July 21, Arbuthnot and Graves appeared in Narragansett Bay with about twenty sail, not all of them of the line, but formidable enough. The French heavy guns had not yet been landed to be emplaced in the forts which the British had left, but which the French engineers found "badly constructed . . . the breastworks not having the proper thickness." Clinton was rumored to be on his way to besiege them with ten thousand troops. The news from France, brought by the frigate *Alliance* to Boston on August 16, was even worse, for it told of Rochambeau's second division blockaded in Brest by thirty-two British ships of the line.

With the help of the Rhode Island and Connecticut militia, the former British lines were hastily repaired and perfected. Even so, "our position," said Deux-Ponts, "would not have been easy, if we had had to do with a bold and skilful enemy." Luckily the British were lethargic. Rear Admiral Graves contented himself with anchoring at Martha's Vineyard in order to intercept the expected arrival of Rochambeau's second division, which never came; while Clinton, forever fearful of a Washington move against New York, remained behind his ramparts.

Fresh French fears, however, were aroused when news came of Admiral Rodney's appearance in New York with ten ships of the line on September 13. Word of this reached Rochambeau on September 18 while he was on his way to Hartford to attend a conference with Washington. After the talks, he hurried back to Newport to make what preparations he could to receive an attack by Rodney, Graves, and Clinton in overwhelming force. Deux-Ponts' mind was filled with forebodings of a "noble defeat" and of the glory to be won by "sacrificing oneself" in a losing cause. But all that Rodney did was to send four of his line ships to reinforce Graves. Clinton had been convinced that the French position in Rhode Island was much too strong to attack.

For a while the anxious French had hopes that De Guichen might save the day for them by coming north in pursuit of Rodney. But any such expectations were dashed by the arrival of the *Gentille* from Cap Français on September 30 with the information that De Guichen had gone back to Europe. This disheartening news came simultaneously with that of "the infamous treason of General Arnold." There was little in the situation which could be called encouraging. Rhode Island was completely blockaded by sea; and there would be no maritime supremacy until spring at the earliest. Washington was so threatened by Clinton that he could not even come to pay them a welcoming visit. The French forces entered upon a long and trying period of what Lafayette was to call "shameful inactivity." He felt responsible for having besought Vergennes and the King to send Rochambeau's troops to America; and now, without the second division, they could do nothing decisive on land, and De Ternay even less by sea.

The Marquis even went so far as to pretend to believe that the death of the Chevalier de Ternay from fever and high blood pressure in December, 1780, was actually caused by his mortification at his being unable to accomplish anything with his squadron. Many of the younger French officers, bored and disgusted with the chilly winter existence in Newport, sought permission to go south to join Greene, where there seemed to be some promise of action, glory, and warmth. When permission was refused, a few managed to occupy their time in travels about the New World. Otherwise, there was nothing to do but to go into winter quarters and wait, while their leaders bombarded Versailles with all manner of urgent appeals for a fleet, for money, for clothing, and for the second division.

Affairs could hardly be going worse for the American cause than in the winter and spring of 1780-81. It was the time of the mutinies, of which it may be said that the wonder was that they had not occurred before. "Money was gone and provisions were disappearing; pay had been in arrears for a year or more, and disputes arose between men and officers regarding terms of enlistment." The mutinies were finally subdued "by a mixed policy of force and compromise." Once more Washington had succeeded in holding what was left of the army together; but his language was close to despair when he told John Laurens: "Day does not follow night more certainly than it brings with it some additional proof of the impracticality of carrying on the war without the aid you were directed to solicit . . . We are at the end of our tether . . . Now or never our deliverance must come."[3]

Even in these darkest hours in the spring of 1781 there were interludes of hope. When a coastal storm seemed to break up Arbuthnot's blockade of Newport De Ternay's temporary successor Destouches made a brave sortie to the Chesapeake to co-operate with Lafayette in the effort to entrap the traitor Arnold. Destouches, whose ships were uncoppered, outmaneuvered Arbuthnot, but left the latter in possession of the Chesapeake. At least the French sailors had the satisfaction of striking a stout blow, inconclusive as it was, against British sea supremacy.

Then on March 6 Washington at last found it possible to make a formal visit to the French encampment in Rhode Island, where he was received with the honors accorded a Marshal of France. "It is impossible," wrote the Swiss Baron Gaspard de Gallatin, "to express the joy and enthusiasm with which the Americans looked upon the guarantor and defender of their liberty; they have an incomparable veneration and respect for him. . . . Rich and poor gathered that evening to drink, sing and dance. The city was illuminated with as many as ten candles per window; the Tories who failed to manifest public joy by illuminating had their windows broken by the populace. Count de Rochambeau gave a superb ball on the following evening, to which all the city's ladies of consequence were invited. General Washington opened the ball by dancing the minuet with all the grace of which a handsome gentleman is capable."[4]

The coming of spring, 1781, did not seem to promise to Washington himself anything but a continuation of the winter's bitter frustrations. On May 1, just a little over five months before Cornwallis surrendered, and about four months before the decisive naval battle of the Chesapeake, he summed up in his diary "the wants and prospects" of his army after six years of war: "Instead of having magazines filled with provisions, we have a scanty pittance scattered here and there in the different States. Instead of having our arsenals well supplied with military stores, they are poorly provided, and the workmen all leaving them." There was "no regular system of transportation established on credit," so that "military impress" had to be used, "hourly oppressing the people—souring their tempers—and alienating their affections." Worse still, the regiments of recruits requisitioned by Congress had not been provided. "Scarce any State in the Union has, at this hour, an eighth part of its quota in the field and little prospect, that I can see, of ever getting more than half." These deficiencies meant, he concluded, that instead of "having the prospect of a glorious offensive campaign before us, we have a bewildered and gloomy defensive one—unless we should receive a powerful aid of ships—land troops—and money from our generous allies and these, at present, are too contingent to build upon."[5]

Yet it was just five days later, on May 6, 1781, that the dark picture was drastically altered by the arrival in Boston of the *Concorde*, bringing the new French naval commander, Commodore Count de Barras St. Laurent, accompanied by the returning Vicomte de Rochambeau. They brought the heartening news that John Laurens' mission (backed by the pleas of Franklin, Lafayette, both Rochambeaus, and Washington) had been a remarkable success in two important particulars. He had been refused the sending of any second division (the limit in men was six hundred replacements for the first); but he had been granted a loan of six million *livres;* and could report that a fleet of twenty ships of the line commanded by Admiral de Grasse had left Brest on March 21, 1781, bound for the West Indies. They had accompanied it in the *Concorde* for a number of days.

But the really earthshaking news was contained in a paragraph of a letter from Minister of Marine de Castries to Rochambeau: "As De Grasse is master of his movements, with authority to unite or separate his forces, I trust he may control the American coasts for some time to come, and that he may co-operate with you if you are preparing any enterprise in the North."[6] Although Rochambeau had received a letter from De Grasse intended "for himself alone" saying that the admiral would come north in July or August "to release the squadron of M. de Barras," he hastened to send the inspiring news to Washington, asking him: "If the fleet from the West Indies should arrive in these waters, an event which will probably be announced beforehand by a frigate, what operations will George Washington have in view, after a juncture of French forces with his own?" Washington replied that since the garrison in New York had twice been reduced by sending reinforcements to the South, it would be advisable to merge the French and American armies on the Hudson above New York "to be ready to take advantage of any opportunity which the weakness of the enemy may afford. Should the West Indian fleet arrive on the coast . . . either to proceed to the operations against New York or against the enemy in some other quarter as circumstances should dictate."[7]

Once more Washington demonstrated both his strong preference for New York as the prime objective and his flexibility of mind in regard to other openings, should they occur. It should be remembered that the American leaders were not yet aware of Cornwallis's invasion of Virginia. It is easy, therefore, to understand Washington's conviction that New York was the place where naval superiority could be used most effectively to end the war. It was the center of enemy power and their principal base of supply. Once captured, or even strongly besieged, an anxious Clinton would almost surely be induced to strip the southern posts of British troops, thereby relieving Greene. New York's defenses were strong but not impregnable. Washington

believed that, in spite of D'Estaing's experience with the balky
pilots, a French fleet could cross the bar, and easily overpower
Graves's squadron unless strongly reinforced by Rodney. Once
New York was occupied, the enemy detachments in the South
would surrender or be overwhelmed. New York supplied the
shortest and surest pathway to victory.

On the other hand, it was easy for the supreme commander to
point out the obstacles to any plan to drive Phillips out of Virginia by meeting De Grasse at the Chesapeake. Washington cited
"the insurmountable difficult and expense of land transportation
—the waste of men in long marches (especially to the climate,
etc.) with other reasons too numerous to detail."[8] The same
objective of taking the pressure off Greene and Lafayette could
be achieved more economically by attacking New York. Washington said that he expected to have an army of ten thousand
men for the purpose within a few weeks. That would be enough,
when the French arrived from Newport, to give the allies the
requisite numerical superiority over Clinton. The best reason
of all for attacking New York was that he and his army were
already poised above it, and had been waiting for months running
into years to take the offensive.

The great change at this point in the war was psychological.
For six long years the initiative had been continuously in the
hands of the British commanders. With Washington it had
always been a question of evading or parrying the next stroke
of the enemy. It had been his assignment to guess what Howe
or Clinton or Cornwallis would do next, and then to find some
means of countering it. Now the shoe was on the other foot.
It was Clinton who must try to figure out what the French and
American allies were up to, and how to cope with their offensive.
The prospect of controlling the sea made all the difference.

These developments made imperative a conference between
the American and French commanders, which took place at
Wethersfield, Connecticut, near Hartford, on May 21, 1781,
attended by Washington and Rochambeau and their aides. De
Barras was expected but could not attend, for a British squadron
had appeared off Block Island. During the conference an intercepted letter from Germain to Clinton was brought in, showing
that the British strategy for 1781 was to contain the allied

armies in the North, conquer and occupy the southern provinces, and then to use them as a base for the invasion of the North.

At Wethersfield it was decided in substance, first, that Rochambeau's army should march to the Hudson; secondly, that the plan with the highest priority was the attack upon New York; and thirdly, that Rochambeau directly, and Washington indirectly through De la Luzerne, should beseech De Grasse to hasten northwards with ships, troops, and money to join in this attack. Washington returned to his headquarters at New Windsor to forward the preparations against New York. He wrote to Lafayette on May 31 about the Wethersfield conference and its conclusions, making it very clear that his own plan with New York as the certain objective had prevailed. It was the interception of this letter which was to mislead Sir Henry Clinton so deftly that Washington has been accused of planning its interception. To make matters worse for the British, Clinton could not hide his joy at possessing inside knowledge of the Franco-American plans.

Meanwhile Washington had become aware of the serious threat to Lafayette's small army by reason of Cornwallis's junction with Phillips and Arnold in Virginia. The only relief which he had available was General Anthony Wayne's reorganized Pennsylvania Line, amounting to only a thousand men, and a new levy of Pennsylvania, Delaware, and Maryland militia. But this move would leave Washington himself with only five thousand five hundred regulars and almost no militia, since the States were still failing to send in their quotas. Even with Rochambeau's four or five thousand men from Newport, the allies would hardly have a numerical margin great enough to justify a siege of New York.

Rochambeau returned to Newport and on May 28 wrote a letter that was to change the course of history. By this time he had heard of Cornwallis's invasion of Virginia, and was still impressed by the advantages to be gained by countering it directly. It may have been also, on his part, a desire to show Lafayette and others that the Rhode Island army was eager to undertake a difficult march to the new center of action in the South after their year of apparent lethargy. Yet Washington was his commanding officer, and had decided upon the New York attack instead of the one in Virginia. Rochambeau was in duty bound to report to De Grasse the minutes of the Wethersfield conference and he did so. But he did it in such a way that Admiral de Grasse could make a choice between the two localities.

"There are," he informed the Count, "two points at which an offensive may be made against the enemy: Chesapeake Bay and New York. The southwesterly winds and the state of distress in Virginia will probably make you prefer Chesapeake Bay, and it will be there where we think you may be able to render the greatest service, whereas you will need only two days to come from there to New York. In any case it is essential that you should send, well in advance, a frigate to inform De Barras where you are to come and also General Washington, that the first may be able to join you and that the second may co-operate with you with his army."[9]

As for the number of ships which De Grasse might be expected to bring, on the day before Rochambeau wrote, May 27, 1781, Washington received from John Laurens at Versailles a letter informing him that "a fleet of twenty sail of the line was on its departure for the West Indies, twelve of which were to proceed to this coast where it was probable that they might arrive in the month of July."[10] Thus at this date the American expectations in regard to the size of De Grasse's fleet were almost exactly the same as Admiral Rodney's own fatal estimate in August.

Just before the *Concorde* sailed from Boston on June 20 bearing Rochambeau's letters to De Grasse, the *Sagittaire* had come in on June 10, bearing a letter from De Grasse to Rochambeau dated March 29. It said that "The forces I command are sufficient to execute the views as to the offensive which it is to the interest of the allied powers to carry out in order to bring an honorable peace . . ." The admiral said that he expected to be at San Domingo at the end of June, and that it would be July 15, at the earliest, before he could come to the North American coast. He added: "Seeing the short time I can stay in the country, which in any event the season will force me to leave, it is important that everything which can serve in the success of your projects shall not delay action a moment."[11]

Washington learned of Rochambeau's recommendations to

De Grasse on June 9-10, and disapproved of the suggestion that the admiral stop at the Chesapeake on his way north. He asked Rochambeau, if the frigate carrying the dispatches had not sailed, to change that sentence in such a way as to leave the matter entirely to De Grasse's judgment and the intelligence he received on the spot. He reminded Rochambeau of the Wethersfield conclusion that "Sandy Hook was mentioned as the most desirable point." But the ship in question had sailed for the West Indies before Washington's letter was received by Rochambeau.

Referring to Rochambeau's letters to De Grasse of May 26 and June 11, Charlemagne Tower, Jr., says: "They are, with regard to their results, among the most important historical documents of the Revolution, for they laid the basis upon which was established the co-operation of the allied forces in the Yorktown campaign."[12] Nothing could be more misleading, however, than to view the situation of the two allied commanders in July and August as a struggle between Washington, insisting upon New York as the unalterable objective, and Rochambeau, somehow conniving secretly with De Grasse to shift the focus to the Chesapeake. Each general had a strong preference which he urged upon the other, but each was enough of an opportunist to leave the final decision to circumstances. Washington lacked troops, and he had been told that De Grasse lacked time. The two shortages finally doomed his dream of winning New York.

One can trace the effect of events upon Washington's New York plan in his diary and his letters to Lafayette. On July 20 he wrote in the former: ". . . the uncertainties under which we labor . . . have rendered it impossible for me to do more than to prepare, first, for the enterprise against New York as agreed to at Wethersfield, and secondly for the relief of the Southern States if after all my efforts, and earnest application to these States it should be found at the arrival of Count de Grasse I had neither men nor means adequate to the first object . . ." Ten days later Washington confided to Lafayette that ". . . from the change of circumstances with which the removal of part of the enemy's force from Virginia to New York will be attended, it is more than possible, that we shall also entirely change our plan of operations . . . Our views must now be turned towards endeavoring to expel the enemy totally from the Southern States, if we find ourselves incompetent to the siege of New York."[13]

Eight years afterwards, on July 14, 1788, young Noah Webster, who wanted to compose a history of the recent war, wrote to Washington at Mount Vernon asking him pointblank whether "the preparations made at the time for attacking New York were the result of a preconcerted plan between yourself and the Count de Grasse, or merely a feint?" Washington replied that "The point of attack was not absolutely agreed upon . . . because it could not be foreknown where the enemy would be the most susceptible of impression . . ." He averred that "it was determined by me, (nearly twelve months beforehand), at all hazards to give out and cause it to be believed by the highest military as well as civil officers, that New York was the destined place of attack, for the important purpose of inducing the eastern and middle States to make greater exertions in furnishing specific supplies than they otherwise would have done, as well as for the interesting purpose of rendering the enemy less prepared elsewhere . . . it was the fixed determination *to strike the enemy in the most vulnerable quarter* so as to ensure success with moral certainty, as our affairs were then in the most ruinous train imaginable . . . I can only add, that it never was in contemplation to attack New York, unless the garrison should first have been so far disgarnished to carry on the southern operation, as to render our success in the siege of that place as infallible as any future military event can ever be made." (Italics his.)[14]

Washington in 1788 may have allowed his hindsight to influence his memory somewhat. The exact degree of his sincerity in urging that New York be attacked is hard to determine. Plainly the initiative had passed into the hands of Admiral de Grasse. It was the timing of his arrival which would decide the enemy's "most vulnerable quarter." Had he been able to appear before August 16, when Rear Admiral Graves returned from his wild-goose chase to Massachusetts Bay, the French fleet would have found New York completely bare of naval protection; and the war might have been won by the capture of Clinton's army rather than that of Cornwallis. Even after Graves had come back, during the period from August 16 to the date of Hood's arrival, August 28, the city was defended by only five effective line ships.

But the size of Washington's army, as compared with that of Clinton, and the strength of the New York defenses were another matter, as Washington discovered when he carried out a reconnaissance in force along the Harlem River front on July 22-23. In his letter to De Grasse of June 11, Rochambeau had been obliged to say: "I cannot conceal from you that Washington has not half the troops he counted on having, and I believe, though he is reticent on this, that he has not at present six thousand men . . ."[15] By August 1, 1781, Washington himself was writing in his *Diary:* "Everything would have been in perfect readiness to commence the operation against New York, if the States had furnished their quotas of men agreeable to my requisitions." Furthermore, the prospects for filling the ranks were so poor that he "could hardly see a ground upon which to continue my preparations against New York . . . and therefore I turned my views more seriously (than I had before done) to an operation to the Southward . . ." and "a hope of Count de Grasse's bringing a land force with him."[16]

Washington's waning prospects of having a large enough army to overpower Clinton's forces in New York received a further setback on August 14, 1781, when transports from Bremen brought twenty-six hundred German reinforcements to that city. Previously, on July 4, Clinton had profited by a peculiar arrangement in Florida which made the Americans very angry at the Spaniards. When a Spanish expedition under Don Bernard de Galvez, with the help of a French squadron commanded by Commodore de Monteil, finally captured Pensacola, Florida, the British garrison of about twelve hundred men were paroled on terms forbidding their use in St. Augustine and Jamaica only. A large part of them were promptly shipped to Clinton in New York.

These accretions raised the total strength of Clinton's army to upwards of ten thousand men, of whom perhaps five thousand could be used for an offensive. Germain's order forbidding Cornwallis to send any of his men to New York had blasted Clinton's long-cherished plan to retake Philadelphia. But there remained the inviting target of Rhode Island, where a combined assault with Rear Admiral Graves might overwhelm De Barras's small fleet and the tiny remaining garrison. In Clinton's mind this was "a most important enterprise" twice delayed, once until Arbuthnot's departure and again by Graves's strange dash toward Boston. Then when Graves had returned, there had to be a further wait while the *Robust* and *Prudent* were being repaired. With Hood's coming on August 28, just as Clinton and Graves, with transports loaded, were about to leave for Newport, the whole Rhode Island scheme collapsed, since, in Clinton's words: "Intelligence brought me that evening over Long Island assured us that Monsieur de Barras' squadron, with transports, storeships, etc., had sailed from Newport on the 25th for the Chesapeake." The Rhode Island expedition, it seemed, had "unfortunately been too long delayed." Graves and Hood sailed off to fight the battle of the Chesapeake; and at about the same time the news came that "the allied army had suddenly broke up its camp on the 29th."[17]

23

WASHINGTON AND
ROCHAMBEAU MARCH SOUTH

"If all these apparently fortuitous occurrences were the result of previous arrangement and premeditation, they display a generalship to which military annals have furnished no parallel."
—Paul Allen

Great decisions made by leaders at the summit, in order to become effective, have to be accompanied by smaller decisions made by their subordinates. This was true of the campaign which culminated at Yorktown. The British failed to achieve harmonious teamwork among their chiefs, while the French and American allies, who might have been expected to quarrel over matters of precedence, co-operated handsomely. This was due in large part to the way in which several French officers of high rank agreed willingly to accept orders from generals and admirals to whom they were technically superior. That proud European aristocrats deigned to act in this manner was something of a surprise.

One of them was the Count de Barras, friend of D'Estaing and commander of the Rhode Island squadron. The question was, what should he do with his seven ships of the line after Rochambeau's army left Newport? In his letter to De Grasse, written on May 26, 1781, Rochambeau had said that Washington had been pressing De Barras "to go with the French troops to Chesapeake Bay. M. de Barras has shown the impossibility of this . . . He says that as soon as the army leaves, he will go to Boston, following out his orders." Rochambeau was of the opinion that five hundred American militia could hold the works at Newport, "which the enemy does not appear to be in a position to attack."

Three days later the French general added a postscript informing De Grasse that, after several councils of war attended by men from both services, De Barras had decided to remain at Newport with four hundred of De Choisy's men and one thousand American militia, sending the siege artillery and other stores to Providence. One of the councils of war lasted for five hours; and this decision which it reached turned out to be important for two reasons: it made possible De Barras's generous response to the call to join De Grasse at the Chesapeake when it came; and his continued presence in Rhode Island distracted the attention of Clinton and Graves from the real source of danger to themselves.

De Barras had been given discretionary authority by Minister de Castries to cruise for British ships off the Banks of Newfoundland, an area which gave promise of being a lucrative source of prize money. Although he shared with De Grasse the permanent rank of commodore, De Barras was the senior of the two. He knew that if he came south to join De Grasse he would lose his independent command, and would be under De Grasse's orders, since the latter had been given the local and temporary grade of Lieutenant General (or Rear Admiral). This makes all the more remarkable his statement that "No one is more interested than I in the arrival of M. de Grasse in these seas. He was my junior; he has just been made Lieutenant General. As soon as I know that he is within reach of this place, I shall set sail to serve under him; I shall serve in this one campaign more, but not in another."[1]

On June 7, De Barras gave a grand farewell dinner on his flagship *Duc de Bourgogne* to sixty citizens of Newport of both sexes. But he was still hoping to be off for Newfoundland on August 5, when the *Concorde* returned from the West Indies with the electrifying news from De Grasse that he would be leaving San Domingo for the Chesapeake soon after August 1 with his entire fleet of twenty-eight line ships, three thousand troops, and (he hoped) a large sum of money; but that he could stay only until October 15. These joyful tidings were sent on to Washington and Rochambeau, reaching them on August 14. Rochambeau immediately sent his aide Count Fersen to beseech De Barras to make good on his promise to come south with all his ships and the train of siege artillery.

Even as late as August 17 De Barras's mind was not wholly made up, for he wrote to Rochambeau on that date expressing anxiety about coming out to sea with his ships against a possibly superior English fleet in southern waters, and spoke of his other plans to go north along the Maine coast toward Newfoundland. But eventually he was prevailed upon to load De Choisy, his troops, the siege cannons, and fifteen hundred barrels of salt meat on board his vessels, leaving Newport on August 21 with only a few hundred men on guard there.

Long before these events, in the early days of June, the regiments of Rochambeau's army were preparing to break camp in order to join Washington on the Hudson, supposedly to attack New York. As Gallatin says, after so many months of inactivity they were "impatient to see the country, the American army, and to be employed in doing something useful to the American cause." Rochambeau wrote to De Barras about their departure from Newport: it was "without leaving a man behind us, except ten lovesick soldiers from the regiment of Soissonais, who wanted to return to see their sweethearts at Newport, and for whom I am going to send . . ." He was surprised at the smoothness of their progress, which enabled them, as he wrote to Count de Ségur, to make "two hundred miles in eleven days' march; there are not four provinces in the kingdom of France, where we could have traveled with as much order and economy, and without wanting for anything."[2] There were many favorable comments from Americans about the order and discipline of his army. To cause as little inconvenience as possible to the inhabitants along their routes, the brigades departed at one-day intervals. The welcomes they received were cordial. At Plainfield, Connecticut, there was a great concourse of people, among them "many very handsome women," said Count de Gallatin. Windham seemed to him "just like a French village"; and at Bolton they provided music in front of the camp, and there was dancing on the green.

The junction of the two armies took place at Philipsburg,

after a forced march by the second French brigade, on July 6. Rochambeau's men occupied the camp prepared for them about four miles southeast of White Plains, across a valley from the Americans. Gallatin reports that there was, alas, little fraternization of officers or men because of the language barrier. General Washington expressed his thanks "for the unremitting zeal with which Rochambeau had prosecuted his march," with special praise for the regiment of Saintonge for the spirited manner in which "they continued and supported their march without one day's respite." On July 7 Count de Rochambeau reviewed the American army; and on the following day Washington did the same for the French. There were expressions of surprise on the part of some of the French officers at the size of the American contingent. Count de Deux-Ponts said: They told us at Newport that the American army had ten thousand men. It has however only twenty-five hundred or three thousand men. But this," he added, "is not a very big lie for Americans."[3]

During June, 1781, Washington had moved his army down from New Windsor to Peekskill, and began minor operations toward King's Bridge. All these motions convinced Clinton that an attack upon New York was imminent, and that every one of his garrison would be needed to defend the city. By the first of August, however, Washington had become pretty well convinced, as his diary shows, that any such massive assault on New York was out of the question. De Grasse, of course, decided matters for him, as far as coming to New York was concerned. But Washington had still to make his own great decision. His diary says, after the receipt of the news from De Grasse on August 14: "Matters having now come to a crisis—and a decisive plan to be determined on—I was obliged, from the shortness of Count de Grasse's promised stay on this coast—the apparent disinclination in their naval officers to force the harbor of New York— and the feeble compliance of the States to my requisitions for men, hitherto, and little prospect of greater exertion in future, to give up all idea of attacking New York; and instead thereof to remove the French troops and a detachment from the American army to the Head of Elk to be transported to Virginia for the purpose of co-operating with the force from the West Indies against the troops in that State."[4]

Washington had two months and one day to march the two armies some four hundred miles and defeat the enemy before De Grasse's promised naval superiority would disappear. On August 15 he gave the order to the troops to be ready to move. Two days later he wrote to Admiral de Grasse: "It has been judged expedient to turn our attention toward the South." If Clinton was to be kept immobilized, however, everything must be done to simulate a continuing intention to make New York the objective. This required absolute secrecy in the two allied armies; and it was astonishingly well preserved.

Dr. James Thacher with the American army noted in his *Journal* that when orders came to move on August 19, "their real object became a subject of great speculation. Ostensibly the investment of the city of New York is in contemplation—preparations in all quarters for some months past indicate this to be the object of our combined operations . . . General Washington and Count Rochambeau have crossed the North River, and it is supposed for the purpose of reconnoitering the enemy's posts from the Jersey shore. A field for an extensive encampment has been marked out on the Jersey side, and a number of ovens have been erected and fuel provided for the purpose of baking bread for the army. But General Washington possesses a capacious mind, full of resources, and he resolves and matures his great plans and designs under an impenetrable veil of secrecy."[5]

On the same day, as the armies set forth in a heavy rain, Count de Deux-Ponts was equally in the dark about their destination. "We are in perfect ignorance," he wrote, "whether we are going against New York, or whether we are going to Virginia to attack Lord Cornwallis, who now occupies Portsmouth with a considerable force." Betting about the matter, he added, "was running high." He was astonished that their crossing of the Hudson river drew so little attention from the British. "An enemy of any boldness or any skill would have seized an opportunity so favorable for him and so embarrassing for us, as that of our crossing the North River. I do not understand the indifference with which General Clinton considers our movements."[6]

In retrospect it may appear that Washington and Rochambeau were only doing the obvious thing under the circumstances; but at the time their march must have seemed a very arduous, expensive, and risky enterprise. Viewed from the landward side, Cornwallis's concentration of his entire army on a poorly fortified peninsula did offer alluring possibilities. But actually they were almost too good to be true. For surely, before De Grasse could reach the Chesapeake and gain maritime control, Cornwallis would have done the sensible thing, namely—move all or part of his army by sea to New York or Charleston. Word was sent to Lafayette to keep the British general from escaping by land in any direction: a difficult assignment with what forces Lafayette and Wayne had at their disposal. But on the ocean side the allied generals could do nothing but wait for De Grasse's coming, and hope that he would arrive in time.

Washington left Major General Heath to guard West Point and the Hudson highlands with thirty-five hundred men opposing perhaps three times that number; and set out with about twenty-five hundred Continentals under Major General Lincoln with Rochambeau's four thousand French regulars. Hazen's regiment and the Jersey troops were ordered to the heights near Chatham, where a French army bakery had been set up, "to veil our real movements and create apprehensions for Staten Island." Washington gave strict orders that no woman camp-follower (and there were many) was "to ride in waggons or walk in the ranks" or be issued rations during the march south. The American army crossed the Hudson at Kings Ferry, followed by the French from August 22-25. Marching in three columns, the two armies preserved through August 28 the appearance of an attack upon Staten Island and then New York. On August 30 the column on the left flank headed toward Sandy Hook as if to cover the entrance of a French fleet. Not until August 29 did the other columns break away toward Princeton and Trenton, where they were to assemble for the crossing of the Delaware. Washington's *finesse* had worked perfectly. It was not until September 2 that Clinton was fully convinced that an immediate attack upon New York was not to take place.

Undoubtedly the British commander-in-chief had been duped, although he stoutly maintained that "the moment Mr. Washington crossed the North River, I concluded he had dropped his design against New York for the present. But, under the persuasions that influenced me, I could not from thence infer he proposed moving his whole force to the southward, though I judged it possible he might send a detachment thither." Clinton's overpowering obsession was still the safety of New York. His logic seems to have run in this groove: Washington would never think of taking his army south unless he had command of the sea; we know that the Royal Navy *always* retains command of the sea; therefore Washington cannot be moving his army to the South. Like Admiral Rodney, he could not imagine that his opponent would risk his entire force in the pursuit of a distant, and greater objective. According to his arithmetic, "my whole force at that period . . . did not exceed ten thousand men . . . reducing my acting army to at most four thousand . . . how was it in my power to have stopped him even with twice as many troops as he had?"[7] Clinton obdurately insisted that he was facing twelve thousand allies instead of an actual seven thousand.

As already observed, during the last two weeks of August Sir Henry's mind had been focused on his pet project of destroying De Barras at Newport in a joint operation with Rear Admiral Graves. He was well aware that Admiral de Grasse might be expected during the hurricane season in the Antilles. The one thing that was fixed in his mind on that subject was Admiral Rodney's promise, several times repeated, to watch De Grasse's movements "like a lynx," and to maintain inviolate the British supremacy at sea. It was perhaps Clinton's very awareness of Cornwallis's dependence upon seapower, as well as of his own, which kept him from leaving New York to attack Washington and Rochambeau, or even Heath. This does not explain his miserable inertia at the time the allied armies crossed the Hudson. But it does indicate that, on his premises, his later inaction was not a simple case of being hoodwinked. For him to leave New York in pursuit of the enemy would not only expose that city to largely imaginary dangers of attack by Heath; it would, as Professor Wallace says, "forfeit the advantage of sea power which could move him swiftly to either Rhode Island or Yorktown as necessary."

One can see why Clinton, after the event, nursed some of the grievances he did against his fellow commanders. He had Sir George Rodney's promise, not only that De Grasse's motions would be watched and reported, but also that Graves would be reinforced adequately and in plenty of time should the French admiral head his way. The first promise was not well kept, and various misfortunes overtook what gestures Rodney made in that direction. The second promise was fulfilled, but only in part, by Sir Samuel Hood's arrival at New York on August 28 with his fourteen of the line. Even so, Clinton could say that he had been assured in Hood's letter to him of August 25 that his squadron was "equal fully to defeat any designs of the enemy, let De Grasse bring or send what ships he may in aid of those under De Barras."[8] That, alas, turned out to be an empty piece of boastfulness.

Thus many factors, including bouts of ill-health with periods of blindness, added to Sir Henry's confusion. With marked understatement, he wrote to Cornwallis on September 2: "It would seem that Mr. Washington is moving an army to the southward with an appearance of haste." At that same moment Washington was already in Philadelphia on a hot, dusty afternoon, writing an anxious letter to Lafayette. The general had had word on August 29 from a trusted observer at Sandy Hook, Brigadier General David Forman of the New Jersey Militia, that he had sighted a British fleet of eighteen ships, later identified as fourteen of the line and four frigates. Added to Graves's squadron in New York, this would give Rodney about as many as De Grasse was bringing. Said Washington to Lafayette: "But my dear Marquis, I am distressed beyond expression, to know what is become of the Count de Grasse, and for fear the English Fleet, by occupying the Chesapeake (towards which my last accounts say they were steering) should frustrate all our flattering prospects in that quarter. I am also not a little solicitous for the Count de Barras, who was to have sailed from Rhode Island on the 23rd Ulto. and from whom I have heard nothing since that time. Of many contingencies we will hope for the most propitious events . . . If you get any thing New from any quarter, send it I pray you *on the Spur of Speed*, for I am almost all impatience and anxiety." (Italics his.)[9]

The French army arrived in Philadelphia on September 3 and 4, and, having halted to burnish its arms and dust its white uniforms, says Baron de Gallatin, "made a most impressive entrance . . . parading three miles through the city," which he described

as "*fort belle*" with its checkerboard of streets and "*la plus com-
merçante des États-Unis.*"

The Philadelphians, accustomed only to fife-and-drum corps,
were especially delighted by "the complete band of music" in
the parade. According to Count de Deux-Ponts, the French
found that Congress was in session, and "we paid it the honors
which the King ordered us to pay. The thirteen members took
off their thirteen hats at each salute of the flags and of the officers."[10]

Long before leaving the Hudson, grumbling about the lack of
back pay among the Americans was continuous. At Dobbs Ferry
on August 2, 1781, Colonel Ebenezer Huntington of a Connecticut regiment wrote to his brother Andrew Huntington of Nor-
wich, merchant and member of the legislature: "From the repeated promises of His Excellency the Governor and Council
to the Committee, previous to their leaving Connecticut, we have
from time encouraged the officers and soldiers to wait with patience, and that they would without any doubt receive some
money soon; they have waited with earnestness, but are now
almost outrageous; they complain of the ill usage they receive
from the State, the more they suffer the more the State insults
them by their neglect, you have no right to expect their services
a moment longer . . . You obliged them to loan you two years,
and now withhold the interest. They have since the loaning of
the two years served you eighteen months, and have received
three months' nominal pay in Old Continental money (at
seventy-five for one). We have borne till we can bear no longer.
You must pay us in solids, or find other servants, and those who
ask no wages. . . . We are serving with the French Army, where
the officers dine in luxury and give us invitations to their tables,
we cannot go to them, because we cannot return the compliment."[11]

At Philadelphia the complaints reached *fortissimo*. There were
even those who said that that city was the end of the line for
them unless they received at least one month's back pay. Robert
Morris was applied to, but even that financial wizard could not,
from American sources, produce the required sum. Luckily John
Laurens had some French aid available; and Morris was able to
borrow about twenty thousand hard dollars' worth from Ro-

chambeau, who divided between the two armies all the money that was left in his coffers. One more crisis had been surmounted; but the wary Continentals were not overly optimistic about what, in the way of payment, was to come. As Colonel Huntington said to his brother: "If we meet with such treatment from you when our services are so much wanted, what can we expect at the close of the campaign (should it be glorious) when you have no further need of our service, but insult and injury in triplicate proportion from what we have already received."

Washington's tense anxiety about both of the French fleets continued until September 5, the day of the battle of the Chesapeake at sea and far beyond his ken. He was on the road just beyond Chester, Pennsylvania, when a messenger coming from the south met him with dispatches. Soon he was holding in his hands a momentous letter from Admiral Count de Grasse announcing that he had anchored his fleet of twenty-eight ships of the line in Lynnhaven Bay, had made contact with the Marquis de Lafayette, and was landing the more than three thousand French troops he had brought with him from the West Indies. Washington's behavior on receiving this news was for him unprecedented. Up to that moment, said Count de Deux-Ponts, he had impressed all the French by "his dignified address, the simplicity of his manners, and his mild gravity." At Chester, however, "his features, his physiognomy, his deportment—all were changed in an instant. He put aside his character as arbiter of North America and contented himself for a moment with that of a citizen, happy at the good fortune of his country. A child, whose every wish had been gratified, would not have experienced a sensation more lively, and I believe that I am doing honor to the feelings of this rare man, in endeavoring to express all their ardor."[12]

Wheeling his horse about, Washington galloped back to Chester, where he knew the barge in which Rochambeau was travelling would soon arrive. When it came in sight, General Washington was seen on the shore waving his arms and his hat for joy. When Rochambeau landed, it was to be embraced by Washington amid a tumult of rejoicing which spread throughout their armies. General Weedon wrote to Lafayette on September 5 from Fredericksburg: "The business with his Lordship in this State will very soon be at an end, for suppose you know e'er this that he have got him handsomely in a pudding bag with five thousand land forces and about sixty ships including transports . . . if our stars don't most wonderfully deceive us, we shall shortly do his business."[13]

There were more anxious moments ahead for the generalissimo of the combined armies. He pushed on to Head of Elk, hoping to find shipping that would save his troops many miles of marching by land. Captain de Saint-Césaire of De Grasse's fleet was there to meet him, but not nearly enough shipping was available to transport both armies down Chesapeake Bay to join Lafayette and Saint-Simon at Williamsburg. The first detachment, which left on September 9, was so delayed by contrary winds that it did not reach the James River until September 19. Washington set off in search of more ships by way of Baltimore on his way with Rochambeau to spend a few days at Mount Vernon, which he had not seen since May 4, 1775—or for over six years. On the way he learned that De Grasse had sailed out of Lynnhaven Bay on September 5, and had not yet returned. "Being apprehensive that we were not assured of the security of our navigation in the Bay," he sent a hasty stop order to the Head of Elk that no more troops were to leave there until further notice.

This ban was not lifted until September 14, when, upon his arrival at the French camp at Williamsburg, Washington "received the pleasing intelligence that the Count de Grasse, who had put to sea on the 5th in pursuit of the British fleet, had returned to his former station at Cape Henry, having driven the British from the coast, taken two of their frigates, and effected a junction with the Count de Barras."[14] It was Count de Barras who, arriving on September 10, quickly sent transports to the upper Chesapeake to bring down the remainder of the armies.

24

THE SIEGE
AND SURRENDER
AT YORKTOWN

*"The blow was on the whole perhaps the heaviest that has
ever fallen on the British Army."*
—Sir John Fortescue, *A History of the British Army*

It is one of the ironies of historical recording that we have many
more personal accounts of the siege of Yorktown than of the
battle of the Chesapeake which made it possible. The naval encounter had sealed Lord Cornwallis's fate, provided Admiral de
Grasse, who had sworn that he must leave for the West Indies
on October 15, would maintain his blockade of the Chesapeake
long enough to prevent any relief from New York; and provided
the siege, at better than two-to-one odds, which made it, as Washington said, "reducible to calculation," was terminated swiftly.
There was much hard digging of trenches, laborious dragging of
siege guns, and some rugged fighting to be done before the
British army could surrender with honor.

Some time was required for the news of the French sea victory
on September 5 to reach Rochambeau and Washington; and it
took even longer for them to appreciate fully the significance of
what had been accomplished. The allied generals had been
deeply distressed by the news of De Grasse's sudden departure
from Lynnhaven Bay to fight Graves's fleet, his continued absence, and even more by hearing that two British frigates (the
Iris and *Richmond*) had appeared in the Chesapeake four days
afterwards. Could it be that the French admiral had been defeated, and all their promising plans thrown into disarray?

Not until the night of September 14 did Rochambeau receive
from the unhurried Admiral de Grasse a letter giving him a cir-
cumstantial account of the September 5 battle. In his diary
Washington described it as "a partial engagement . . . with Admiral Graves whom he [De Grasse] had driven back to Sandy
Hook," with the result, as he wrote to Governor Thomas Sim
Lee on the following day, that "the Bay is now secure."[1] One
French officer at least, Count de Deux-Ponts, grasped the full
value of De Grasse's achievement, writing in his *Journal* that
"This victory of the Count was of great importance to the allied
army. If the French had been defeated in this action, it would
have left the British in the possession of Chesapeake Bay, and
would have thwarted the plans of General Washington for the
capture of Yorktown, and of the British army."[2] Washington
himself was shortly to see the light. On October 19, the day of
Cornwallis's surrender, the general wrote to Major General William Heath these perceptive words: "The naval engagement appears to have been of much greater importance than was at first
estimated."[3]

One of the principal reasons why De Grasse's sea victory did
not attract more attention was because of a widespread preoccupation with his present and future intentions. The admiral had
been dissuaded from attacking Cornwallis before the arrival of
the northern armies, but he was still bursting with impatience to
use his forces against the British before he had to depart. "The
fifteenth of October is near at hand," he had written to Washington on September 2.

Soon after arriving at Williamsburg, Washington had asked
for an interview with the French admiral, who replied promptly
that he would be delighted to receive Washington and Rochambeau with their staffs on board his flagship, and would send a
small British prize, the *Queen Charlotte*, to transport them. Taking General Knox with them, the generals sailed out on September 17 to the massive *Ville de Paris*, where they were ceremoni-
ously received. It is said that the admiral, already an admirer of
Washington, embraced the dignified Virginian, as tall as himself,
kissed him on both cheeks, and called him "*Mon cher petit gén-
éral!*" causing Knox "to collapse with laughter."

In the course of a long conference, the generals were told once

more that the fleet's stay must be short, not one day beyond the
end of October. De Grasse expressed his willingness to provide
eighteen hundred to two thousand sailors and marines for one
last grand assault upon Yorktown if they should be needed, and
whatever heavy naval guns could be mounted upon land fortifications. But the admiral refused bluntly to consider a second
campaign against Wilmington or Charleston after Yorktown,
pleading the unsuitability of his ships for seaport attacks. North
America was, after all, a side-excursion for him. The rich Caribbean was the real bone of imperial contention. There was a splendid dinner on the *Ville de Paris*, with all the captains of the fleet
in attendance. As the guests departed, all thirty-six battleships
broke out flags, dressed shrouds and tops, and fired "royal"
salutes. Thanks to bad weather, it took the *Queen Charlotte*
three days to return the generals to Williamsburg.

Soon after this allied love-feast Admiral de Grasse was deeply
troubled by reports of British naval reinforcements, under Rear
Admiral Robert Digby, which were said to be about to arrive in
New York and to number from three to ten ships. "The enemy
are beginning to be almost equal to us," he wrote to Washington
on September 23, "and it would be imprudent of me to put myself in a position where I could not engage them in battle should
they attempt to come here with succors."[4] Having been caught
once by Graves at anchor on a lee shore, De Grasse announced
that he was leaving the Chesapeake immediately in order to meet
the returning enemy in the open sea. He would leave only two
of his line ships to blockade the York River, and the four frigates
which he had previously stationed there. He would not take
away Saint-Simon's corps, since his sole purpose in going was to
secure sufficient sea room to maneuver against the British. There
could, of course, be no guarantee that he would be able to return.

Word of his intentions produced consternation and "painful
anxiety" among the land forces; and on September 25 brought
forth fervent appeals from Washington, Rochambeau, and Lafayette, all of them earnestly beseeching him at all costs to remain in the Chesapeake. De Grasse called a council of the flag
officers, who advised him to stay. Another crisis had been narrowly averted. The good news reached Washington on September 27 that the Chesapeake would continue to be secure. Thank-

ing De Grasse, he declared that his action proved "that a great mind knows how to make personal sacrifices to secure an important general good." On the very next day the allied armies began their march to invest Yorktown. Leaving at about five o'clock in the morning, they proceeded together "about seven miles" where the roads parted, the American army taking the right, and the French the left, to within two miles of Yorktown." About noon they met the first British pickets, who were quickly driven back, and by nightfall, "the line being formed, all the troops, officers and men, lay upon their arms during the night."

What distinguished the American army from the French was not only the lack of smartness in appearance, but an almost complete lack of acquaintance with the kind of operation they were jointly to undertake. With the exception of Generals Steuben and Lincoln, none of them had ever been present at a siege of the full-dress variety, and Lincoln had been besieged rather than a besieger. The rest had known war as an endurance contest of marching and countermarching, of improvising and making-do, of unsystematic skirmishing and the avoidance, when possible, of formal battles against prepared positions. The sort of men who composed Washington's army are described by Chevalier d'Ancteville, an engineer officer with Saint-Simon's corps, as: "Six regiments of regulars, disciplined, hardened, and in condition to fight in the line . . . about sixteen hundred men; twenty-five hundred militiamen of the country; and five hundred riflemen or mountaineers . . . these last two troops are not in uniform, they wear baggy breeches with or without shoes . . . good marksmen for skirmishing in the woods, but not for fighting in the line . . . All are sober and patient, living on corn meal and enduring privations or delays without murmuring, they are able to face fatigue and long marches, very valuable qualities which make of them a true light infantry . . . most of them are handsome men . . . There are also one hundred and fifty dragoons well mounted and drilled, and managing their horses well."[5]

These adaptable Americans were about to find themselves in a world new to them: the eighteenth-century world of military science according to the rules laid down by that greatest of military engineers of his century, Sebastian Le Prestre de Vauban (1633-1707). It was Vauban who had himself conducted fifty-three sieges, and had constructed innumerable fortresses to withstand them. He had his counterparts at Yorktown in MM. de Vernon and de Menonville, chief engineer and chief designer of the trenches respectively. Under their direction, both French and American soldiers were soon busy making gabions, fascines, and saucissons to protect the hundreds of diggers. The way to save lives was by pick and shovel.

It was now the superb French siege guns brought by De Barras, and some that had been hauled by land all the way from West Point, which came to the fore. As Napoleon said later: "In a siege it is the artillery that takes a stronghold; the infantry simply assists." It would take time, however, to bring the heavy siege pieces forward and emplace them. Washington declared that it was "of the utmost importance that the Heavy Artillery should be brought forward without a moment's loss of time." Meanwhile to everyone's surprise, including Tarleton's, Earl Cornwallis made almost no attempt to interfere with the preliminary operations against him, or to break out of the iron ring that was being forged about him on land. His lack of enterprise can only be explained by his mistaken confidence in Clinton's promise of a speedy relief expedition from New York. He had sent Colonels Dundas and Tarleton across the mile-wide river to Gloucester with seven hundred men, keeping six thousand in Yorktown, plus a thousand sailors from the shipping.

Yorktown had once been a flourishing tobacco port, but it had become a sleepy hamlet of about sixty houses, situated upon a bluff thirty feet above the York River. It was anything but a fortress capable of withstanding a long siege. Cornwallis did what he could to strengthen its earthworks, aided by about two thousand Negro slaves who had fled from their American owners in the hope of gaining their freedom. The weather continued to be very warm. The Earl had gained the reputation of being the most aggressive, unyielding fighter among the British generals in America. Why he made such a weak defense is hard to explain. Or why he told his soldiers such fairy tales as that the French "had come to the place to procure a quantity of tobacco, and if they could not be supplied here, the fleet would set sail in eight or ten days at the farthest and leave the American continent."[6]

Cornwallis was evidently angry at Clinton, and seems to have

decided to leave everything to his commander-in-chief. His only
real hope was to delay the inexorable advance of the allied hosts
until Clinton could hasten to his relief with four or five thousand
men, at least. On September 29, when the enemy troops were
already "about a cannon's shot" from his outer lines, he received
Clinton's letter of September 24 indicating that the New York
armada would set sail on October 5. On the arrival of that hope-
ful message, Cornwallis decided, as he replied to Clinton that
evening ". . . to retire this night within the works, and I have no
doubt, if relief arrives in any reasonable time, York and Gloucester will both be in possession of His Majesty's troops."

This abrupt abandonment of his outer defenses seemed to
General Anthony Wayne to be "an indication of confused pre-
cipitation." It angered Tarleton, who said it was premature,
especially in view of the need of gaining time by every possible
means. The outer works were strong enough to have been
stoutly contested, at least until heavy artillery was brought
against them. Delay would give Cornwallis a chance to strengthen
his inner works; but he preferred to rely instead upon "the labor
and firmness of the soldiers" to hold the second line of fortifications. The French and Americans lost no time in occupying the
three redoubts which had been presented to them, and in building a fourth.

Yorktown was now to be reduced by purely scientific European methods of siege warfare, which avoided costly frontal attacks by the infantry and permitted the slowly advancing batteries of artillery to do the work. Washington's orderly book
listed fifty-five paragraphs of regulations for the "Service of the
Siege" as prescribed by Vauban and Vernon. Once the town had
been invested, the first step was the construction of lines of
countervallation to protect the camp of the besiegers against sor-
ties by the garrison. The allies expected that Cornwallis would
make "many a severe sortie"; but in fact he made only one, and
that quite futile.

The first move against the British was made on the night of
October 6, which saw the opening of the first parallel (or
trench) at a distance of eight hundred yards. This was undertaken "in the greatest silence" by fifteen hundred fatigue men
guarded by twenty-eight hundred men under arms. Although

the defenders opened fire, the allied losses were "extremely in-
considerable." There was a prescribed ceremony for the opening
of the first parallel during a siege, but a strange piece of ritual
was added to it when a detachment of American light infantry
under Colonel Alexander Hamilton was given the honor of
marching into the trench with massed drums and fifes and flying
colors. After planting the colors on the parapet, "our next maneuver," said Captain James Duncan in his diary, "was rather
extraordinary. We were ordered to mount the bank and front
the enemy and there by word of command go through all the
ceremony of soldiering [Steuben's Manual of Arms], ordering
and grounding our arms. Although the enemy had been firing
a little before, they did not give us a single shot. I suppose their
astonishment at our conduct must have prevented them . . .
Though I esteem Colonel Hamilton one of the first officers in the
American army, I must beg leave in that instance to think he
wantonly exposed the lives of his men."[7] It is altogether likely
that Hamilton's act of bravado marked the last performance in
history of that bit of siege ritual.

Estimates of the probable length of the siege varied considerably. On September 30, Lieutenant William Feltman of the First
Pennsylvania Regiment wrote in his *Journal:* "This day Captain
Davis laid a bet with me of a beaver hat that Lord Cornwallis
and his army would be prisoner of war next Sunday." But on
October 8, he says, "I bet a pair of silk stockings with Captain
Davis that Cornwallis and his army would not be prisoners of
war by this day two weeks."[8] Feltman won the first wager, but
lost the second.

On October 9, an American officer wrote: "Happy day! We
returned the hostile fire." The first French battery on the extreme left began firing during the afternoon, and was soon
joined by an American one on the extreme right. Four more
batteries joined in on October 10; and according to the diary of
a German corporal, Stephen Popp, "The inhabitants of the city
fled with their belongings to the river and hid themselves in sand
and rocks. Still they did not entirely escape, for many of them
were fatally injured through the richocheting of the bombs."[9]
So great was the effect of the bombardment upon the British redoubts that Washington deemed it possible to open the second

parallel about halfway between the first and the enemy lines. This brought the armies so close together that work could not be done upon the batteries of the second parallel during the daylight.

By October 11, fifty-two allied siege guns were firing, and are said to have hurled fifteen thousand shells into Yorktown. Cornwallis wrote to Clinton: "We have lost about seventy men, and many of our works are considerably damaged, with such works, on disadvantageous ground, against so powerful an attack we cannot hope to make a very long resistance." In order to complete their second parallel, however, the besiegers were obliged to storm British redoubts numbered 9 and 10. This was accomplished on the night of October 14. A picked French contingent under Colonel William de Deux-Ponts captured the "Bastion" redoubt (Number 9) in thirty minutes; and a body of American light infantry under Colonel Alexander Hamilton took a smaller redoubt (Number 10) in ten minutes. Dr. Thacher explains the reasons for the difference between the two gallant storming actions: "The Americans removed a part of the abatis with their hands, and leaped over the remainder. The French troops, on coming up to theirs, waited until their pioneers had cut away the abatis, *secundum artem*, which exposed them longer to the galling fire of the enemy."[10] Deux-Ponts was ecstatic: "I never saw a sight more beautiful or more majestic . . . I owe them [his troops] the happiest day of my life." The French casualties numbered ninety-two as against thirty-four for the Americans. It was the last fighting done by Washington's army in the war.

By next morning both redoubts formed a part of the second parallel, and batteries were being constructed for the final assault. Cornwallis wrote to Clinton: "My situation now becomes very critical; we dare not show a gun to their old batteries, and I expect that their new ones will open tomorrow morning. Experience has shown that our fresh earthen works do not resist their powerful artillery, so that we shall soon be exposed to an assault in ruining works, in a bad position, and with weakened numbers. The safety of the place is, therefore, so precarious that I cannot recommend that the fleet and army should run any great risk in endeavoring to save us."

To save any shreds of his military reputation Lord Cornwallis,

as a besieged general, was obliged to order at least one sortie. It
was made on the night of October 15 by four hundred men under Colonel Abercrombie. Their object was to spike the guns of
the new batteries. They succeeded in putting four French and
three American cannon out of action, but all seven were firing
just six hours later. In desperation Cornwallis began to move
troops to the Gloucester side of the river on the night of the
16th, hoping to break through Choisy's forces in the direction of
New York possibly to meet the rescue fleet on the shore; but a
severe storm at midnight spoiled the project, and all the soldiers
returned to Yorktown. The jig was up. "We at that time could
not fire a single gun," Cornwallis reported, "I therefore proposed
to capitulate." At least a week earlier than the allies had expected
Cornwallis had been bombarded enough. He had not exhausted
his provisions; most of his works were still standing; but over a
thousand of his men were suffering from "the ague" and other
diseases.

Four years to a day after the Saratoga surrender a British
drummer mounted a parapet and beat a "parley." There was a
day of dickering over terms: Cornwallis wanted his troops
paroled to England for the duration, but Washington insisted
upon the terms which General Clinton had imposed upon General Lincoln at Charleston. A sharp point of military etiquette
was involved which has not been generally understood. The rules
for the surrender of a fortified place granted "the honors of war"
only when the garrison marched out through the breach which
had been made by the enemy in the main work, proving that it
was possible for the enemy to enter in the opposite direction. If
no breach existed the garrison was deemed not to have made a
gallant defense, and must go out through a gate without receiving the honors of war. To have flags flying and drums beating
indicated that the garrison had acquitted itself well, and was still
able to defend itself against insult and humiliation.

When the honors of war had been earned it was customary
for the band of the defeated army to play a march air of the opponent, perhaps as a return gesture of honor between equals for
having been recognized as gallant foes. What had happened at
the siege of Charleston, which was not strictly a fortress any
more than Yorktown, was that General Lincoln's army had been

denied the honors of war by General Sir Henry Clinton, and had
been forced to match out with colors cased and without being
permitted to play a British air. This was an insulting reflection
upon the character of their defense of that city. When the same
article was proposed to Major Ross, representing Lord Cornwallis at Yorktown, he said: "This is a harsh article." To which
Lieutenant Colonel Laurens, speaking for the allies, replied:
"Yes, sir, it is a harsh article." Despite protests, the article stood;
and, as nearly everyone knows, the British air played at the surrender ceremony was: "The World Turned Upside Down."

At the Yorktown Centennial Celebration in 1881, the Honorable Robert C. Winthrop gave a vivid description of the scene
at the surrender: "A mile of ten full regiments of French, a legion of cavalry and a corps of Royal Engineers, with white uniforms and facings of yellow, and violet, and crimson, and green,
and pink, with the *fleur de lis* proudly emblazoned on the white
regimental standards, with glittering stars and badges on their
officers' breasts, and with dazzling gold and silver laced liveries
on their private servants. Opposite them, the American 'regulars,'
if we had anything which could be called regulars, clad in their
old Continental uniforms in possible condition, many in home-
spun, worn by battle, coats out at the elbows, shoes out at the
toes, in some cases, no coats, no shoes at all."[11]

The British prisoners, said Lieutenant Feltman, who was present, "all appeared to be much in liquor." They were wearing
new uniforms, which would otherwise have had to be surrendered. In every possible way they tried to show their contempt
for the Americans. Lord Cornwallis had previously announced
that he would "die sword in hand" before surrendering. He pled
an indisposition, sending his sword by General O'Hara, who
tried to find General Rochambeau in order to surrender to a
Frenchman, not an American. He was, however, guided to
Washington and turned over to General Lincoln, who had been
placed in charge of the proceedings in order to make up for his
abasement at Charleston. Claude Blanchard was indignant at the
shabby behavior of the British: "Throughout the whole *triste
cérémonie* the English exhibited *morgue* and not a little insolence. Above everything else they showed contempt for the
Americans."[12] Earl Cornwallis went so far as to decline an invi-

tation to dine that evening with Washington and accepted one from Baron de Vioménil instead.

The siege of Yorktown was the last of its kind conducted on American soil, "remarkable for the completeness of its execution," says Colonel John W. Wright, U.S.A., "colored by fortitude and deeds of valor, and accompanied by the rolling of drums and waving banners. Yorktown was one flickering glimpse of war in his ancient panoply."[13] The cost in battle casualties, in spite of the heavy rain of shot and shell over a small area, was surprisingly small. The British killed, wounded, and missing numbered 552, while the French lost 253 and the American regulars (no reliable figures were kept for the militia) 130. The toll from disease on both sides was much heavier.

One might have thought that, after such great exertions, the men of the allied armies would have been given a rest. What actually happened was that they were swiftly put to work filling up and smoothing over the parallels which they had so laboriously excavated. The point was that Clinton and Graves might possibly come back with strength enough to turn the tables and besiege them. There was no desire to supply the enemy with trenches and batteries ready-made. It was a very fatiguing business, but the joy of victory was in the air.

When the British fleet did return, too late to do anything about changing the result, they brought the grand total of ships of the line and heavy frigates in the waters off the Chesapeake to seventy-two. This, in terms of numbers and firepower, was by far the largest assemblage of naval armament that had ever been seen up to that time. But not another shot was fired. The *coup de Grasse* had been delivered. The French admiral had been "the arbiter of the war." As Washington fully recognized in his letter to De Grasse on October 20: "The surrender of York from which so great glory and advantage are derived to the allies, *and the honor of which belongs to Your Excellency*, has greatly anticipated our most sanguine expectations." (Italics mine.)[14]

In a sentence which has often been quoted, Washington also stated to De Grasse: "You will have observed that, whatever efforts are made by the land armies, the navy must have the casting vote in the present contest."[15]

25

APPORTIONING
THE BLAME AND PRAISE

"Yesterday a British fleet had a rich and most glorious harvest of glory in view, but the means to gather it were omitted in more instances than one."
— Sir Samuel Hood, September 6, 1781

No one wanted to be the scapegoat for the loss of the battle of the Chesapeake or of Cornwallis's army or of America. The handiest candidate was, of course, Rear Admiral Graves. In a letter which he wrote to Lieutenant General Simcoe, he had said: "The 5th of September was, I confess, a moment of ambition to me."[1] The depth of his disappointment was revealed in his somewhat apologetic report to Lord Sandwich, written on September 14, 1781, before he had reached New York. Observing that he had been outnumbered by the French, Graves wrote: "Yet I think that had our efforts been made together, some of their van, four or five sail, must have been cut to pieces. The signal was not understood. I do not mean to blame anyone, my Lord. I hope we all did our best." He acknowledged that "the mutilated state of the squadron [after the engagement] prevented my keeping the wind of the enemy, as well as several shifts of wind in their favor." His ships had been "brought to such a state of damages that we could only think of preserving the best appearance."[2]

When George III read this report, he wrote to Sandwich on October 14, 1781, long before the news of Cornwallis's capitulation reached London: "Lord Sandwich will not be surprised that after the knowledge of the defeat of our fleet, for there is no looking on the admiral's account in another light, and worst of all the retreat to New York, that I nearly think the empire ruined. I am not of a desponding disposition; I have endeavored to serve my country. If evils must ensue, I am ready to meet them. He that has a good conscience is always in a situation that others are not aware of. This cruel event is too recent for me to be as yet able to say more."[3]

Graves's defense was greatly helped by the ill-advised and unjust charges made in a speech by Lord Denbigh in the House of Lords on November 17, 1781. He alleged that the admiral had received "repeated advices from Rodney in May, July, and August last" of an intended French naval expedition to the Chesapeake, "with a recommendation to collect his whole strength" and to meet Hood off the Capes of Virginia." He charged further that Hood had arrived there, sent a frigate to inform Graves, and "waited afterwards for nine days for his coming, and, being then tired, sailed with his whole squadron for New York . . . found Graves at Sandy Hook, not even preparing to sail; and that at last, when the admiral moved from thence towards the Chesapeake, he left four ships of force behind him."[4]

Admiral Rodney compounded this nonsense, some of which was of course founded upon his ignorance of what had happened to the dispatches he had sent to Graves, by his letter from Bath to George Jackson on October 19, 1781, berating Graves for acting "in direct opposition to the orders and letters of his superior," and also condemning Sir Peter Parker, commanding in Jamaica, for detaining the *Torbay* and *Prince William*, as well as for failing to send some of his own ships to the Chesapeake. Rodney maintained that Graves's "mode of fighting I will never follow. He tells me that his line did not extend so far as the enemy's rear. I should have been sorry if it had . . . by contracting his own line he might have brought his nineteen against the enemy's fourteen or fifteen, and by a close action totally disabled them before they could have received succor from the remainder, and in all probability have gained a complete victory . . . If they intend the war should be concluded, there *must be* but one General and one Admiral commanding in chief in America and the West Indies." (Italics his.)[5]

The controversy over Graves's conduct therefore began with

a mixed volley of just and unjust criticisms, to which his eldest brother William Graves endeavored to reply in two letters designed for publication in the London *Morning Chronicle* of January 21 and 22, 1782. Even after some enlightenment about the fate of the *Swallow* and the *Active*, Admiral Rodney insisted, speaking in his own defense in the House of Commons, that "I had sent to the commander-in-chief in America, desiring he would collect his whole force, and meet me with it off the Capes of Virginia . . . but no answer was sent either to Sir Samuel Hood or myself, for I was then so ill, that I was coming home . . . If the admiral in America had met Sir Samuel Hood near the Chesapeake, the probability was, that De Grasse would have been defeated, and the surrender of Lord Cornwallis prevented."[6]

Even had all of Rodney's messages to Arbuthnot and Graves been delivered, they were not nearly so specific as he insisted upon dreaming that they had been. In his crucial dispatch on July 7, 1781, there was not the slightest hint that he understood that De Grasse's fleet was aiming for the Chesapeake, nor of any written instructions to Hood "to guard the mouth of the Chesapeake . . . and keep his frigates cruising off the coast to the southward, that he might have timely notice of the enemy's approach . . . No one of which [orders] has been regarded." His remarks to Parliament, says Chadwick, "are but the imaginings of what ought to have been advised by himself but were not advised in any such terms."[7]

When Rear Admiral Digby arrived in New York in late September, 1781, to relieve him, Graves complained to the Admiralty of "being relieved by a junior officer, and sent to another station [Jamaica] where I can only be second and possibly third in command . . . [which] implies such a disapprobation of my conduct as will certainly discredit me in the opinion of mankind . . ." This was written on September 26, 1781, and of course the orders had been issued before anyone in London was aware of the battle of September 5. On March 25, 1782, Philip Stephens replied that the Admiralty entertained "no disapprobation of your conduct, for nothing could be more distant from their thoughts."[8]

Graves insisted that "calumnies in the newspapers" required his return to England. On July 25, 1782, he sailed from Jamaica on the disastrous voyage in the *Ramillies* at the head of "the craziest squadron that ever put to sea" consisting of the captured *Ville de Paris* and eight other line ships, of which only two reached England after a violent storm. Despite all the charges he was given further employment, although not promoted to vice admiral until 1787, nor to full admiral until 1794. In the end he received an Irish peerage as Baron Graves and a pension of one thousand pounds a year.

Such leniency of treatment aroused the ire of the English naval historian Michael Lewis. After blaming Graves for missing "two golden opportunities," he writes: "And what did they do to Graves on his return. Shoot him? Cashier him? Certainly not. They did not even try him. He was re-employed, rose to high rank, and ultimately gained a peerage. And why not? He had faithfully kept their rules, their Instructions, their inviolable line. He had lost no engagement, no ships—none was lost on either side. He had merely lost America."[9]

In another of his books, the same historian says: "In the whole history of sailing-warfare no rigid adherence to the line was ever more fatal than that of Thomas Graves on the afternoon of the 5th of September, 1781. Then, in the course of a few brief hours, he twice held the main western fleet of France in the hollow of his hand, and with it, perhaps, the issue of the whole war, possibly, even, the future of the whole world, since the existence of the United States was at issue, too."[10] Captain James declares that in approaching the French fleet at the Chesapeake, "Graves was in a position beyond the wildest dreams of a sea-commander. His whole fleet was running down before the wind, and his enemy was before him, working slowly out of harbor. He had only to fall upon their van with full force and the day was his."[11]

So far, then, it all seems like plain sailing: Graves is the villain because he stuck to the line approach and let at least "two golden opportunities" slip through his fingers, as Sir Samuel Hood pointed out at length in his "Sentiments Upon the Truly Unfortunate Day." Hood, who freely admitted that he "thought meanly" of his superior, appears at first to be, along with Rodney, who was later to be credited with "breaking the line" at the Saintes, a champion of much more supple tactics. But a strange anomaly appears when one examines the theories held by the three admirals in contrast to their practices upon the field of battle.

On September 6, 1781, the day after his disastrous engagement with De Grasse, Graves issued a remarkable memorandum to his fleet beginning with the sentence: "When the signal for the line of battle ahead is out at the same time with the signal for battle, it is not to be understood that the latter signal shall be rendered ineffectual by a too strict adherence to the former."[12] He went on to say that the line signal should be interpreted as preserving "the line of extension for the fleet . . . parallel to that of the enemy during battle," but "keeping as near the enemy as possible."

Whereupon Sir Samuel Hood wrote upon the back of his copy of the memorandum: "It is the first time I ever heard it suggested that too strict adherence could be paid to the line of battle; and if I understand the meaning of the British fleet being formed parallel to that of the enemy, it is, that if the enemy's fleet is disorderly and irregularly formed, the British fleet is, in compliment to it, to form irregularly and disorderly also. Now, the direct contrary is my opinion; and I think, in case of disorder or irregularity in the enemy's line, that the British fleet should be as compact as possible, in order to take the critical moment of an advantage opening and offering itself, to make a powerful impression on the most vulnerable part of the enemy. According to Mr. Graves's Memo., any captain may break the line with impunity when he pleases."[13]

Here Sir Samuel Hood appears as a devout believer in the literal observance of the line, while Graves is cast in the role of a willing modifier of the doctrine. As Captain James points out: "If that memorandum of the 6th of September had been issued two days earlier, a very different turn might have been given to the course of events." The evidence about what was in the minds of the two admirals is so contradictory that, as Julian S. Corbett says: "It suggests some such conundrum as: When is a line of battle not a line of battle?"

The partisans of Graves were sure that the man who lost the battle of the Chesapeake was Hood. Rear Admiral Graves's cousin Thomas Graves was present as captain of the *Bedford*, and wrote in his signal book this comment on the memorandum:

"N.B. The foregoing order was given the day after the action with the French fleet of twenty-four sail of the line, in consequence of the second in command not bearing down and engaging the enemy, which was his duty; but kept his wind, by which means a most glorious victory was lost, and with it the loss of Lord Cornwallis's army in Virginia."[14] The American Rear Admiral Chadwick agrees that "Hood did not wholeheartedly aid his chief;" and his fellow-admiral Robison declares flatly: "Had Hood been a man of less influence, he—like Palliser and Lestock—would have been court-martialed for not doing his *utmost* to engage the enemy. In fact, he did nothing . . ." (Italics his.) [15]

We are left with the "disturbing" thought that Graves's theory was considerably more progressive than either Hood's or Rodney's, but that "he lacked the genius" to put his principles into practice. He found "the weapon" of the *Fighting Instructions,* thinks Corbett, "too rigid and heavy for the strength of his wrist." In his famous *Essay on Naval Tactics*, Mr. John Clerk of Edinburgh declares that "the receipe for a good admiral is found in the person who combines theory with practice, is blessed with a clear head, and has his heart in the right place."[16] Although Graves's theory was probably a good one, and his heart was undoubtedly in the right place on September 5, 1781, he had anything but a clear head.

Whatever each admiral intended on September 5, there can be no doubt that they were miserably served by the antiquated British system of naval signalling. At this distance the vexing question about which signal was flying at what hour cannot be solved, but the passionate statement of Captain Thomas White of one of the ships in Hood's squadron is impressive. He said: "I could not fancy that what I that day saw was a mere chimera of the brain, and that what I believed to be the signal for the line was not a Union Jack, but an *ignis fatuus* conjured up to mock me."[17] In part the English failure was in the technology of communication.

Later in his career, Hood was fortunate enough to have a number of chances to show his mettle as an independent commander, and used them brilliantly. This makes all the more mysterious his omission to do his full duty at the Chesapeake.

But the officer whose reputation suffered the least from any criticism was Admiral Rodney, thanks in part to his being in Parliament when the news of Yorktown, "the most melancholy Great Britain ever received," Hood called it, reached London.

Rodney had made four or five serious blunders in the campaign: his coming to New York; his overlong preoccupation with "putting the guttings of St. Eustatius into the belly of the *Sandwich*"; his erroneous stationing of Hood off Martinique; his vital miscalculation of De Grasse's strength in going north; and his use of the *Gibraltar* for his homeward voyage. Yet all these faults of omission and commission were erased in an instant by his dazzling victory over De Grasse at the Saintes in April, 1782. John Adams once remarked that the British public "went mad over naval victories," and for the second time Rodney was to profit by their wild enthusiasm. He had done much to lose the American colonies. At the Chesapeake, as Randolph G. Adams has said, England for once failed to "muddle through." But Rodney managed nevertheless to win for England "the last victory" in the fifth Anglo-French war, and in the West Indies. That was what seemed most important in 1782.

Just the reverse fate overtook Admiral de Grasse, his unlucky opponent and prisoner. In his instance, defeat wiped out most of the credit he had acquired at the Chesapeake, just as victory at the Saintes made Englishmen forget the earlier blunders of Rodney. De Grasse returned to France from captivity in England, where he had the ill-luck to be popular, to be greeted with almost universal obloquy. Almost none of his contemporaries had a good word to say in his behalf. His fall had been too precipitous. He retired to his chateau of Tilly, where his depressed spirits were lifted temporarily by the receipt of the cannon voted to him by Congress as "a feeble proof to posterity of the immeasurable services that Your Excellency rendered to the United States of America." During the French Revolution the cannon were melted down and made into coins.

De Grasse is a man to whom America owes much, but knows little, probably because of his short and meteoric stay in the country. Lafayette and Rochambeau both have their statues in Jackson Park opposite the White House, but the only monument bearing De Grasse's name (along with theirs) in this country did not rise at Yorktown for exactly one hundred years after Congress on October 29, 1781, had authorized it. Not until 1930 did an American, A. Kingsley Macomber, present a statue of De Grasse to France, where it stands in the gardens of the Trocadéro at Paris.

Another participant in the Yorktown debacle (for the British) was fortunate in his opportunities to redeem himself in the wars of the French Revolution and in India, namely—Earl Cornwallis. Far from being in disgrace, he arrived in England as something of a hero, conferred with North and Germain, and had a private audience with the King. "Neither the government nor the general public," says Stevens, "blamed him for the disaster that had overtaken his command." In a House of Lords debate over a possible inquiry into the loss of the army at Yorktown, the Duke of Grafton asserted that it "was the common language in France, that Lord Cornwallis's army was *sold*." (Italics his.)[18] It was Sir Henry Clinton who was assigned most of the blame for supposedly "failing to support" Cornwallis's invasion of Virginia, which he had neither ordered nor countermanded. The public remembered only that he was commander-in-chief in America. It was said that he came back to England "laughed at by the rebels, despised by the British, and cursed by the loyalists." Although he was reputed to have had "a very kind reception from the King," Parliament did not even bother to call him on the carpet to listen to his version of Yorktown. Abnormally sensitive to criticism and wounded by what seemed to him ingratitude, Clinton spent the rest of his life defending his every act in America. But the more he protested his innocence, the more his quarrelsomeness, his inertia, and his lack of military imagination became apparent.

Behind the mediocre British admirals and generals stood an absurdly complicated and inefficient administration which maintained separate stations and commands in competition with one another. The British public showed a good deal of intuitive wisdom in directing its wrath about Yorktown against the King's ministers rather than against the commanders in the field. At the top there was an appalling deficit of enlightened leadership. "We had," says Michael Lewis, "no William Pitt, nor any war-leader of even moderate ability. Fortunately, however, the French did not produce one either, which is perhaps the chief reason why we did not succumb."[19]

In addition to their appalling ineptitude in administering an empire, the chief shortcoming of king and ministers was their total and profound misunderstanding of the forces on the march in America. The latter were never stated better, philosophically, than by Captain Levi Preston: "We had always governed ourselves, and we always meant to. They didn't mean we should."[20] Over against this yearning for self-rule, which in the late twentieth century has led to the creation of literally scores of new nations, the English governing class had nothing to offer but a graceless insistence upon dependence and subordination to the mother country.

The web of responsibility for losing the American colonies spreads beyond and behind the ministers to a British society ill-prepared to exercise the responsibilities of empire. Landed aristocrats like Germain and Sandwich were intent upon serving the established interests of a relatively settled social order. They envisaged the colonies as merely "tenancies of the Crown," and their inhabitants as inferiors to be kept in their places. Unhappily for them, across the Atlantic the winds of political change were blowing up a storm. But their backs were turned in that direction; their faces were only toward the past and their precarious present. With an understatement that is more British than American, Charles M. Andrews comments: "It can hardly be said that the Englishmen of the ruling classes were governed in their colonial relations by any ideals that were destined to be of service for the future of the human race."[21]

So unprepared was England for the tidings from Yorktown, and so weak and disorganized was the opposition to the North government, that it was not until the end of January, 1782, that the principal ministerial target of criticism, Lord George Germain, was removed from office at the price of a peerage, and "was received into the quiet bosom of the House of Lords." Lord Sandwich was the next candidate for political oblivion; but with the government's majority steadily shrinking, it became apparent that Yorktown had doomed the whole North ministry. When the news of Cornwallis's surrender first reached him, it was reported that North "received the news as one might a ball in the breast. He reeled, threw out his arms, exclaiming wildly, as he paced up and down the apartment for a few minutes, 'Oh, God! It's all over!' " He recovered swiftly, however, and it was not until March 20, 1782, that he surprised the House of Commons by resigning.

George III told North: "It is you who desert me, not I you." The king talked darkly of abdicating rather than countenancing American independence. Stubborn to the last, he was the "final obstacle"; but without granting independence, he found that he could not have a parliamentary government. Over a century was to elapse before England's rulers fully grasped the fallacy of colonialism, and began voluntarily to set their remaining overseas subjects free. "The lesser breeds," it is true, have not always displayed much gratitude for their years of tutelage.

When it came to apportioning praise for the Yorktown victory, George Washington received so much that he is threatened with the fate of Aristides called "the Just," who became a bore. Nevertheless Washington was the man whose perseverance made Yorktown possible, and who had no small part in making it actual. He stands before the world as the model leader of a movement for independence, and for at least three reasons: his inspiring tenacity in times of prolonged adversity; his insistence upon respect for civil authority, even in the form of a weak Congress; and his unswerving fidelity to the ideal of a union of States rising above petty local interests. To keep his dimensions human it should be noted that he was not a very good judge of other generals in his army (Arnold for example), and he was probably not as able a professional tactician as Cornwallis. Only the early Arnold and Greene and possibly Lafayette deserve comparable mention.

What Washington contributed to the brilliant combined operation in Virginia was chiefly his "naval genius," his adaptability in planning and executing, his willingness to take a risk, and his *finesse*. Without French help, both on sea and on land, it is hard to see how he could have brought the war to a decision. Yorktown is one instance where statistics are truly eloquent and not misleading. Of the allied forces on land, nine thousand five hundred were French. The exact size of the naval personnel present is hard to determine, but in fifty armed vessels and twenty-six transports there must have been between twenty thousand and twenty-two thousand Frenchmen. The American soldiers numbered thirty-five hundred regulars and about two thousand militia. The French furnished ninety pieces of heavy ordnance, the Americans sixty.

The American Revolution is perhaps the world's prime example of independence achieved by a copious amount of what today would be called foreign aid. As in our time, it was probably motivated by a mixture of enlightened self-interest and sympathy for national ideals. It was also accompanied on both sides by the sort of suspicions and recriminations with which we have become too familiar. The French complained that they were expected to do all the fighting and the paying; the Americans groused about winning their own independence and the need for "paying for it with American blood."

What did the struggle cost the French and Spanish governments in hard cash? Up to the year 1783, the French archives show expenditures on behalf of the United States of America of 1,507,500,000 *livres*. After an exhaustive study of the matter, Professor Marion of the Collège de France placed the total figure at two billion *livres*. If the costs of the war with England as America's ally are included, another 1,200,000,000 *livres* would have to be added. It is extremely hard to translate that sum into modern values, but two billion *livres* would come to about half a billion of today's dollars, perhaps much more. The drain on the treasury of Louis XVI surely aggravated the financial crisis at the time of the French Revolution, but that uprising had other causes in addition. The Spanish government placed its monetary share in the American Revolution at 8,000,000 *reales* with another 1,000,000 *reales* spent by the Spanish colonies.

American independence of Great Britain resulted from a complex galaxy of causes; the astonishingly pervasive ineptitude of the King's ministers and officers; the internal political division in England over the coercion of the colonies; the excessive hopes of aid from Americans loyal to George III; Britain's diplomatic isolation in Europe; the strategic logic of geography; the foresight of French statesmen in furnishing many kinds of aid to the rebels; the wise and tenacious leadership of Washington; and the unsung heroism, drastically underestimated by the British, of his "amateur soldiers pitted against professionals."

All these factors and more came together in the climax of the six years of struggle which was staged at Yorktown, Virginia. From a camp nearby on October 20, 1781, the day after the surrender, the Marquis de Lafayette wrote to the Count de Maurepas: "*La pièce est jouée . . . et le cinquième acte vient de finir*." ("The play has ended . . . the fifth act has just been finished.")

Nearly a century and a half later, Captain W. M. James, R.N. was to write: "Yorktown has often been described as one of the decisive battles of the world, but it was the naval skirmish off the Chesapeake that was decisive."[22] But even at the time there were those who perceived the same truth. On January 24, 1782, a nameless correspondent wrote to the *Political Journal* of London: "In a word, the fate of Lord Cornwallis and of America perhaps may be said to rest upon the merits and demerits of the action of the 5th of September, and not upon those of any circumstances, either previous or subsequent."[23]

APPENDIX

Orders of battle of the two fleets,
Battle of the Chesapeake,
September 5, 1781

BRITISH (19)[a]

Frigates	Ships	Guns	Commanders
	Alfred	74	W. Bayne
Santa Monica	*Belliqueux*	64	James Brine
Richmond	*Invincible*	74	Charles Saxton
Solebay	*Barfleur*	90	Sir Samuel Hood, Rear Admiral of the Blue
La Nymphe			Alexander Hood
Adamant	*Monarch*	74	Francis Reynolds
Salamander,	*Centaur*	74	J. Inglefield
fire ship	*America*	64	S. Thompson
Sybil	*Resolution*	74	Lord R. Manners
La Fortunée	*Bedford*	74	Thomas Graves
	London	90	Thomas Graves, Rear Admiral of the Red
			D. Graves
	Royal Oak	74	J. P. Ardesoif
	Montagu	74	George Bowen
	Europe	64	S. Child
	Terrible	74	Hon. W. C. Finch
	Ajax	74	N. Charrington
	Princessa	70	Francis S. Drake, Rear Admiral of the Blue
			C. Knatchbull
	Alcide	74	C. Thompson
	Intrepid	64	A. J. P. Molloy
	Shrewsbury	74	Mark Robinson

[a] The fleet approached the Chesapeake in the above order, but entered action in reverse order, headed by the *Shrewsbury*.

After the battle and the return to New York, the *Terrible*, 74, was replaced by the *Prudent*, 64; and the *Torbay*, 74, and *Prince William*, 64, joined the fleet from Jamaica. Rear Admiral Robert Digby added the *Prince George*, 90, *Canada*, 74, and *Lion*, 64, for the fruitless voyage back to the Chesapeake.

French (24)[b]
(*approximately in the order of engaging*)

Ship	Guns	Commander
Pluton	74	D'Albert de Rions
Marseillais	74	Castellane Majastres
Bourgogne	74	Comte de Charitte
Diadème	74	M. Montecler
Réfléchi	64	De Boades
Auguste	80	De Bougainville, chef d'escadre
Saint-Esprit	80	Chabert Cogolin
Caton	64	Comte de Framond
César	74	Coriolis d'Espinouse
Destin	74	Comte du Maitz de Goimpy
Ville de Paris	110	Rear Admiral Comte de Grasse Vaugirard de Rosnay, Chief of Staff
Victoire	74	Chevalier D'Albert Hippolyte
Sceptre	74	Comte de Vaudreuil
Northumberland	74	Marquis de Briqueville
Palmier	74	D'Arros Argelos
Solitaire	64	Chevalier de Cicé Champion
Citoyen	74	Comte de Thy
Scipion	74	Clavel Ainé
Maganime	74	Chevalier de la Bègue
Hercule	74	Chevalier Turpin du Breuil
Languedoc	80	Baron de Monteil, chef d'escadre
Zélé	74	Chevalier Gras Préville
Hector	74	Renaud d'Allen
Souverain	74	Chevalier de Glandèves

[b] In addition, *Glorieux*, 74, *Triton*, 64, and *Experiment*, 50 were detached to blockade the James and York rivers. After the battle, Comte de Barras brought from Newport *Duc de Bourgogne*, 80, *Neptune*, 74, *Conquérant*, 74, *Éveillé*, 64, *Provence*, 64, *Jason*, 64, *Ardent*, 64, and two frigates. De Grasse had seven frigates—*Andromaque, Rallieuse, Surveillante, Concorde, Gentille, Diligente*, and *Aigrette*—and captured two more—*Iris* and *Richmond*—after the battle of September 5.

NOTES

Introduction

1. Jacob H. Patton, *Yorktown, A Compendious Account* (New York, 1837), p. 33. See also Paul Allen, *A History of the American Revolution* (Baltimore, Md., 1822), II, pp. 442–43.

2. Captain Dudley W. Knox, U.S.N., *The Naval Genius of George Washington* (Boston, 1932), p. 87.

Chapter 1. The Stage—and Some Properties

1. Major General J. F. C. Fuller, *The Conduct of War* (New Brunswick, N.J., 1961), p. 76.

2. Hoffman Nickerson, *The Turning Point of the Revolution* (Boston, 1928), p. 47.

3. Gerald S. Graham, *Empire of the North Atlantic: The Maritime Struggle for North America* (Toronto, 1958), pp. 197–98.

4. Elizabeth S. Kite, "Colonel John Laurens Brings the Needed Aid from France," *Légion d'Honneur*, VIII (1937–38), p. 233.

5. John Campbell, *Lives of the British Admirals* (London, 1813), VIII, p. 25.

6. G. R. Barnes and J. H. Owen, eds., *The Private Papers of John Earl of the Sandwich, First Lord of the Admiralty, 1771–1782* (London, 1832–38), IV, pp. 178–79. (Cited hereafter as *Sandwich Papers*.)

7. Fleming MacLiesh and Martin L. Krieger, *The Privateers* (New York, 1962), p. 46.

8. William L. Clowes, *The Royal Navy* (London, 1898), III, p. 354.

Chapter 2. The Actors—Though Not in Order of Their Appearance

1. *Sandwich Papers*, II, p. 6.

2. Lieutenant Commander Leland F. Lovette, U.S.N., *Naval Customs, Traditions and Usage* (Annapolis, Md., 1939), p. 68.

3. Campbell, *Lives*, VII, pp. 18–19.

4. J. H. Plumb, "The World Beyond America," *American Heritage Book of the Revolution* (New York, 1956), p. 19.

5. Graham, *Empire*, p. ix.

6. Rear Admiral S. S. and Mary Robison, *A History of Naval Tactics from 1530 to 1930* (Annapolis, Md., 1942), p. 140.

7. Julian S. Corbett, ed., *Fighting Instructions, 1530–1816* (London, 1905), p. 285.

8. Edward K. Chatterton, *Battles by Sea* (London, 1925), p. 134.

9. David Hannay, ed., *Letters Written by Sir Samuel Hood in 1781–83* (London, 1895), p. viii. (Cited hereafter as *Hood Letters*.)

CHAPTER 3. ARCHITECTS OF DEFEAT: GEORGE III AND LORD NORTH

1. See Herbert Butterfield, *George III and the Historians* (Rev. ed., New York, 1959); C. L. Mowat, "George III: The Historians' Whetstone," *William and Mary Quarterly*, 3rd series, XVI (1959), pp. 171–78; Edmund S. Morgan, "The American Revolution: Revisions in Need of Revising," *William and Mary Quarterly*, 3rd series, XIV (1957), pp. 3–15.

2. Sir George O. Trevelyan, *Early History of Charles James Fox* (London, 1880), p. 119.

3. Butterfield, *Geo. III and Historians*, p. 76.

4. Arthur S. Turberville, *English Men and Manners in the Eighteenth Century* (New York, 1957), p. 78.

5. W. Bonham Dunne, ed. *The Correspondence of King George the Third with Lord North from 1768 to 1783* (London, 1867), p. xiii.

6. W. Baring Pemberton, *Lord North* (London, 1938), p. 29.

7. Herbert Butterfield, *George III, Lord North and the People, 1779–80* (London, 1949), p. 3.

8. Captain William M. James, R.N., *The British Navy in Adversity: A Study of the War of American Independence* (London, 1926), p. v.

9. George H. Guttridge, *English Whiggism and the American Revolution* (Berkeley, Calif., 1942), p. 1.

10. *Sandwich Papers*, I, p. 63.

11. Sir Lewis B. Namier, *England in the Age of the American Revolution* (London, 1930), p. 4; Trevelyan, *C. J. Fox*, p. 117.

12. Pemberton, *North*, p. 129.

13. Sir Nathaniel W. Wraxall, *Historical Memoirs of His Time* (Rev. ed., London, 1836), II, pp. 7, 11; Namier, *England in the Age*, p. 181.

14. *Sandwich Papers*, I, p. 102; III, pp. 41–42, 61.
15. Robert Beatson, *Naval and Military Memoirs of Great Britain, 1727 to 1783* (London, 1804), IV, pp. 33–36; Rear Admiral Sir Charles Ekins, R.N., *The Naval Battles of Great Britain from 1744 to the Peace of 1814* (London, 1824), p. 341n.
16. Pemberton, *North*, p. 7.
17. Wraxall, *Memoirs*, II, p. 142.
18. Ian R. Christie, *The End of North's Ministry, 1780–82* (London, 1958); Pemberton, *North*, p. 107.
19. *Sandwich Papers*, II, p. 239.
20. Pemberton, *North*, pp. 111–12.
21. *Political Magazine and Parliamentary Journal*, II (London, 1782), p. 10.
22. Pemberton, *North*, pp. 3–4, 188.

CHAPTER 4. ARCHITECTS OF DEFEAT: LORDS GERMAIN AND SANDWICH

1. Alan Valentine, *Lord George Germain* (Oxford, 1962), pp. 17, 18, 20.
2. *Ibid.*, pp. 71, 72.
3. H. Manners Chichester, "George Sackville Germain," *Dictionary of National Biography* (London, 1898), XXI, p. 230.
4. Valentine, *Germain*, p. 100.
5. Margaret Spector, *The American Department of the British Government, 1768–1782* (New York, 1940), p. 20.
6. *Ibid.*, pp. 75, 85.
7. Valentine, *Germain*, pp. 116, 289.
8. *Ibid.*, p. 260.
9. George H. Guttridge, "Lord George Germain in Office," *American Historical Review*, XXXIII (1927–28), p. 38.
10. *Ibid.*, p. 42.
11. *Political Magazine*, II, p. 6.
12. Erich Eyck, *Pitt Versus Fox: Father and Son, 1735–1806*, trans. Eric Northcott (London, 1950), pp. 133–34; Pemberton, *North*, pp. 60–61.
13. Sir John Knox Laughton, ed., *Letters and Papers of Charles Lord Barham* (London, 1907–8), II, p. viii. (Cited hereafter as *Barham Papers*.)
14. James, *British Navy*, p. 16.
15. Valentine, *Germain*, p. 126; Clowes, *Royal Navy*, III, p. 467.
16. Robert G. Albion, *Forests and Sea-Power* (Cambridge, Mass., 1926), pp. 282, 287.
17. *Sandwich Papers*, I, pp. 69–70.

18. *Ibid.*, I, p. 236.
19. *Ibid.*, IV, p. 291.
20. Gerald S. Brown, "The Anglo-French Naval Crisis, 1778: A Study of Conflict in the North Cabinet," *William and Mary Quarterly*, 3rd series, XIII (1956), p. 16.
21. *Sandwich Papers*, II, pp. 258, 259; III, pp. 163, 170.

CHAPTER 5. ARCHITECTS OF DEFEAT: GENERALS CLINTON AND CORN-
        WALLIS

1. Valentine, *Germain*, pp. 157, 158.
2. Frederick Wyatt and William B. Willcox, "Sir Henry Clinton: A Psychological Exploration of History," *William and Mary Quarterly*, 3rd series, XVI (1959), pp. 6, 17, 20, 25.
3. Valentine, *Germain*, p. 212.
4. Sir John Fortescue, *A History of the British Army* (London, 1911), III, p. 210.
5. William B. Willcox, ed. *The American Rebellion: Sir Henry Clinton's Narrative of His Campaigns, 1775–1782* (New Haven, Conn., 1954), p. 142.
6. *Ibid.*, pp. xlviii, li.
7. Wraxall, *Memoirs*, I, p. 380.

CHAPTER 6. ARCHITECTS OF DEFEAT: ADMIRALS RODNEY, HOOD AND
        GRAVES

1. Dudley Pope, *At Twelve Mr. Byng Was Shot* (Philadelphia, Pa., 1962), p. 286.
2. Chatterton, *Battles*, p. 135.
3. Wraxall, *Memoirs*, I, pp. 324–25.
4. *Sandwich Papers*, III, p. 155.
5. Wraxall, *Memoirs*, I, p. 325.
6. Major-General Godfrey B. Mundy, *The Life and Correspondence of the late Admiral Lord Rodney* (London, 1830), I, p. 192.
7. *Sandwich Papers*, III, p. 155.
8. Robison, *Naval Tactics*, p. 317; *Sandwich Papers*, III, pp. 160, 215.
9. David Hannay, *Rodney* (London, 1891), pp. 136–37; *Sandwich Papers*, III, p. 229.
10. *Ibid.*, III, p. 264.
11. *Ibid.*, III, pp. 261–62.
12. *Wraxall*, Memoirs, I, p. 124.
13. Mundy, *Life of Rodney*, I, p. 403.
14. *Sandwich Papers*, III, pp. 228–29.
15. *Ibid.*, III, pp. 161–62.

16. *Hood Letters,* pp. x, xii, xiii–xv.

17. *Ibid.,* p. 56.

18. Rear Admiral French E. Chadwick, U.S.N., ed., *The Graves Papers and Other Documents relating to the Naval Operations of the Yorktown Campaign* (New York, 1916), p. 9 (cited hereafter as *Graves Papers*); *Sandwich Papers,* III, pp. 238–39.

19. *Ibid.,* III, p. 267.

20. William B. Willcox, "The British Road to Yorktown: A Study in Divided Command," *American Historical Review,* LII (1946–47), pp. 3–4.

CHAPTER 7. ARCHITECTS OF VICTORY: LOUIS XVI, CHOISEUL, AND VERGENNES

1. Wraxall, *Memoirs,* I, p. 114.

2. Claude Farrère, *Histoire de la Marine Française* (Paris, 1934), p. 241.

3. Edward S. Corwin, *French Policy and the American Alliance of 1778* (Princeton, N.J., 1916), p. 2.

4. *Ibid.,* pp. 15, 23, 29.

5. Thomas Balch, *The French in America during the War of Independence of the United States, 1777–83* (Philadelphia, Pa., 1891), p. 57.

6. Graham, *Empire,* p. 108.

7. John R. Alden, *The American Revolution, 1775–1783* (New York, 1954), p. 181.

CHAPTER 8. ARCHITECTS OF VICTORY: LAFAYETTE AND ROCHAMBEAU

1. Louis Gottschalk, *Lafayette Comes to America* (Chicago, Ill., 1935), p. viii.

2. *Ibid.,* p. 97.

3. *Ibid.,* pp. 144–45, 146–47.

4. Henry Steele Commager and Richard B. Morris, eds., *The Spirit of 'Seventy-Six* (Indianapolis, Ind., 1958), II, p. 1211.

5. Jean-Edmond Weelen, *Rochambeau: Father and Son,* trans. Lawrence Lee (New York, 1936), p. vii.

6. Stephen Bonsal, *When the French Were Here* (New York, 1945), p. 43.

CHAPTER 9. ARCHITECTS OF VICTORY: DE GRASSE AND WASHINGTON

1. G. Lacour-Gayet, *La Marine militaire de France sous le règne de Louis XVI* (Paris, 1905), pp. 406–7; *Graves Papers,* p. 247.

2. Lacour-Gayet, p. 255.

3. Maurice Thiéry, *Bougainville: Soldier and Sailor* (London, 1932), p. 270.

4. Captain Joachim Merlant, *Soldiers and Sailors of France in the American War for Independence, 1776–1783* (New York, 1920), p. 164; J. C. Shea, ed., *The Operations of the French Fleet, etc.* (New York, 1864), p. 21.

5. Merlant, *Soldiers and Sailors*, pp. 171–72.

6. Knox, *Naval Genius, passim.*

7. *Ibid.*, p. 70.

8. *Ibid.*, pp. 54–55.

9. *Ibid.*, p. 64.

10. *Ibid.*, pp. 61n., 70.

CHAPTER 10. THE ACTION: ENGLAND'S UNSOLVED PROBLEM

1. James, *British Navy*, pp. 17, 34.

2. *Ibid.*, p. 421.

3. Nickerson, *Turning Point*, p. 417.

CHAPTER 11. HOW CORNWALLIS GOT TO YORKTOWN—BRITISH VICTORIES IN THE SOUTH: CHARLESTON AND CAMDEN

1. Willcox, *The American Rebellion*, p. 137.

2. Valentine, *Germain*, p. 340.

3. Willcox, *The American Rebellion*, p. 141.

4. *Ibid.*, pp. 151, 153.

5. *The Siege of Charleston by the British Fleet and Army, Etc.* (Albany, N.Y., 1867), pp. 18, 28, 35; Willcox, *The American Rebellion*, p. 159.

6. Willcox, *The American Rebellion*, pp. 164n., 167, 170, 171n.

7. *Ibid.*, pp. 163n., 184.

8. Commager and Morris, *Spirit of 'Seventy-six*, II, p. 1106.

9. *Siege of Charleston*, p. 168; Commager and Morris, II, p. 1109.

10. *Siege of Charleston*, pp. 129–30.

11. Beatson, *Naval Memoirs*, V, p. 23.

12. *Siege of Charleston*, p. 204n.

13. Willcox, *The American Rebellion*, p. 175n.; *Siege of Charleston*, p. 188.

14. *Siege of Charleston*, pp. 81, 86.

15. *Ibid.*, p. 172.

16. Beatson, *Naval Memoirs*, V, p. 28; *Siege of Charleston*, pp. 21, 82, 210.

17. Willcox, *The American Rebellion*, p. 442.

18. Sir Henry Clinton Papers, William L. Clements Library, Ann Arbor, Mich.

19. Willcox, *The American Rebellion*, p. 186.
20. *The Annual Register of World Events* (London, 1781), II, pp. 18, 19.

CHAPTER 12. CORNWALLIS VERSUS GREENE: COWPENS AND GUILFORD COURT HOUSE

1. Valentine, *Germain*, p. 370.
2. Willcox, *The American Rebellion*, p. 226.
3. Burke Davis, *The Cowpens-Guilford Courthouse Campaign* (Philadelphia, Pa., 1962), p. 25.
4. *Ibid.*, pp. 31, 33.
5. Lieutenant Colonel Banastre Tarleton, *A History of the Campaigns of 1780 and 1781* (Dublin, 1787), p. 217.
6. Willcox, *The American Rebellion*, pp. 95n., 247.
7. Fitzpatrick, John C., ed. *The Writings of George Washington from the Original Manuscript Sources, 1745–1799* (Washington, D.C., 1937), XX, p. 183. (Cited hereafter as *Writings of Washington*.)
8. *Political Magazine*, II, pp. 639–40.
9. Davis, *Cowpens-Guilford*, pp. 105, 141.
10. Commager and Morris, *Spirit of 'Seventy-six*, II, p. 1166.
11. Julian P. Boyd, ed., *The Papers of Thomas Jefferson* (Princeton, N.J., 1950), V, p. 111.
12. Davis, *Cowpens-Guilford*, p. 166.
13. Willcox, *The American Rebellion*, p. 271.

CHAPTER 13. CORNWALLIS AND LAFAYETTE IN VIRGINIA

1. Davis, *Cowpens-Guilford*, p. 180.
2. John R. Alden, *The South in the Revolution* (Baton Rouge, La., 1957), p. 260.
3. Willcox, *The American Rebellion*, p. 279n.
4. *Ibid.*, p. 278.
5. John C. Miller, *Triumph of Freedom* (Boston, Mass., 1948), p. 551.
6. Louis Gottschalk, *Lafayette and the Close of the American Revolution* (Chicago, Ill., 1942), pp. 213–14.
7. H. J. Eckenrode, *The Story of the Campaign and Siege of Yorktown* (Senate Document 318, 71st Congress, 3rd Session, Washington, D.C., 1913), p. 222.
8. Gottschalk, *Lafayette and Close*, p. 228.
9. Willcox, *The American Rebellion*, p. 284.
10. *Ibid.*, p. 284.

11. Benjamin F. Stevens, *The Campaign in Virginia: The Clinton-Cornwallis Controversy* (London, 1888), I, p. 13.

CHAPTER 14. CORNWALLIS GOES TO YORKTOWN

1. James, *British Navy*, p. 281.
2. Gottschalk, *Lafayette and Close*, p. 280.
3. *Ibid.*, p. 288.
4. Merlant, *Soldiers and Sailors*, p. 163.
5. Gottschalk, *Lafayette and Close*, p. 282.
6. Abbé Claude C. Robin, *New Travels Through North America* (Philadelphia, Pa., 1783), p. 54.
7. Henry C. Baird, ed., *The Journal of William Feltman of the First Pennsylvania Regiment, 1781–82, including the March into Virginia and the Siege of Yorktown* (Philadelphia, Pa., 1853), p. 12.
8. Frank Moore, ed., *Diary of the American Revolution from Newspapers and Original Documents* (New York, 1860), II, p. 485.

CHAPTER 15. DE GRASSE AND SAINT-SIMON DECIDE TO COME NORTH

1. Clowes, *Royal Navy*, III, p. 447.
2. E. E. Gilliam, "The French Colony of San Domingo, Its Rise and Fall," *Magazine of American History*, XX (1888), p. 471.
3. Clowes, *Royal Navy*, III, p. 468.
4. Campbell, *Lives*, VII, p. 11.
5. *Calendar of Correspondence relating to the American Revolution of Brigadier-General George Weedon, Richard Henry Lee, Hon. Arthur Lee, and Major-General Nathanael Greene* (Philadelphia, Pa., 1900), p. 1511. The entry is incorrectly listed as from Henri de Saint-Simon.
6. Washington Papers, Library of Congress, p. 162, folios 21, 731.
7. Corwin, *French Policy*, p. 293; Henri Doniol, *Histoire de la Participation de la France à l'Établissement des États-Unis d'Amérique* (Paris, 1890), IV, pp. 548, 684.
8. *Ibid.*, V, p. 448; see also Jared Sparks, *The Writings of George Washington* (New York, 1837–39), VIII, p. 76n.
9. Charles Lee Lewis, *Admiral De Grasse and American Independence* (Annapolis, Md., 1945), p. 115.
10. Doniol, *Histoire*, V, pp. 475–76.
11. *Ibid.*, V, p. 477; C. L. Lewis, *Admiral De Grasse*, pp. 123–24.
12. C. L. Lewis, *Admiral De Grasse*, pp. 133–34.
13. *Journal of an Officer in the Naval Army in America in 1781 and 1782* (New York, 1874), p. 151.
14. *Ibid.*, p. 151.
15. Shea, *Operations*, pp. 63, 150.

16. Thomas White, *Naval Researches: A Candid Inquiry into the Conduct of Admirals Byron, Graves, Hood and Rodney* (London, 1830), p. 75.

17. Karl Gustaf Tornquist, *The Naval Campaigns of Count de Grasse During the American Revolution, 1781–1783*, trans. A. Johnson. (Philadelphia, Pa., 1942), p. 51.

18. James Brown Scott, *De Grasse à Yorktown* (Baltimore, Md., 1931), pp. 201–2.

19. *Journal of an Officer*, p. 152.

20. Tornquist, *Naval Campaigns*, p. 54.

21. *Ibid.*, pp. 54–55.

22. *Ibid.*, pp. 55, 57–58.

CHAPTER 16. RODNEY DALLIES AT SAINT EUSTATIUS

1. *Barham Papers*, I, p. 98.

2. Mundy, *Life of Rodney*, II, pp. 2, 13, 97.

3. *Ibid.*, II, pp. 29, 30, 73.

4. Beatson, *Naval Memoirs*, V, p. 160n.

5. *Barham Papers*, I, p. 95.

6. Beatson, *Naval Memoirs*, V, pp. 177–78.

7. *Hansard* (Journals of the House of Commons), XXII (London, 1781), pp. 221–22.

8. Beatson, *Naval Memoirs*, V, p. 175; Mundy, *Life of Rodney*, I, p. 156.

9. J. Franklin Jameson, "St. Eustatius in the American Revolution," *American Historical Review*, VIII (1902–3), pp. 706, 707.

10. Mundy, *Life of Rodney*, II, pp. 13, 139.

11. Miller, *Triumph*, p. 591.

12. *Sandwich Papers*, IV, p. 151.

13. *Political Magazine*, III, p. 91.

14. Helen Augur, *The Secret War of Independence* (New York, 1955), pp. 324–25.

15. Mundy, *Life of Rodney*, II, pp. 23, 69, 97; Beatson, *Naval Memoirs*, V, p. 178.

16. Hannay, *Rodney*, pp. 160–61.

CHAPTER 17. HOOD, NOT RODNEY, TO THE RESCUE

1. *Barham Papers*, I, p. 98.

2. *Sandwich Papers*, IV, p. 153.

3. *Hood Letters*, pp. 21–22.

4. *Sandwich Papers*, IV, p. 132.

5. *Graves Papers*, pp. 18–19.

6. Miller, *Triumph*, p. 194.

7. *Graves Papers*, p. 39.
8. *Ibid.*, pp. 46–47.
9. *Hood Letters*, p. 18.
10. *Graves Papers*, p. 48.
11. *Ibid.*, pp. 27, 32.
12. *Sandwich Papers*, IV, pp. 136, 152.
13. *Ibid.*, IV, pp. 66, 135.
14. *Graves Papers*, pp. 58–59.
15. Willcox, *The American Rebellion*, p. 328.
16. *Barham Papers*, I, pp. 122–23.
17. *Sandwich Papers*, IV, pp. 174, 198.
18. *Graves Papers*, p. 34.

CHAPTER 18. THE BATTLE OF THE CHESAPEAKE: FIRST PHASE

1. *Graves Papers*, p. 61; *Sandwich Papers*, IV, p. 181; William Graves, ed., *Two Letters Respecting the Conduct of Rear-Admiral Graves* (Morrisania, N.Y., 1865), p. 7 (cited hereafter as *Two Letters*).
2. *Sandwich Papers*, IV, p. 181.
3. *Graves Papers*, p. 67.
4. *Political Magazine*, III, p. 153.
5. *Ibid.*, III, p. 44.
6. Scott, *De Grasse*, p. 205.
7. *Graves Papers*, p. lxxiv.
8. Robert de Loture, *Washington Nous Voici! La France au Secours de l'Indépendence Américaine* (Paris, 1934), p. 141.
9. R. de Kerallain, "Bougainville à l'armée du Comte de Grasse, guerre de l'Amérique, 1781–1783," *Journal de la Société des Américanistes de Paris*, XX (1928), p. 53.
10. *Graves Papers*, pp. 228–29.
11. Shea, *Operations*, p. 69.
12. Kerallain, *Bougainville*, p. 19.
13. *Sandwich Papers*, IV, pp. 181–82.
14. Shea, *Operations*, p. 69.
15. *Political Magazine*, III, p. 620.
16. *Two Letters*, p. 7; *Graves Papers*, p. 62; *Political Magazine*, II, p. 622.

CHAPTER 19. THE BATTLE OF THE CHESAPEAKE: SECOND PHASE

1. *Graves Papers*, p. 165.
2. Beatson, *Naval Memoirs*, V, p. 273.
3. *Ibid.*, V, p. 274.
4. *Graves Papers*, pp. 62, 69.

5. *Ibid.*, p. 70.
6. Shea, *Operations*, p. 70n.
7. *Ibid.*, pp. 71, 72.
8. *Graves Papers*, p. 72.
9. Kerallain, *Bougainville*, p. 19n.
10. Shea, *Operations*, p. 73; *Graves Papers*, p. 113.
11. Tornquist, *Naval Campaigns*, pp. 62–63.
12. Julian S. Corbett, ed., *Signals and Instructions, 1776–1794* (London, 1908), p. 54; Ekins, *Naval Battles*, p. 122.
13. Tornquist, *Naval Campaigns*, pp. 59–60.
14. *Ibid.*, p. 59.
15. *Political Magazine*, II, p. 623.
16. *Graves Papers*, p. 62.
17. Scott, *De Grasse*, p. 205.
18. *Graves Papers*, p. 73.
19. *Ibid.*, pp. 62, 73.
20. *Sandwich Papers*, IV, p. 182.
21. *Graves Papers*, p. 204.
22. Scott, *De Grasse*, p. 205.
23. *Graves Papers*, p. 232.
24. Shea, *Operations*, p. 158.

CHAPTER 20. THE BATTLE OF THE CHESAPEAKE: THIRD PHASE

1. Shea, *Operations*, p. 157.
2. *Graves Papers*, p. 91.
3. *Political Magazine*, II, p. 631.
4. "Journals of Henry Duncan, Captain, R.N., 1778–1781" in John Knox Laughton, ed., *The Naval Miscellany* (London, 1902), I, p. 202.
5. *Graves Papers*, p. 86.
6. Sir John Knox Laughton, *From Howard to Nelson* (London, 1899), p. 379.
7. Tornquist, *Naval Campaigns*, p. 62.
8. Kerallain, *Bougainville*, p. 19.
9. Tornquist, *Naval Campaigns*, pp. 65–66.
10. *Graves Papers*, p. 64.
11. *Political Magazine*, II, p. 623.
12. *Ibid.*, II, p. 668.
13. Kerallain, *Bougainville*, p. 22.
14. Knox, *Naval Genius*, p. 99.
15. *Graves Papers*, p. 92.
16. *Ibid.*, p. 78.
17. *Political Magazine*, II, p. 154.

18. *Graves Papers*, p. 65.

19. *Political Magazine*, II, p. 53.

20. Scott, *De Grasse*, p. 206.

21. Loture, *Washington*, p. 145.

22. *Ibid.*, p. 146. Lieutenant de Loture errs in his identification of the *Richmond* as one of the two buoy-cutting frigates. The work was done, as pointed out above, by the *Medea* and the *Iris* on the previous day.

23. *Graves Papers*, pp. 92, 93.

24. Bonsal, *When the French*, p. 135.

25. *Graves Papers*, p. 83.

CHAPTER 21. "TOO LITTLE, TOO LATE"

1. *Political Magazine*, II, p. 623.

2. *Hood Letters*, p. 43.

3. William Heath, *Memoirs of Major-General Heath During the American War* (Boston, Mass., 1789), p. 110.

4. Willcox, *The American Rebellion*, p. 334.

5. *Political Magazine*, II, p. 613.

6. Willcox, *The American Rebellion*, p. 329.

7. *Ibid.*, p. 336.

8. *Ibid.*, p. 571.

9. *Hood Letters*, p. 36.

10. *Graves Papers*, p. 97.

11. Willcox, *The American Rebellion*, pp. 173–74.

12. *Ibid.*, pp. 341, 342.

13. *Hood Letters*, pp. 37, 38.

14. Willcox, *The American Rebellion*, pp. 372–73.

15. Albion, *Forests*, p. 310.

16. *Graves Papers*, pp. 97–98.

17. *Hood Letters*, p. 37.

18. *Graves Papers*, p. 119.

19. *Ibid.*, p. 121.

20. *Ibid.*, p. 138.

21. *Political Magazine*, III, p. 632.

CHAPTER 22. ROCHAMBEAU WRITES A LETTER

1. Count William de Deux-Ponts, *My Campaigns in America* (Boston, Mass., 1868), p. 88.

2. Mathieu Dumas, *Memoirs of His Own Time* (Philadelphia, Pa., 1839), I, p. 40.

3. Gottschalk, *Lafayette and Close*, pp. 167, 211–12.

4. Warrington Dawson, "*Un garde Suisse de Louis XVI au service de l'Amérique: le Baron Gaspard de Gallatin*," *Le Correspondant*,

No. 1633 (August 10, 1931), p. 673. (Cited hereafter as *Gallatin*.)

5. John C. Fitzpatrick, ed., *The Diaries of George Washington, 1748–1799* (Boston, Mass., 1925), II, pp. 207–8. (Cited hereafter as *Washington Diaries*.)

6. Charlemagne Tower, Jr., *The Marquis de Lafayette in the American Revolution* (Philadelphia, Pa., 1895), II, p. 283.

7. *Graves Papers*, pp. lvi–lvii.

8. *Washington Diaries*, II, p. 218.

9. Doniol, *Histoire*, V, pp. 475–76.

10. *Washington Diaries*, II, p. 230.

11. *Graves Papers*, p. lviii.

12. Tower, *Marquis de Lafayette*, II, p. 400.

13. Colonel H. L. Landers, U.S.A., *The Virginia Campaign and the Blockade and Siege of Yorktown* (Washington, D.C., 1931), pp. 148–49.

14. *Ibid.*, pp. 136–37.

15. *Graves Papers*, p. lix.

16. *Washington Diaries*, II, pp. 248–49.

17. Willcox, *The American Rebellion*, p. 327.

CHAPTER 23. WASHINGTON AND ROCHAMBEAU MARCH SOUTH

1. Balch, *The French in America*, p. 147.

2. Merlant, *Soldiers and Sailors*, p. 159.

3. Deux-Ponts, *My Campaigns*, p. 117.

4. *Washington Diaries*, II, p. 253.

5. Commager and Morris, *Spirit of 'Seventy-Six*, II, p. 1214.

6. Deux-Ponts, *My Campaigns*, pp. 122 and n., 123.

7. Willcox, *The American Rebellion*, pp. 328–29.

8. *Ibid.*, p. 562.

9. *Writings of Washington*, XXIII, p. 77.

10. *Gallatin*, p. 682.

11. "Letters of Ebenezer Huntington, 1774–1781," *American Historical Review*, V (1899–1900), p. 727.

12. Deux-Ponts, p. 126n.

13. Commager and Morris, *Spirit of 'Seventy-Six*, II, pp. 1218–19.

14. Knox, *Naval Genius*, p. 102.

CHAPTER 24. THE SIEGE AND SURRENDER AT YORKTOWN

1. *Washington Diaries*, XXIII, p. 115.

2. Deux-Ponts, *My Campaigns*, p. 131.

3. Douglas Southall Freeman, *George Washington: A Biography* (New York, 1954), V, p. 513.

4. Landers, *Virginia Campaign*, p. 180.

5. Warrington Dawson, "The Chevalier d'Ancteville and His

Journal of the Chesapeake Campaign," *Légion d'Honneur*, II (October, 1931), p. 89.

6. Baird, *Journal of William Feltman*, p. 18.

7. Colonel John W. Wright, U.S.A., "Notes on the Continental Army," *William and Mary Quarterly*, 2nd series, XII (1932), p. 100.

8. Baird, *Journal of William Feltman*, pp. 16–17.

9. "With Cornwallis at Yorktown," *American Heritage*, XII (October, 1961), p. 61.

10. James Thacher, *A Military Journal during the American Revolution* (Boston, Mass., 1827), p. 276.

11. Patton, *Yorktown*, p. 51.

12. Bonsal, *When the French*, p. 166.

13. Colonel John W. Wright, U.S.A., "Notes on the Siege of Yorktown," *William and Mary Quarterly*, 2nd series, XII (1932), p. 249.

14. Bonsal, p. 170.

15. *Graves Papers*, p. lii.

CHAPTER 25. APPORTIONING THE BLAME AND PRAISE

1. *Two Letters*, p. 22.
2. *Sandwich Papers*, IV, p. 182–83.
3. *Ibid.*, IV, p. 181n.
4. *Two Letters*, p. 3.
5. *Graves Papers*, p. 135.
6. Mundy, *Life of Rodney*, II, p. 166.
7. *Graves Papers*, p. 136.
8. *Ibid.*, p. 163.
9. Michael Lewis, *The History of the British Navy* (Fair Lawn, N.J., 1937), pp. 145–46.
10. Michael Lewis, *The Navy of Britain* (London, 1948), p. 491.
11. James, *British Navy*, p. 290.
12. *Barham Papers*, I, p. 127.
13. Corbett, *Signals and Instructions*, pp. 260, 261n.
14. *Ibid.*, p. 261n.
15. Robison, *Naval Tactics*, p. 334.
16. Ekins, *Naval Battles*, p. xiii.
17. Clowes, *Royal Navy*, III, p. 500n.
18. *Political Magazine*, III, p. 115.
19. Michael Lewis, *History of British Navy*, p. 138.
20. *American Historical Review*, XLVIII (1942–43), p. 123.
21. *American Historical Review*, XXXI (1925–26), p. 232.
22. James, *British Navy*, p. 299.
23. *Political Magazine*, III, p. 44.

BIBLIOGRAPHY

Books and articles consulted in addition to those cited in the Notes.

ADAMS, RANDOLPH G., "A View of Cornwallis's Surrender at York-town," *American Historical Review*, XXXVII (1932–33), pp. 25–49.

AITON, ARTHUR S., "Spain in the American Revolution," in *Bicentennial Notes on George Washington, No. 2* (Port Huron, Mich., 1913).

ALLEN, GARDNER, *A Naval History of the American Revolution*, 2 vols. (Boston, Mass., 1913).

American Military History, 1607–1958 (Washington, D.C., 1958).

ANDREWS, CHARLES M., "The American Revolution: An Interpretation," *American Historical Review*, XXXI (1925–26), pp. 219–32.

ARMSTRONG, ORLANDO K., *The Fifteen Decisive Battles of the United States* (New York, 1961).

BAMFORD, PAUL W., *Forests and French Sea Power, 1660–1789* (Toronto, Ont., 1956).

BARNETT, JOHN, *Fighting Admirals* (London, 1910).

BASYE, ARTHUR, "The Secretary of State for the Colonies, 1776–1782," *American Historical Review*, XXVIII (1922–23), pp. 13–23.

BEDOYÈRE, MICHAEL DE LA, *George Washington* (Philadelphia, Pa., 1945).

BEMIS, SAMUEL F., *The Diplomacy of the American Revolution* (New York, 1935).

BIRD, HARRISON, *March to Saratoga: General Burgoyne and the American Campaign* (London, 1963).

BLANCHARD, CLAUDE, *Guerre d'Amérique* (Paris, 1831).
BOWMAN, ALLEN, *The Morale of the American Revolutionary Army* (Washington, D.C., 1943).
British Army Maps of Yorktown (Bay City, Mich., 1931).
British Maps of the American Revolution (Ann Arbor, Mich., 1936).
BUCHSER, JOHN J., *Yorktown Cradle of the Republic* (Hampton, Va., 1937).
BUTLER, RICHARD, "General Richard Butler's Journal of the Siege of Yorktown," *Historical Magazine*, VIII (1864).
CALLAHAN, NORTH, *Daniel Morgan: Ranger of the Revolution* (New York, 1961).
———, *Henry Knox, General Washington's General* (New York, 1958).
CALLENDER, GEOFFREY, *The Naval Side of British History* (London, 1924).
CARRINGTON, HENRY B., *Battles of the American Revolution, 1775–1781* (New York, 1876).
CHANNING, EDWARD, *A History of the United States, III* (New York, 1912).
CHASTELLUX, (FRANÇOIS JEAN) MARQUIS DE, *Travels in America in 1780, 1781 and 1782* (London, 1787).
CHEVALIER, L. ÉDOUARD, *Histoire de la Marine Française pendant la Guerre de l'Indépendance Américaine* (Paris, 1877).
CHIDSEY, DONALD B., *Victory at Yorktown* (New York, 1962).
CLINTON, SIR HENRY, *Observations on Earl Cornwallis's Answer* (London, 1783).
CLOSEN, BARON LUDWIG VON, *The Revolutionary Journal of Baron Ludwig von Closen*, trans. Evelyn M. Acomb (Chapel Hill, N.C., 1958).
CONTENSON, BARON LUDOVIC DE, *La Société des Cincinnati de France et la Guerre d'Amérique, 1778–1783* (Paris, 1934).
CORNWALLIS, EARL CHARLES, *An Answer to that Part of the Narrative of Lieutenant-General Sir Henry Clinton, K. B., Which Relates to the Conduct of Lieutenant-General Earl Cornwallis* (London, 1783).
COUPLAND, REGINALD, *The American Revolution and the British Empire* (London, 1930).
CRICOURT, ADOLPHE, *Histoire de l'Action Commune de la France et l'Amérique pour l'Indépendance des États-Unis* (Paris, 1876).
CROMOT DU BOURG (MARIE FRANÇOIS JOSEPH MAXIME) BARON, "Diary of a French Officer 1781," *Magazine of American History*, IV, Nos. 3–6, VII, No. 4 (1880–81).

CUMBERLAND, RICHARD, *Character of the late Lord Viscount Sackville* (London, 1785).

CURTIS, E. E., *The British Army in the American Revolution* (New Haven, 1926).

DAWSON, H. B., *Battles of the United States by Sea and Land* (New York, 1858).

DE MOND, ROBERT O., *The Loyalists in North Carolina during the Revolution* (Durham, N.C., 1940).

DOYLE, JOHN A., "The War of Independence," Ch. VII in *Cambridge Modern History, VII* (Cambridge, Eng., 1907).

DRAPER, LYMAN C., *King's Mountain and Its Heroes* (Cincinnati, Ohio, 1881, and New York, 1929).

EDLER, FRIEDRICH, *The Dutch Republic and the American Revolution* (Baltimore, Md., 1911).

FERSEN, COUNT AXEL DE, "Letters of de Fersen Aide-de-Camp to Rochambeau Written to His Father in Sweden, 1781–1782," *Magazine of American History*, III (1879).

FISHER, SYDNEY C., *The Struggle for American Independence*, 2 vols. (Philadelphia, Pa., 1908).

FLEMING, THOMAS J., *Beat the Last Drum: The Siege of Yorktown, 1781* (New York, 1963).

FORCE, PETER, ed., *American Archives*, 4th series, 6 vols. (Washington, 1837–46).

GALLOWAY, JOSEPH, *A Letter to the Right Honorable Lord Viscount H - - d on his Naval Conduct in the American War* (London, 1779).

GANOE, WILLIAM A., *The History of the United States Army* (New York, 1943).

GIBBES, ROBERT W., *Documentary History of the American Revolution*, 2 vols. (New York, 1853–57).

GIPSON, LAWRENCE H., *The British Isles and the American Colonies: Great Britain and Ireland. 1748–54* (New York, 1958).

GORDON, WILLIAM, *The History of the Rise, Progress, and Establishment of the Independence of the United States* (London, 1788).

GOTTSCHALK, LOUIS, *Letters of Lafayette to Washington* (New York, 1944).

GREENE, GEORGE W., *Life of Nathanael Greene: Major-General in the Army of the Revolution*, 3 vols. (New York, 1871).

GUTHRIE, WILLIAM D., "Reflections Suggested by the National Celebration of the Sesquicentennial Anniversary of Yorktown, 1781–1931," *Légion d'Honneur*, II (1931), pp. 63–77.

GUTTMACHER, MANFRED S., *America's Last King: An Interpretation of the Madness of George III* (New York, 1961).

GUTTRIDGE, G. H., "The Whig Opposition in England during the American Revolution," *Journal of Modern History*, VI (1934), pp. 1–12.

HATCH, CHARLES E., JR., *Yorktown and the Siege of 1781* (Washington, D.C., 1954).

HOOD, DOROTHY, *The Admirals Hood* (London, 1911).

HOSTE, P. PAUL, *A Treatise on Naval Tactics*, trans. Captain J. D. Boswell (Edinburgh, 1854).

JAMES, ADMIRAL SIR WILLIAM, *The Influence of Sea Power on the History of the British People* (Cambridge, Eng., 1948).

JOHNSON, WILLIAM, *Sketches of the Life and Correspondence of Nathanael Greene* (Charleston, S.C., 1822).

JOHNSTON, HENRY P., *The Yorktown Campaign and the Surrender of Cornwallis* (New York, 1881).

Journals of the Continental Congress, 34 vols. (Washington, D.C., 1904-37).

LAFAYETTE, MARQUIS DE, *Memoirs, Correspondence and Manuscripts of General Lafayette* (New York, 1837).

Lafayette in Virginia: Unpublished Letters, ed. by Gilbert Chinard (Baltimore, Md., 1928).

LA LOGE D'AUSSON, COMTE DE, *Yorktown, ou Comment la France Royale Libéra l'Amérique* (Paris, 1931).

LANCASTER, BRUCE, *Lexington to Liberty* (New York, 1955).

LANDERS, H. L., *The Battle of Camden, South Carolina* (Washington, D.C., 1929).

LASSERAY, COMMANDANT ANDRÉ, *Les Français sous les Treize Étoiles, 1775–1783*, 2 vols. (Paris, 1935).

LAUZUN, (ARMAND LOUIS DE CONTAUT) DUC DE, *Memoirs of the Duc de Lauzun* (New York, 1912).

LEE, HENRY, *Campaign of 1781 in the Carolinas*, etc. (Philedelphia, Pa., 1824).

———, *Memoirs of the War in the Southern Department of the United States* (Washington, D.C., 1827).

LELAND, WALDO, "Letters from Lafayette to Luzerne, 1770–1783," *American Historical Review*, XX (1914–15), pp. 383–95.

"Letter from De Vergennes to Lafayette, August 7, 1780," *American Historical Review*, VIII (1902–3), pp. 306–8.

"Letter from the Marquis de Lafayette to Dr. Samuel Cooper, 1781," *American Historical Review*, VIII (1902–3), pp. 89–91.

Lives of the Most Celebrated British Admirals (Edinburgh, 1808).

LOCKER, EDWARD R., *Memoirs of Celebrated Naval Commanders* (London, 1822).

LOSSING, BENJAMIN J., *The Pictorial Field Book of the Revolution*, 2 vols. (New York, 1879).

MACKENZIE, FREDERICK, *Diary of Frederick Mackenzie . . . . during the Years 1775–1782*, etc., 2 vols. (Cambridge, Mass., 1930).

MAHAN, ALFRED THAYER, *The Influence of Sea Power upon History, 1660–1783* (Boston, Mass., 1890).

MATHIESON, WILLIAM L., *England in Transition: 1789–1832: A Study of Movements* (London, 1920).

Messager de New-York, Le, Yorktown Number, Oct. 15, 1931 (New York, 1931).

MOULTRIE, WILLIAM, *Memoirs of the American Revolution*, 2 vols. (New York, 1802).

MUMBY, FRANK A., *George III and the American Revolution* (Boston, Mass., 1925).

NOAILLES, VICOMTE DE, *Marins et soldats français en Amérique pendant la Guerre de l'Indépendance des États-Unis, 1778–1783* (Paris, 1903).

Original Papers relating to the Siege of Charleston, 1780 (Charleston, S.C., 1898).

PAULLIN, CHARLES O., *The Navy of the American Revolution* (Cleveland, Ohio, 1906).

PECKHAM, HOWARD H., *The War for Independence: A Military History* (Chicago, Ill., 1958).

PENNYPACKER, MORTON, *General Washington's Spies on Long Island and New York* (Brooklyn, N.Y., 1939).

PERKINS, JAMES B., *France in the American Revolution* (Boston, Mass., 1911).

PRATT, FLETCHER, *The Battles That Changed History* (Garden City, N.Y., 1956).

RICHMOND, ADMIRAL SIR HERBERT, *Statesmen and Sea Power* (Oxford, Eng., 1946).

RITCHESON, CHARLES R., *British Politics and the American Revolution* (Norman, Okla., 1954).

ROSS, CHARLES, ed., *Correspondence of Charles, First Marquis Cornwallis* (London, 1859).

RUSSELL, PETER, "The Siege of Charleston: Journal of Captain Peter Russell, December 25, 1779–May 2, 1780," *American Historical Review*, IV (1898–99), pp. 478–501.

Seamanship and Naval Tactics, A System of (Philadelphia, Pa., 1799).

SHAFROTH, JOHN F., *The Strategy of the Yorktown Campaign* (Menasha, Wis., 1931).

Sketch of the Reign of George the Third from 1780 to the Close of the Year 1790, A., 4th ed. (London, 1791).

SIMMS, WILLIAM GILMORE, *The Life of Nathanael Greene* (Philadelphia, Pa., 1849).

SPARKS, JARED, *Correspondence of the American Revolution*, 4 vols. (Boston, Mass., 1853).

STEDMAN, CHARLES, *The History of the Origin, Progress and Termination of the American War*, 2 vols. (London, 1793).

STEUBEN, BARON DE, *Regulations for the Order and Discipline of the Troops of the United States*, 10th ed. (New York, 1794).

STONE, EDWIN M., *Our French Allies* (Providence, R.I., 1884).

SWEM, E. G., *Views of Yorktown and Gloucester Town, 1755* (Newport News, Va., 1946).

TRAMOND, JOHANNES, *Manuel d'Histoire Maritime de la France* (Paris, 1916).

TREACY, M. T., *Prelude to Yorktown: The Southern Campaign of Nathanael Greene, 1780–1781* (Chapel Hill, N.C., 1963).

TREVELYAN, GEORGE O., *The American Revolution*, 6 vols. (London, 1905).

TROUDE, O., *Batailles Navales de France, II* (Paris, 1868).

TURNER, EDWARD R., "The King's Closet in the 18th Century," *American Historical Review*, XLV (1939–40), pp. 761–76.

UHLENDORF, EDWARD A., *Revolution in America: Letter and Journals of Major Baurmeister of the Hessian Forces, 1776–1784* (New Brunswick, N.J., 1957).

————, *The Siege of Charleston: The Von Jungkern Papers* (Ann Arbor, Mich., 1938).

VAN DOREN, CARL, *Secret History of the American Revolution* (New York, 1941).

WALLACE, WILLARD R., *Appeal to Arms: A Military History of the American Revolution* (New York, 1951).

WALN, ROBERT, JR., *Life of Marquis de Lafayette* (Philadelphia, Pa., 1825).

WALPOLE, HORACE, *Memoirs of the Reign of King George the Third*, 4 vols. (London, 1894).

WARD, CHRISTOPHER, *The War of the Revolution, II* (New York, 1952).

Washington and Comte de Grasse, Correspondence of, August 17– November 4, 1781 (Washington, D.C., 1931).

WHITLOCK, BRAND, *Lafayette*, 2 vols. (New York, 1929).

WILD, EBENEZER, "Journal of Ebenezer Wild, 1776–81," *Proceedings of the Massachusetts Historical Society*, 2nd ser., VI (1800–01).

WILLCOX, WILLIAM B., "Rhode Island in British Strategy, 1780–81," *Journal of Modern History*, XVII (1945), pp. 304–31.

———, "British Strategy in America, 1778," *Journal of Modern History*, XIX (1947), pp. 97–121.

WRIGHT, MARCUS J., "Lafayette's Campaign in Virginia," *Publications of the Southern History Association*, IX (1905).

WRONG, GEORGE M., *Washington and His Comrades in Arms* (New Haven, Conn., 1921).

INDEX